WITHOUT A BADGE

WITHOUT A BADGE

UNDERCOVER IN THE WORLD'S DEADLIEST CRIMINAL ORGANIZATION

Jerry Speziale

with MARK SEAL

KENSINGTON BOOKS

www.kensingtonbooks.com

Some names have been changed to protect
the privacy of individuals connected to this story.

To my wife, Maggie, the love of my life and my best friend. With you at my back, I found the strength to go anywhere and do anything. I love you, now and always.
—Jerry Speziale

To my wondrous wife, Laura, who lights my path and shows the way.
—Mark Seal

Contents

1

The Junkie

I'm standing on the corner of 119th Street and Park Avenue in Spanish Harlem, anxiously awaiting the 1:00 A.M. opening of a shooting gallery. My clothes, rescued from a Salvation Army bin, are smeared with dog feces. My hair, long and braided in cornrows, is dotted with dirty beads. My arms are pocked with track marks.

It's the middle of the night, but it's rush hour on this dark corner beneath the El platform, on a street reeking with urine and teeming with junkies. Every ear is tuned to the moment when somebody whistles, signaling the opening of the shooting gallery. I'm hopping up and down, hands in my sweatshirt, asking everybody, "What's out?" Meaning what variety of heroin, coke, or crack will be served up when the gallery opens.

"Yo, dude, when they gonna bust this door open?" I ask. "How much longer we gotta wait?"

The other junkies gather round. They know me as Crazy Jerry from Jersey, a loud, in-your-face guy who's always screaming obscenities, picking through garbage, and generally acting deranged, and they're hoping that maybe I'll share my bag with them. But once that whistle cuts through the night, it's every man for himself. We all rush toward the graffiti-covered door of a dilapidated tenement.

"Line up! Line up!" commands a grimy, rail-thin Spanish ghetto guy in a dirty T-shirt. We all do as told, fifty suddenly obedient junkies in a line, each rolling up our sleeves to show the doorman our tracks, proof that we're not cops. I shove up my sleeve when it's my turn.

"Just gimme the dope!" I say, acting panicky. The mangy guy at the door backs away from my stench and ushers me inside.

I step into a crack-clouded, urine-scented, gutted shell of a building with lightbulbs hanging from sockets. It's a smoky den of needles, guns, and dope, the floors littered with a dozen addicts sampling the wares. I thrust a fistful of cash at the dealer, a shirtless skeleton wearing only cut-off jeans and a do-rag, and cop my bag, ignoring his young Dominican bodyguards with their shaved heads and automatic pistols. Then I rush back out into the night like any junkie who's eager for a fix.

But it's all a masquerade, designed to help me "get over"—pass as a junkie and make a buy. My stained clothes are just a costume. My track marks were made with theatrical makeup. My cornrows are beauty parlor extensions. My high is from the NYPD-sanctioned beers I tossed down to take the edge off the evening. Crazy Jerry from Jersey is Jerry Speziale, undercover cop. Through the Kell transmitter wire taped up the middle of my back and the microphone snaking up the front of my chest, I signal the backup cops, who rush in for a bust.

Everybody warned me, "White guys can't get over." But for the last three years, I've been getting over nightly, helping our unit become the most productive in NYPD history. We're the NYPD Street Enforcement Unit, a citywide narcotics unit dedicated to fighting street-level drugs. Going undercover is the quickest way for an NYPD cop to achieve the coveted gold detective's shield. But the last three years have taken their toll. I've been shot, robbed, run over by a cab, pushed off of a roof, beaten by rogue cops who didn't recognize me . . . and much more. Worst of all, the work has ceased to be satisfying.

It's one bust after another after another, sometimes ten times a night, and we never seem to make a dent in the traffic. We bust 'em one at a time, a street at a time, sometimes a neighborhood at a time, two hundred cops leaping out of city buses in massive raids. I score in shooting galleries, tenement flats, street corners, makeshift labs . . . every imaginable variety of sordid locale, where the difference between life and death is how fast I can score and get out the door, without ever letting anyone make the connection between Crazy Jerry from Jersey and the busts that follow. Each night is an endless stint of theatrics, during which I'm acting crazy but silently praying, "Please, God, don't let them make me."

Meaning ID me as a cop.

Because if they do, I'm dead.

———

As dawn breaks on another all-nighter, I'm driving home in my fifty-dollar orange VW Cheech and Chong mobile, still dressed in my costume, reeking of dog feces, sweat, beer, and crack. When I pull into the beautiful new town house community where I live with my wife, Maggie, who is about to give birth to our first child, the morning smells like bacon and eggs.

None of our neighbors know that I'm a cop. I park the Bug and trudge toward our front door. Just then, I see my wife and a neighbor, a young woman who's pushing a baby in a stroller. "Pretty soon, Maggie," I hear the woman tell my eight-months-pregnant wife. "Yours will be here before you know it." They stop in midsentence and stare at me as if I were something out of a horror movie.

Maggie, who wholeheartedly supports me in my police career, is nonetheless repulsed by my appearance. Ashamed, she quickly looks away and breaks down crying.

And I know I've got to find a way to rise above the grind of busting junkies on the street.

I've got to find a way to get to the source.

———

Years before, Maggie had saved me.

My father was a New Jersey barber. He ran a shop called Gerard's in the city of Paterson. When we moved into the borough of Totowa, he had another shop where he worked by himself. When we moved to Wayne, he eventually ran a shop with six or seven haircutters called Mario Gerard's. My mother worked as a law firm paralegal. And I was—well, I wouldn't say I was a juvenile delinquent, but I was definitely a wild and energetic kid.

I wasn't robbing banks or sticking up stores. I was just the type of guy who would get on a snowmobile in the winter and taunt the cops into trying to chase me. Or find a thousand ways to drive my only sister, Debbie, who was four years younger than me, crazy. Or I'd get my dirt bike and hang out at the shopping mall looking for mischief. I became a member of a small-time street gang called the T-Bowl Gang. The gang was named for the local bowling alley, the T-Bowl. We'd get in fights with other gangs from other towns. By the time I was fourteen, I was already off on the wrong foot, drinking booze, getting in trouble, tearing up my town.

At fourteen, I also got a part-time job, working every night after school. The Wayne Hills Mall was going up, and I went down and worked construction. By the time I had my driver's license at seventeen, I got a job driving a tow truck as a highway "recovery specialist," the authorized wrecker for the New Jersey State Police. Clearing wrecks. Towing deadbeats.

Then I met Maggie Reinhardt, and she became the light of my life.

I met Maggie when she was fifteen and I was eighteen. She worked for a modeling agency and they were doing a fashion show for a boutique in the Wayne Hills Mall. She was walking through the mall, and I was hanging out in front of an arcade with my "T-Bowl" gang jacket, when I saw her for the first time.

"Did anybody ever tell you you're beautiful?" I yelled across the mall.

Maggie looked at me and gave me the finger and said, "Get lost!"

Those were our first words.

Finding out about Maggie was my first real investigation. I went to Wayne Hills High School and Maggie went to Wayne Valley High School. Her family was straitlaced. Her father had just passed away at forty-two of a heart attack. He had worked for Winer Industries, selling clothes to JC Penney and all the resale shops. His death left his family okay financially, but emotionally there was a big hole in their home. Maggie was devastated.

One night her school had a bonfire. I parked across the street and said "Hi" to Maggie as she passed, and she said "Hi" back. I found a mutual friend and convinced her to get Maggie to meet me. I parked my tow truck outside Maggie's house as our friend walked in, and pretty soon Maggie emerged.

"Do you want to go for a ride with me?" I asked her.

"Sure," Maggie said, and we went on our first date. We towed a car and then went to McDonald's, where the drive-through attendant alerted Maggie's brothers where she was and who she was with. Her brothers went into Full-Alert Status. They'd heard I was a badass, and they were determined to rescue their sister from me. But it didn't work. We started dating and in 1985, Maggie and I got married.

With Maggie, I found my focus: to have a family and a great job. I loved law enforcement, and law enforcement straightened me out, and all that came from Maggie.

═══

I've always loved action. As a kid growing up, my big dream was to become a fireman. I became a maniacal fire buff, always hanging around the fire department. My dad would walk me up to the firehouse and I would sit on a fire engine. But it was my uncle Tony, my mother's brother, who pointed me toward my career.

Uncle Tony was a New York State Trooper. He was one of the original undercovers on the New York State Police; he helped bust the Hell's Angels. He wore this big Afro and a leather jacket with chains and earrings and drove an old Cadillac Seville. I always looked up to Tony. I was entranced by all of his undercover adventures.

Sometimes, Tony and his partner would come to my grandmother's (Tony's mother's) house, the two of them looking like desperados, and they'd take their guns out of their waistbands and show them to me. How cool was that? To masquerade as a badass to bust the bad guys? I saw myself in that role . . . someday.

By the time I got out of high school I was focused on becoming a cop. I took the New York State Police test, and I scored fairly well. By then, uncle Tony was a sergeant in the state police detective bureau and a representative for the Troopers' Union. He knew me as this wild kid who probably would have destroyed his career if he vouched for me to get on the New York State Police.

Uncle Tony could have gotten me on with one phone call. He worked in Albany and he knew the superintendent. The guy was once his partner. But Tony didn't help me. I never got called for my background, never got called for my physical, never got called at all.

My alternative was the NYPD or staying local. My father knew some politicians and a captain at the Passaic County Sheriff's Department, Joe Vacardipone. Joe was well liked by the sheriff. I had already taken the NYPD test and begun the process of applying there, but my father thought New York City was too tough and dangerous. He talked to Joe, and Joe got me an interview at Passaic County. Damn, if they didn't sign me on.

In 1981 I had my first job in law enforcement. The position, corrections officer. I was working in the jail with hardened criminals, moving them throughout the facility, taking them to court and to the gym, doing odd jobs around the place.

Then the NYPD called. It was 1982 and the department desperately needed new officers. The drug wars were raging and record levels of crime had left the force shell-shocked and riddled with vacancies. Officers were retiring or just quitting in record numbers. The NYPD, trying to keep pace with demand, was bringing in three thousand new recruits at a clip.

When I got the call, I almost dropped the phone. I had been accepted in the next class at NYPD! I was supposed to be signed in that same Friday and was told to report to induction with my New York State driver's license and be ready for service. This was what I'd wanted, but now that I had it, I didn't know what to do.

Pretty soon there was a chorus. Maggie, my parents, everybody all told me to forget about New York. "Hey, listen, you've got a great job here," they said. "You're safe in Jersey. There's no real danger. You just started. Don't leave for New York City. We don't want you to do this."

I might have followed their advice. But then, on the day of my acceptance, I was talking to John Turre, a canine officer at the Passaic County Jail with ten long years on the job. "I got called for the NYPD and they want me to go Friday. What would you do?" I asked John.

He looked at me and said, "Kid, get the hell out of here."

I went home and told Maggie that I'd decided to go with the NYPD. She tried to talk me out of it, but I was determined. Without telling her, I got up the next morning and drove over the George Washington Bridge and got sworn in, one more rookie headed to the Police Academy.

After the swearing-in ceremony, I got a New York City driver's license and, because I was required to have a residence in New York

City, found a dirty, rat-infested apartment in an old walk-up in Brooklyn. It was in a basement and it had a bathroom that was shared with three other guys. One of my roommates was a Middle Eastern refugee who played the mandolin all night long. The bathroom was so filthy I had to take a shower with my sneakers on. When I got home and told Maggie what I'd done, she looked at me as if I had just said I was leaving her.

That night, she drove into the city with me to help me bring my stuff. She walked in, took one look at this filthy excuse of an apartment, and began begging and pleading with me not to stay there. But it was too late. I was a member of the NYPD, and I was ready to go wherever my new job would send me.

———

I was assigned to patrol in the Bronx, stationed in what they call an A House. A precinct is called a house, and the department rates them alphabetically—an A House, a B House, and a C House. C Houses would be located in low-crime areas like Staten Island. B Houses would be somewhere where there wasn't much happening, maybe out in Queens in a neighborhood like Forrest Hills.

A Houses were different, dangerous. They were in places like the South Bronx, Harlem, Washington Heights, or the Lower East Side. A Houses were the worst of the worst, and I absolutely loved it. I'd work twenty-five jobs a night, probably five to eight of them involving shots fired or a man-with-a-gun. It was nonstop action, all night long. I'd go from job to job to job. It was high crime and fast paced.

Then in 1986, I got my chance to shine. I was in the four–six precinct in the Bronx with another patrol officer, my buddy John Lynn. He was a really easygoing guy who loved the outdoors and snowmobiles, motorcross and mountain bikes. Even though we each only had two years on the job, we were considered "hair bags," meaning veteran officers in the precinct.

John and I were a radio car team, but that night the brass broke us up. We were experienced guys who knew our precinct boundaries, and they wanted each of us to work with a rookie. They put me with a guy named James Clark, a young, Irish-looking kid with light brownish red hair that he wore short and combed back. He was quiet, and even quieter now that he was a brand-new boot on the street with a partner that was anything but conventional.

Because John and I were friends—we went on vacations together, and we were really close—we had an unwritten rule that we would back each other up on whatever job we got with our respective rookies.

I got an alarm call to Webster Avenue, went there, and found nothing going on, so I called it in as an accidental trip or a faulty alarm. Then I heard over the radio, "Ten-thirty in progress," which means a robbery was going down. A guy with a gun was holding up somebody in a vestibule. I heard that "Forty-six King"—John Lynn's unit—was headed to the scene. I was "Forty-six Eddie," so I said over the radio, "This is Forty-six Eddie, I'm going on a back," meaning a backup.

We raced to the scene. Rookie Jimmy Clark was driving our old Dodge Diplomat, and the farther we drove, the worse the neighborhood got. Tenement buildings on dirty streets with garbage strewn along the sidewalks. The buildings all looked the same—vestibule-type jobs with dingy little courtyards in the middle. The smell of urine wafted up from the street. It was, in short, junkie heaven.

I radioed John Lynn; he was almost there, and I was still a ways away. I asked John to give me a description when he got there. Once he got to the front of 1790 Weeks Avenue and walked into the courtyard and then into the vestibule, John encountered one Benjamin Clark, who was acting mighty strange. His eyes looked all buggy. He had a horrendous case of the shakes. He was drenched in sweat and hell-bent on robbery and homicide.

We were about to be introduced to our future.

Benjamin Clark was standing in a big, downstairs vestibule, in the middle of one stairway going right and a second stairwell going left. Lurking in the shadows, Clark would wait for people to walk through the doorway, then line them up on the wall to rob them. He was screaming, "Get on the wall! Spread-eagle!" when John Lynn found him. He already had a few people against the wall. One of the witnesses said that when Clark heard sirens heading his way, he fired a gunshot into the floor and said, "Fuck them! I'm ready!"

Clark fired on John and hit him through his holster, grazing his hip. John shot back at Clark and then ducked into a doorway to reload his gun. My rookie partner was driving and he started to pass the building. "It's right there!" I shouted. I opened the door and leaped out of the moving car, just as I heard John yell, "Ten-thirteen, shots fired! Ten-thirteen, shots fired!" In the courtyard, I could smell the gun smoke. John's young partner had run back out of the building when John came under fire, and was hiding in the garden.

One of the people lined up on the wall was a woman named Lisa Gist. When John came in, Gist tried to escape and Clark shot her in the back of the head. She went down and her body blocked the door. She was bleeding profusely, but she was coherent, saying, "Help me. Help me."

That's what I heard when I rushed into the building.

"John? John?" I was yelling. I saw him hiding behind the door, while Clark was reloading his gun. I fired a shot and hit Clark in the ankle. Clark took off, bolting up the stairwell, with me hot on his trail.

The next officer on the scene was another rookie, a brave woman named Crystal Rodriguez, and she followed me up the stairs. Just as we made the turn for the fourth floor, Benjamin Clark fired again. His shot hit the cinder-block wall, and a big chunk bounced off and hit me in the head.

I thought I'd gotten shot in the head, and I'll never forget that feeling. Maggie was pregnant with our daughter, Franki, and I had this vision that I was never going to see my daughter or my wife again. That gave me the strength to fight.

Crystal and I took cover, trying to shoot up the stairs, while shots rained down on us. One hit Crystal in the badge, another right in the rim of her vest. She looked at me and said, "I think I'm hit." I threw her into the arms of another officer who was coming up the stairs, then ran back up after Benjamin Clark.

All I could see was his muzzle flash blazing down from the darkness above. The next thing I knew, I felt a fiery pain in my forearm, and this time I knew I'd been hit.

I ran back down the stairs. It was 4:00 A.M. by then and I started calling for more assistance: helicopters, emergency services, SWAT teams, everybody.

We set up a perimeter around the building. But crazy Benjamin Clark went up to the roof, jumped to the top of an adjoining building, took off his pea coat, and walked out the front door as if he were just a normal person wondering what the hell was going on. He was walking down the sidewalk when a sergeant yelled out to him, "Hey, pal, get out of here, there's some nut shooting."

I spotted Clark and jumped up and down yelling, "That's him! Police!" When he didn't surrender, I fired my gun at him and he started shooting again.

I emptied six shots into him, but he didn't stop. He started stutter-stepping, dancing like a deer. He'd turn around and shoot, and then he'd go down on his knee and he'd get up and run and turn around and shoot again. I reloaded and fired six more and although some found their target, the guy didn't even flinch. He began running again, with me hot on his heels.

By then a dozen cops were shooting at Benjamin Clark. It was like the gunfight at the O.K. Corral, just a crazy rain of blood and bullets. Clark never stopped firing at us until about twenty of us emptied our guns into him and Benjamin Clark bounced all over the street like a rubber ball.

When he finally fell, we found all these vials with little white rocks in them, scattered around his body, and we thought, *What the hell is this?* They looked like miniature white peanuts. We'd never seen crack before.

Although we didn't realize it at the time, Benjamin Clark was our first taste of a revolution that would soon put the NYPD to a bloody test. By 1988, the department would be buried in a wave of coke and crime. And just as Benjamin Clark was the first foot soldier of what would be an epidemic of crack that would ravage New York City, I knew I had found my calling as a cop.

———

When they wheeled me into the hospital, the attendants wanted to call my wife. I told them absolutely, positively no.

"My wife is having a troubled pregnancy, you push me to a phone and I'll personally tell her that I've been shot," I said. I wanted Maggie to hear my voice so she would know that I was okay.

All through my hospital stay, I thought of three things—Maggie, our baby, and becoming an undercover cop. I had already interviewed to become a narc and hoped to be accepted as a "Ninety-Day Wonder," a member of the ninety-day program in which NYPD would take successful street cops from busy precincts and try them out for ninety days in undercover work. If you were accepted into the program, after three years of undercover assignment you would get your gold detective's shield, pushing the normal route of seven years down to three.

Becoming an undercover narc was a fast track for getting to detective, but being a narc was the toughest job in the city. Buying drugs and hanging with dope dealers wasn't a favorable assignment; the brass knew that everybody wasn't cut out for it. When I applied to do my ninety days, I expected to be accepted right away, because there weren't a lot of guys crazy enough to do it.

The shooting made up my mind for me.

While I was in the hospital, then-mayor Ed Koch paid a visit, along with Police Commissioner Patrick Murphy and other members of the brass. I remember them circling my hospital bed, surveying the damage. One of them said to me, "What do you want to do with your career?"

I didn't hesitate. "I wanna be a narc," I said. I told them that I'd put in for my ninety days and they looked at me as if I had ten heads. I'd just survived a blazing gun battle, and they were giving me the chance for some cushy assignment; asking to become an undercover narc was like trading a winning lottery ticket for a postage stamp. Any sane guy would have said he wanted to work at Police Plaza and push papers around all day. But I wanted to be an undercover.

When I returned to my precinct after sick leave, there was a telephone message waiting. I'd been accepted as a "Ninety-Day Wonder," and I would be assigned to the Street Enforcement Unit, a citywide command in Manhattan.

———

What did I know about being an undercover narcotics agent? Absolutely nothing. There were no schools for hanging out in shooting galleries or masquerading as a junkie, and the NYPD had no formal training for this type of work. Everything was on-the-job training. I learned fast. First lesson: It all comes down to listening, eavesdropping, wire-tapping.

Every undercover develops his own technique and "front," or style of masquerade. The best undercovers I've seen, whether in a police department or a federal agency, are the ones that really believe in what they're doing and throw themselves completely into playing the part.

When you're totally into your role, you actually believe that you're a junkie—or a drug smuggler. That's why the psychological affects are so strong and so serious. You become that person for a time.

That's what happened to me. For the next few years I carried out variations on my Crazy Jerry routine. In New York's most crack-infested neighborhoods, I posed as a low-level drug user to set up buys and busts. Working with the NYPD Organized Crime Control Bureau, Street Enforcement Narcotics Unit, I was involved in taking down thousands of street dealers. But I was frustrated, because I could see that I was still just skimming the surface of the drug trade. I was far from the source of the problem.

Three years after going undercover, I got a promotion to one of the fifteen DEA task force groups on Christmas Eve, 1989. The New York Drug Enforcement Task Force (NYDETF) is the longest-standing drug enforcement task force in the nation, dating back to 1975. To get into a task force, agents weren't recruited by the DEA but by whatever agency the officer originally belonged to. Each agency—the DEA, the NYPD, and the New York State Police—recruited their own members and assigned them to the DEA task force.

Whatever your branch of service, in order to get into the DEA task force, you first had to be a detective. Then you had to have extensive narcotics street and major drug case experience. Then, and only then, could you be considered for an interview before a board consisting of the individual task force's captain, other agents from the DEA, and representatives from the three individual agencies whose members were recruited to serve.

It turned out to be a very sweet gig. I got a take-home car and thousands upon thousands of dollars in overtime pay. Plus, our task force turned out to be the most prestigious unit in New York City law enforcement. Pretty soon, every New York City narc's dream was to become a member of the DEA task force. But only eighty of five thousand detectives got the call. You had to be a superstar in the narcotics division and it would take a while before you would even be considered

For fifteen months, I was assigned to Group 77, the aggressive newcomer in a group of mostly older guys. I started pushing for wiretaps. I'd learned all about wiretaps from an expert named Frank Bose, who I called Grandpa. We had worked together in the Harlem Narcotics Unit when I was an undercover, and we had gone on to Group 77 together. Grandpa had worked for the Tandy Corporation as a technician, developing cellular telephones back in the pioneering days of cellular technology. He was like Mr. Gadget, complete with the lab coat and the complicated tools, and I couldn't have asked for a better mentor. He was an electrical genius.

I'd wanted to do wires when I first came to the task force, but aside from Grandpa, none of the other members of the group wanted to do anything. Grandpa and I set up our first wiretap on a Colombian trafficker. But we could only get one side of the conversation, his outgoing calls only. The DEA's technicians told us it wasn't possible to pick up both sides of a telephone conversation because the technology wasn't available.

Grandpa and I fought that prevailing logic. We went over and had lunch with some of the guys at Cellular One at the switching station in New Rochelle, New Jersey. We brought them NYPD T-shirts, hats, and coffee mugs. I basically served as Grandpa's gofer, carrying his toolbox, while he walked around the switches in his lab coat and met with the technicians, everyone trying to figure out how we could hear both sides of a cell phone conversation. Eventually, we accomplished our goal through what's called a "loop extender," a device that places a loop in the circuit that routes the call over a dedicated line to the wiretap equipment for monitoring.

From there I learned how the switch worked, how the cell sites worked, and about the technology. Then I started doing one wiretap after another. As the technology improved, so did my skills at keeping up with the improvements. When Skypagers became popular among drug dealers, I would learn how to tap them, too.

———

From the beginning, I wanted to bust the world, while most of the other members of my team wanted to sit around and read the *New York Post*. At 4:00 P.M., they would say, "Let's go out and see if we can find some drug dealers." At 6:00 P.M., it was quitting time. I huffed and puffed all day long, begging everybody to help me kick down doors and clean up the streets. The group's apathy was appalling, considering that we were at war in New York City.

Violent crime was soaring. Coke and crack were flooding the

streets. The enemy was from an area of South America known as the "White Triangle," with Cali, Colombia, at its apex. The trafficking organizations, or "cartels," which made their home first in Medellín on the coast and then two hundred miles south in Cali, posed a major challenge to U.S. law enforcement.

Starting where the Medellín groups stopped after being taken down by the Colombian National Police in the early 1980s, the Cali cartels made great efforts to pass themselves off as legitimate businessmen. Sophisticated, wealthy, and ruthless, these traffickers had access to the latest technologies, and soon developed an infrastructure much like that of an organized crime or terrorist organization.

But while traditional Mafia families corrupted officers and judges, the Cali cartels corrupted entire institutions of government. During the late 1980s and early 1990s, the cartels generated billions of dollars in drug revenues per year, littering the streets of New York with both coke and the corpses of those who double-crossed them.

The police powers of New York decided to go after the Colombian drug cartels by creating a new "group." They already had fifteen special drug enforcement groups, some of them created as far back as 1975, each comprising agents and officers from the NYPD, the New York State Police, and the DEA. There were maybe fifteen guys to every group. In 1990, they decided to create the new division expressly to go after the Cali drug cartels. Instead of bringing in new members, they asked each of the existing divisions to give somebody up for a new group.

The supervisors of the existing groups were reluctant to give up their best guys to a brand-new operation with no credibility. You don't give up your Mickey Mantle. You give up your liabilities, your loose cannons, your renegades, your wild men. When the "give up" period came, the members of my old group said, "Hasta la vista, Jerry."

I was sent to the new group, which was called Group 93.

2

Group 93

The first meeting of Group 93 was at DEA headquarters on Fifty-seventh Street and Eleventh Avenue. Eleven of us came shuffling into the building's lobby like kids on the first day of school, all wide-eyed and wondering what the hell we'd gotten ourselves into. One by one, we filed in, a ragtag group of renegades, orphaned by our respective departments, all of us eager to prove our former bosses wrong. In our T-shirts and blue jeans, we looked like a gang of bikers, not a soon-to-be-elite drug-enforcement unit.

"Okay, welcome, everybody," said a five-foot, ten-inch bulldog whose voice boomed as loud as thunder. He introduced himself as Eddie Beach, our new supervisor. "Welcome to Group 93," he continued. "We're going to get to work immediately. But first things first. Lemme show you your new office."

Eddie Beach led us to an offshoot of a hallway that looked like an exit. There was an old door with an ancient combination lock. He unlocked the door and we all walked in, and for a minute we all just looked at each other dumbfounded. Somebody had to be joking. This wasn't an office at all; it was an old bulk-evidence storage room. Windows? Forgetaboutit. It was just a dank, dark room with giant holes in the sheetrock from years of banging bulk evidence against the walls. There was dust everywhere.

"This sucks," said Mikey Monge, who, with his fluent Spanish, would turn out to be one of Group 93's greatest undercovers.

15

"How we gonna work from this hellhole?" added Jerry Vetrano, who we called "Jerry V." He was one tough, mean cop and would become a big source of our group's moxie and muscle.

"We're gonna fix it up!" I said.

We all chipped in whatever money we had in our pockets and walked over to a hardware store on Fifty-second Street and got some paint and plasterboard. We mended the holes, painted the walls, and mopped the floor. When we were done, it was still basically a closet. But it didn't matter; we weren't planning to spend much time there.

"It's not much," I said. "But it's a start."

So there we were, twelve guys sitting in a closet, trying to figure out how to go after the big drug dealers. We had no clue. But we had a hell of a combination of men to figure it out. In time our group would evolve as agents came and went, but from the beginning two of us always remained, me and my boss and partner, Eddie Beach.

Eddie Beach was a former New York State Police detective whose forte was busting members of the Italian Mafia. He was so stocky and thick that you could break a bat over him and the bat would splinter. He always wore a very serious expression beneath a full head of thick grayish hair that he pushed straight back. In that dark gray mop there was a streak, like a bird feather, of white gray.

Eddie always spoke in a gruff voice—when he used it, which was rare. He was a man of very few words, but he wasn't anybody's fool. He'd graduated from Fordham University, where he was a member of the hockey team and an excellent student. Now that he was a dedicated family man and a DEA group supervisor, he left nothing to chance.

From the beginning, everybody called me "Craze," short for Crazy Jerry from Jersey. But I wasn't the only nut in Group 93. That first day, after our meeting, all of us retired to a bar. By then we were all on the way to being a team.

All of us came to the group with a sigh of relief. We were happy to get away from our former groups, the groups that gave us up, groups we saw as tired, complacent, and ineffective. We shared two common denominators. First, we were all aggressive. Second, every guy in the room had an odd personality. We were all misfits who, somehow, fit together perfectly. Because we were all crazy.

Crazy enough to go after the world's most powerful criminal organization.

We knew we were after the Cali drug cartels, but we had no idea where to start. In the beginning, I would have been happy scoring a dime bag on 110th Street from anybody claiming to be a Colombian. I was so green that I thought of busting the cartels just as I thought of any other drug bust.

I started looking for snitches.

Snitches—or confidential informants—are what make drug busts happen. You give them what they want, usually either cutting them a deal to reduce the criminal charges against them or breaking them out of jail, and they give you what you need—information. In thinking about busting the cartels I envisioned a typical snitch, some low-life, street urchin, dirt merchant—a man or woman who wore the same clothes months on end and was lucky to get stuck in a thunderstorm for a shower.

The typical snitch in my experience was an addict whose habits long ago conquered his conscience; a guy who would give up his mother for fifty bucks and a dime bag of coke. When snitches got pinched, they had to squeal on somebody—or else. "Skels," that's what we called 'em. Skeletons. We were always worried about searching them. "You got any needles on you?" we'd ask. Nobody wanted to get stuck by an addict's needle.

In 1989, the new members of Group 93, working out of our evidence locker of an office, were unable to come up with any street snitches connected to the Colombian drug cartels. So we asked each of our old units to lend us one. I went to Bobby Mistretta, an Italian stallion on the New York Joint Drug Enforcement Task Force. In those days, Bobby wore his blond hair to his shoulders, sported a pinky ring, and drove a Mercedes. I asked—no, begged—for him to lend me a snitch to get me started.

"Come on, Bobby, just loan me somebody, anybody," I said.

After thinking about it for half a second, Bobby said, "Okay, I'll loan you Gloria." He said she was a Colombian—and that was good enough for me.

Next thing I knew, Bobby and I were flying down to the Miami suburb of Kendall, Florida, and walking up to a low-rise ranch house. The doors were open. We walked around back to the pool, where the music was cranked up loud. Gloria was hosting a party. I love drug parties, where an undercover agent's actions can speak louder than words. I'm the ultimate party boy, always ready to jump up and boogie on the garbage can, if I can dance my way into some scumbag's trust.

Gloria's shindig was the typical dope dealer's ball; a crowd of layabouts on lounge chairs, guzzling frozen margaritas, shoehorning coke, and getting high. But things began to get weird. Gloria, who was on federal probation for drug smuggling, kept interrupting our interview to make out with another woman.

Bobby shrugged. "What can I say, Craze?" he said. "Didn't I tell you she was a lesbian?"

As the day dragged on, the party got louder and wilder. Gloria kept telling us what a great informant she'd make and how much she could do for the government if we let her off her probational leash. I was ready to split, figuring Gloria and all of her tips would turn out to be as wacky as she was. But then she gave us a name, a friend of hers, who, she said, was the wife of a "major" Colombian drug trafficker. Her friend was doing fifteen years to life at the all-women Bedford Hills Correctional Facility in Bedford Hills, New York.

"Estella Ochoa," Gloria said. "She wants to cooperate."

"Slow your roll," said Eddie Beach, who served as both my supervisor and my partner. He was the boss, handling the administrative aspects of our group. But he was also expected to be a working member on the street, responsible for keeping a lid on crazy agents like me.

Eddie was the 01, as we called it. Then you'd have the 02 and the 03. The longer you were there, the closer your number would move down to the 01 spot. He carried that 01 designation like a heavy load as we drove out to the Bedford Hills Correctional Facility, every inch of his big bulldog body trying to exude cool.

That's what Eddie always said: Slow your roll, meaning keep a lid on your adrenaline, your energy, your enthusiasm, your craziness. Eddie and I were polar opposites. He was from the New York State Police and I was from NYPD. He carried a notebook in which he wrote down everything including the time and contents of his breakfast, while I kept everything spinning in my head. He was burly and methodical and I was thin and wild. We were the brains of Group 93. We ran the operation.

"Slow your roll," Eddie said again as we got closer to the prison in Bedford Hills. It was a wet wintery day. No snow, but rainy. That cold brisk New York rain that blows straight into your bones. I figured that Estella Ochoa, coming from wacky Gloria, had to be another flake at best. But, I also figured, what the hell? At least she was Colombian.

Estella Ochoa was doing fifteen years, mostly thanks to her husband, Tony Ochoa. He had been busted for five hundred kilos (a thousand pounds) of coke in the home he shared with Estella in Queens, New York. Because her husband decided to fight the case, and because he lost, Estella wasn't getting an easy knock. He got twenty-five years to life, and she got fifteen. She couldn't do anything about it; the penalty for ratting on a Colombian drug dealer isn't just divorce, it's death.

I assumed we'd bust her out of jail in exchange for information—or at least we'd promise to bust her out and see what she'd give up. The women's prison at Bedford Hills is adjacent to the legendary Sing Sing men's lockup. I didn't even know where it was, but Eddie did because it was in his upstate jurisdiction when he served as a New York State Trooper.

We drove up a winding wooded road, rounded a bend, and came up over the crest of a hill. From there, I could see the two-story brick building. There were two big fenced gates with these massive brick pillars every few feet. We parked our car in the lot and started walking toward the guard booth, where we flashed our badges and told the guard who we wanted to see.

The guard led us to a locker, where we stored our guns. Then we walked through a couple more gates until we got to the front of the facility, where another officer behind a glass window checked us out again. Finally we were led through the steel doors into the dayroom, where we met Estella Ochoa.

I was worlds away from Harlem, eager to make a difference, avidly chasing the Kilo Fairy, the drug cop's term for a major hit. Walking through those steel doors, I imagined Estella as just another skel, some worn-out nag in prison rags with her hair in a bun. But then the dayroom door opened. Estella Ochoa stepped into the interrogation room, and . . .

Wow.

Hair dark as a Brooklyn blackout. Eyes like twin pools of black ink. Curves in places where some women don't even have places. Breasts that pushed the limit of the prison issued fabric. All packed tightly into a dark green prison jumpsuit like a burlap bag full of bobcats.

I rolled my tongue off the floor and tried to speak. But no words came.

Eddie Beach pulled out his notebook. "What can you do for us?" he asked Estella with a just-the-facts-ma'am stare.

"I could get you in and take them down," she said.

She swore she could give us the goods on the Ochoa family, whose members, she promised, were major operators in the Cali drug cartels. She was about as blank about the structure of the cartels as I was, but she at least knew one major player. "Julio Ochoa," she purred.

Although her husband was in jail, she said his brother, Julio, was still trafficking big time. If we freed her, Estella promised, she would fly back to Colombia, reconnect with her husband's brother, get him to deliver a big boatload of coke, and help us make our first step toward busting the cartels.

"Believe me, I can do it," she said, staring at us earnestly .

And I'm thinking, *Yes. Unlock these doors and let this beautiful Colombian bird fly out of the cell and south to Bogotá, where, back in the organization, she'll seduce its members with her beauty.*

That's how green I was.

I told her to pack up her things because we were busting her out immediately, and she'd be on the next flight to Bogotá—all of which I fully planned to do. Eddie didn't interrupt or disagree. I left that jail as if I'd just met the answer to all of my prayers, and I didn't slow my roll until I reached the special narcotic prosecutor's office—which had handled the case of *State of New York vs. Anthony Ochoa*—at Eighty Center Street in downtown Manhattan.

Still high on Estella's promises, I marched into the office of the Honorable Sterling Johnson and told him that we needed to let Estella Ochoa out of jail in exchange for her helping us bust the Cali drug cartels.

The special narcotics prosecutor laughed me out of his office.

"Forget about it!" he said. "You don't know what you're talking about."

I never saw Estella Ochoa again.

All that came out of our meeting were some beautiful memories and, of course, a name. Julio Ochoa.

———

Within the hour of getting kicked out of the special prosecutor's office, I was sitting at the computer in the Group 93 evidence locker, looking up NADDIS , the Narcotics and Dangerous Drugs Information System. It's an intelligence database controlled by DEA on all investigations and intelligence. The database has been around since the inception of the agency, which was originally the Bureau of Narcotics and Dangerous Drugs, BNDD, before it was called DEA. You can find just about anything about anybody in the drug world on NADDIS, and I relied on it regularly.

At the computer, I typed in the words *Ochoa, Julio* and *Colombia.* I hit *enter* and gasped. It was like seeing Estella Ochoa all over again—pages and pages of violations. Julio Ochoa was a USDA prime drug trafficker. A major-league violator. Sixteen NADDIS pages detailed his involvement in hundreds of cases.

Scrolling through the pages was like taking a trip around the world. He'd done major deals in Miami, LA, Fort Lauderdale, West Palm Beach, Houston, Dallas, San Antonio, and countless international points beyond. Best of all, Julio Ochoa had already been infiltrated by a CI—a confidential informant.

Negotiated with confidential informant SG1-2002 in Sao Paulo, Brazil, regarding two thousand kilos of cocaine destined for NYC, one document read. The informant's number—SG1-2002—leaped off the screen. I figured that this CI, already having dealt with Julio, could put me inside the cartel.

That's how green I was.

NADDIS doesn't give CI's names, only numbers. For the names you have to go to the case's controlling agent. So I called the DEA's Confidential Informant's Desk in Washington DC. "Who's the controlling agent for SG1-2002?" I asked.

A few minutes passed as an agent looked up the number. "He's an informant out of the Miami and Brasilia offices," the agent said. "He's controlled in Miami by Special Agent Morgan Holley and in Brasilia by Special Agent John Gratez."

I called Brasilia. No John Gratez. Transferred to nobody knows where. So I called Morgan Holley, a young DEA agent in the Miami office. "I'm Jerry Speziale, New York task force. Can you give me any information on CI SG1-2002?"

I could hear Morgan Holley take a long breath.

"Paul Lir Alexander," he said. "Unbelievable. Outstanding. Incredible CI. An international freelance informant with contacts everywhere. Works for big money. Even did intelligence work for the Mossad. . . ."

I was salivating.

"But there's one problem."

"What's that?"

"He's blacklisted. He was doing some stuff for us in Brasilia, where he not only got involved in a corruption scandal but was also suspected of dealing coke while working as a CI. The Brazilian press exposed him as an informant, and the story spun out of control. The press kept putting heat on Tom Cash."

Oh, boy. Tom Cash was the legendary, explosive special agent in charge of the Miami field division, a big, loud southern Floridian who scared the hell out of every agent beneath him. I once inadvertently parked in Cash's parking space—and he almost tore my throat out.

Paul Lir Alexander had a great deal going in Brazil, Morgan Holley told me, but his business wasn't just working undercover with the DEA. He was also doing a big cocaine business with the Cali cartels. He had created a rip-roaring graft scheme with the chief (and very crooked) narcotics officer of the South District of Rio de Janeiro. Paul and the corrupt chief cut a deal to split profits from selling whatever drug shipments Paul helped the chief narc intercept.

Everything was profitable—and safe—for both parties. When the corrupt chief was replaced by a new chief narcotics officer, the former chief offered the same deal to the new guy. But the new narc turned out to be a Boy Scout. A "sting" operation was set to trap Paul, but Paul's informants tipped him off and he fled to Miami. So Paul got off scott-free, except for the DEA blackball.

"The press kept asking Cash, 'Who is this Paul Alexander?' and 'What's he doing?' 'Is he working for the U.S. government?'" said

Holley. "Cash finally said, 'Get him off our books. Make him disappear so we don't have to answer any more questions.' So Paul gets blacklisted. He's ordered to change his name and generally disappear . . . forever. He recedes into the shadows never to be heard from again."

Until now. The minute I heard Paul's name, I knew I had discovered my drug enforcement destiny. I had to find Paul Lir Alexander and bring him back into the fold. "I gotta find him!" I told Morgan Holley. "I've got to talk to him to see if he can help me bring down Julio Ochoa."

"Listen, get over it," Holley said. "The guy's damaged goods."

But I wouldn't listen. "I'll find him," I said. "What's his name again?"

"Paul Lir Alexander," Holley said. "But he's also Pedro Chamoro. Jose Oscar Arguello. David Coleman. He has a dozen different names and aliases. You're never gonna to find him, and you're gonna destroy your career if you ever do."

———

I bet Eddie Beach a month of lunches that I'd find Paul Lir Alexander. I raced back to the computer and began searching the DEA database, Nexis/Lexis, ChoicePoint and a dozen different search engines, for any information about Paul Lir Alexander. Before long, I had assembled a list of old addresses, some utility and electric bills, as well as post office boxes he'd used at Mailboxes USA and Mail Boxes, Etc., two of the many post offices of choice for the international drug trade.

I flew to Miami, one of Paul Lir Alexander's last known residences, and went to work knocking on doors, making connections, and mailing out postcards to Paul with what I considered some irresistible bait: *My name is Jerry Speziale, New York task force, and I want to clear your name.*

I left messages with his ex-wife, his neighbors, with bartenders, dry cleaners, supermarket clerks, any path on which Paul Lir Alexander might have traveled. Somehow I felt certain this big fish was going to take my bait.

3

Paul

It was the end of another perfect day on the Florida coast. A cool breeze came in off the sea, and as it mingled with hot air still rising from the Miami Beach sand, the world seemed to sigh in relief at the setting of the sun.

On the flagstone porch of a modern, glass-wrapped beach house, Paul Lir Alexander sat drinking Pellegrino mixed with orange juice. Paul ignored the crimson and salmon sunset that reached up over the palms behind the house. He ignored the sleepy wash of waves over the sand, and the happy laughter of children nearby. His attention was focused, as always, on business.

A long time ago, Paul had learned the best way to make big money from the massive cocaine trade in his native Brazil. Smuggling wasn't the answer. He knew plenty of smugglers, and most of them ended up dead long before they got rich. It was much safer to be a crooked cop, but there was a limit to the wealth one could build by taking bribes.

The best way to make money from cocaine was not from selling coke, but selling information to the highest bidder. In the early nineties, the highest bidder was the government of the United States. The deal was always the same, 20 percent of all cash seized as a direct result of whatever information the confidential informant provided. Not long ago, Paul Alexander had gotten very rich this way.

Paul enjoyed the lifestyle of a wealthy entrepreneur with a dozen different South American businesses—shoes, entertainment, tourism.

You name it, he did it. But most of all he fancied himself an intellectual, an anthropologist with a master's degree in economics who loved dusty books and Byzantine researches. His favorite subject was American law enforcement.

Paul Alexander was an importer/exporter, and his main client was the Cali cocaine cartel. He was fiercely loyal to this organization, and he'd gained a reputation for his willingness to take extraordinary risks. *El Parito Loco*—that's what they called him. The Crazy Bird. He was crazy enough to do what few Cali men ever dreamed of doing, do business with the investigative power of the American government with one hand and the deadly Cali cocaine cartel with the other.

A month passed. Eddie Beach was ready to start collecting on his lunches. But I refused to give up.

One day, the unit phone rang in our office. I picked it up.

"Why you look for me?"

The five words were spoken in a cool, calm, calculated Brazilian accent, a slow and steady monotone like a record being played at the slowest speed. His question was totally different from the typical snitch call, which is usually, "Hey, yo-yo, it's me! Cool from down the street!"

It had to be Paul.

"Paul, Paul it's me, Jerry! Jerry Speziale! I want to clear your name! When can we get together?"

All he said was, "Tonight, seven o'clock, Sheraton Center. Lobby."

And he hung up.

That night the hotel was, as always, full of tourists and conventioneers. I paced the lobby in my usual office uniform—tight red Lou Costello Gym T-shirt, jeans, sneakers, and a golden Christ head on a neck chain. The lobby was a sea of faces and I was wondering how I'd recognize Paul Lir Alexander, when I felt a tap on my shoulder.

I turned around and saw a short, pale, and expressionless guy in his early thirties, all dressed up for dinner. He wore expensive-looking shoes, a dark well-cut suit with banker's suspenders, and a fancy shirt and tie. He looked more like an overworked, middle-aged American businessman than an infamous Brazilian CI, just a flabby little milquetoast of a man whose face had gone slack from too much work and worry. His black hair was parted perfectly to the side with almost imperceptible hair plugs supplementing his receding hairline. He carried a black leather attaché case. He stared at me through horn-rimmed glasses, and all he said was, "Cop, come with me."

I followed him outside to the street, where a stretch limo was waiting. On the drive downtown, I talked about my successes in the drug war, about my awards, commendations, and medals, about how I got over as an undercover narc in Harlem, about how I masqueraded for three years as a junkie to bust whole neighborhoods of dealers. I thought I was impressing Paul when I told him I was one of only eighty out of five thousand NYPD detectives to be promoted into the New York Drug Enforcement Task Force, and how I finally felt ready to take on Colombian kingpins like Julio Ochoa, then get to work on the Cali cartels and rid the streets of New York of coke forever. I didn't stop gabbing until we got all the way to Little Italy, where we went into an Italian Mob restaurant. We sat down to dinner, surrounded by tables full of swarthy men and overdressed women.

That's when Paul finally spoke.

"No, no, no," he said, shaking his head. "Let me explain something to you, Jerry. You act like a cop. You talk like a cop. You think like a cop. You *smell* like a cop. If you think you're going to get close to the cartels, you're crazy. They'll smell you a mile away, and they will kill you."

"If you could just call and get a conversation going with Julio Ochoa," I said. "Maybe we can get the two thousand kilos that you were negotiating with him about in Brazil."

I thought the cartel was some small club, where everybody knew everybody. I thought Paul could just call Ochoa and set him up for a bust, just like I'd set up Rojeto and Paulie and a thousand other junkies in Harlem.

Paul shook his head again. "You don't have the first clue about the cartels," he said.

The waiter arrived. I ordered a drink and multiple courses for dinner. Paul drank iced tea and asked for a tuna salad. He was all discipline and self-control, while I was all intake and outbursts.

"Julio Ochoa, Julio Ochoa," I repeated like a mantra.

"Jerry, please," Paul said. "Forget Julio Ochoa. He's about as significant as a gnat on the ass of a mosquito when it comes to the enormity of the cartels. He's probably just an investor with customers in the States. This is a global operation, Jerry, with infinite operatives."

But I was still stuck in Jersey. "If we could bust Julio Ochoa, it would at least give us a start in busting the organization," I said.

I took another slug of vodka while Paul stared at me like you'd stare at some pitiful mutt on a street corner.

"The cartels are not an organization, Jerry," Paul said in a low whisper. "They're an *association* of drug traffickers."

I realized it was time to keep my mouth shut and let him talk.

"There are various distribution cells throughout the world that operate independently and are given cocaine shipments from the cartels on consignment," Paul continued. "They guarantee these shipments with their lives, and the lives of their families back in Colombia. These cells, like all the associates of the cartels, have compartmentalized operations. So the partners on one deal—the manufacturers, transporters, money launderers, and so forth—may never be partners on another deal again. There's a purchasing department, a payroll department, a distribution department, all designed to keep everything separated—and every aspect is designed to be impossible to infiltrate."

The waiter stopped by to ask if we needed anything. Paul shook his head no. "Who invented all this?" I asked.

"The families of the Cali cartel," Paul said. "Everyone associated with the distribution of cocaine—investors, transporters, producers—all have to be approved by one of the families near Cali, Colombia, where the majority of the world's cocaine is grown, produced, and distributed."

He started counting out the families on each of the manicured fingers on his right hand. When he raised his hand, I got a close-up of his wristwatch, a bejeweled Rolex that looked like it could tell time in a dozen languages.

"The two Rodriguez-Orejuela brothers, Chepe Santacruz-Londono, Pacho Herrera, and Victor Patino. These five and others control all the cocaine shipments that come out of the Valle de Cali, the valley outside of Cali, the second largest city in Colombia. And the families control the coke world with an iron fist. Anyone who wants to move a load out of Cali, or anywhere else in Colombia, has to get blessings from the families. No one circumvents the families. If they do, they've signed their death warrant. If anyone gets caught doing a load without permission of the cartels, without the permission of the families or their representatives, they will be killed, or their loads will be stolen—or most likely both."

Of course, I was impatient. I thought, *Why not just bust the families?* But Paul was way ahead of me.

"Forget about it," he said. "They have attorneys around the world and use the U.S. discovery laws to figure out how law enforcement has infiltrated them in the past, and how they might be infiltrated in the future. And they've designed strategies to prevent being infiltrated again."

I felt a bird in the hand was better than a flock of traffickers in the bush. I wanted to bust Julio Ochoa right then and there, immediate gratification, just like I'd gotten every night as Crazy Jerry in Harlem. So I interrupted Paul a dozen times.

"No, Jerry, you're not listening to me," Paul would say at each interruption. "Please pay attention!"

He held up a hand and waited for silence before saying another word.

"Here's how it works," he said. "There's a group of investors like you or me, or okay, this Julio Ochoa, and we want to become involved in a load. We have to go to a representative of one of the Cali families to be sanctioned to move the load. The families get a piece of the action because they control everything. One of the Cali families controls the laboratories producing the product, another controls the ports and all the loading, another family has the planes and pilots for transportation. . . . But to move the loads they need legwork—infinite associates and foreign cells handling production, transportation, and distribution."

Listening to Paul, I began to see the international dimensions, the magnitude and sophistication of the operation. The reports we'd written about the structure of the drug trade were useless. We hadn't scratched the surface.

"Okay," I said. "How do we break through and bust these guys?"

"The way into the cartel isn't though Julio Ochoa, whoever he is,"

Paul said. "The only way to bust the cartel is to become part of it. To become associated with it."

"And how do we do that?" I asked.

"By providing a service that they need," he said.

"So what do they need?" I asked.

"First, they need investors," Paul said. "Through my contacts, we could invest in a shipment of cocaine with the cartels. When the load arrives in the U.S., we'd be privy to where it's being stored because we own a portion of the shipment. But that's risky. And we only have one shot. The kilos are going to come in, and once we bust the buyers, we've got to lock them up—and we've blown our cover forever."

"Right," I agreed. "But it's impossible. I could never get the government to approve a million dollars to invest in an illegal cocaine shipment that I might never see."

Paul slid his chair a little closer to mine and raised two fingers. "Number two, we could become money launderers. We pick up money for a load, charge a percentage, and launder the money through the banking system. We could then follow the bank leads to the accounts where the money was wired and wait until these accounts get fat. Then we'd issue seizure warrants and reap millions."

"That's beautiful, Paul!" I exclaimed. "We'll make big money hits and big coke seizures at the same time!"

He held up his hand to stop me. "Not so fast. Every deal is designed to keep the money separated from the drugs. So if there's a loss on the drug side, it won't spread to the money side—and vice versa. Years ago, they kept both the cash and the coke in stash houses, but after being busted a few times they made sure that the money-laundering cells never store the proceeds in the area where the drug cells are storing the coke. The money-laundering cells don't commingle with the drug distribution cells. So the only seizure you'd be making is of money. As money launderers, we'd never bust anybody. Because the accounts are going to be in bogus names."

Paul leaned back in his chair and up went three fingers. "The third way in is transportation," he said. "That's what the cartels need most. We could become transporters. That's where the real money is. That's also my area of expertise. It's what I know best."

"Okay, tell me more."

"We'd pose as transporters, creating a front as international importers and exporters, opening our own businesses in South America so we look legitimate. We'll have the cartels fly us shipments of cocaine to midpoints in Central America, where we'll provide airstrips and refueling facilities. From that midpoint, we'd be responsible for taking the loads and bringing them into the U.S. for delivery to the customers of the cartel. We could then arrange to have the customers busted when they pick up the loads."

He told me that he already was involved in South American diamond mines, shoe factories, and entertainment companies. So setting up the dummy corporations wouldn't be difficult.

"It's a big job," Paul said. "First, we have to go to Guatemala—"

"Why don't we start in Houston?" I said. "I've got great contacts there." When Eddie Beach and I were still in Group 77, we did a wiretap on a cell phone on a Miami-based smuggler who regularly traveled to Houston. We spent a month in Houston, working with the local branch of the DEA.

"No, it must be Guatemala, the only main transshipment point for the Colombian traffickers," Paul said. "That's where we'll take control of the cartel's shipments. Once we're in Guatemala, we'll have to rent some farmer's field out in the jungle and build an airstrip to land the smuggler's planes."

Now my head was swimming. "Rent a farm?" I asked. "Are you kiddin' me? I could never even begin to get approval for that!"

That interruption was apparently the last straw for Paul. He tried to signal for the check, but I stopped him before he could catch the waiter's eye. I promised to stop interrupting, and Paul continued telling me about how to bust the cartels.

"We will have to personally receive planes on our airstrips," he said. "We'll off-load tons of cocaine, refuel the planes to return to Colombia, and then be responsible for transporting the loads into the U.S. and delivering them to the distribution cells. Then, once we deliver the drugs to the stateside distributors, we walk away with the money and the backup teams seizes both the drugs and the distributors."

I loved it. I was ready to fly south immediately—and to hell with regulations and permissions from the brass. But Paul held up his hand before I could say a word.

"There's only one catch, and it's a big one," he said. "It's absolutely imperative that we always shift the blame for the bust to the other parties involved in the deal. Because whoever's holding the load when the deal goes down is dead."

"I know we've got an embassy in Guatemala," I said. "But I'll be honest with you. I don't even know what airline flies down there, much less how to begin to pull off this type of operation. If you'll show me, I'll do whatever I have to do, even if I have to spend my own money and break every rule in the book."

"Please, slow down," Paul said. "Let's take it point by point. First, you've got to listen to me. All right?"

"All right."

I soon realized that Paul didn't really want his old job back, and he didn't seem to give a damn about clearing his name. He wanted money, *big* money, 20 percent of all cash seizures. He was also motivated by ego. The more time I spent with Paul, the more I became convinced that ego was the key to his personality. He just believed that he was the best at whatever he did and he was eager to prove it.

"I don't work for nothing," he said. "I want you to pay me, and I want you to pay me *very* big. I plan to work for the government for a couple of years, and then retire a multimillionaire."

The most I had ever paid a drug informant in the past was two hundred dollars. Getting cash from the NYPD was like pulling teeth. I didn't tell Paul that. I said, "Yes! Of course! No problem, Paul!"

"Point by point," Paul said again. "Second, please go back and see if you can remove me from the blacklist. If you can, I'll be willing to take the gamble and try to train you."

"Train me?" I asked.

Paul looked me up and down, as though appraising livestock.

"I'll show you what to wear, how to speak, and how to act. You'll have to follow my every word, and forget everything you've learned from these idiot agents. After we go through how to dress, which will be exclusively Armani, and how to talk, which will include Spanish, and not like a gringo, I'm going to get you a passport. I'm going to teach you how to travel, and how to fly a plane and build a landing strip in the middle of the jungle. I'm going to teach you how to set up businesses, about importing and exporting and about currency and commodities in different countries."

My head was swimming. I had rarely left the New York City area. But I was ready to follow wherever Paul led me.

Paul signaled the waiter for the check. "I'm going to recreate you, Jerry," he said before we left the restaurant. "I'm going to make you into an international drug trafficker, and if you listen to me and follow all of my rules, point by point, you will become the most famous narcotics agent in the world." He shot me a grin. "But first, of course, you must get me off the blacklist."

"Piece of cake, partner!" I lied. "I'll take care of it first thing in the morning."

4

Coke Dealer
Charm School

First thing next morning, I grabbed a DEA manual and discovered—what a surprise!—it's *impossible* to reinstate a blacklisted informant *unless* you can prove he once again has credibility and can become an asset to the government. So, I decided, that would be my story. Paul could be an invaluable asset in the war against drugs.

The first part was easy. I banged out some fancy creative writing that made Paul look as innocent as a Sunday school teacher, yet at the same time so well connected to the Colombian drug lords that he could bring down the entire cartel with a few phone calls.

The second part was not so easy. I had to get John Maltz, special agent in charge of the New York Drug Enforcement Task Force, to sign off on my request. A legendary street narc for most of his thirty-year career, Maltz had the body of Hulk Hogan and a hairdo to match. He was one mean SOB; but, thank goodness, I was one of his boys.

Because he was the chief, and had to sign off on my official activities, I was constantly in his office while everyone else was petrified to go near it. He liked my energy and enthusiasm—or so I thought.

When I went in to see Maltz about the matter of Paul Lir Alexander, I felt like a kid on my way to the woodshed for a whipping. But I stuffed the fear down deep in my gut and revved up my roll to full-tilt boogie.

"Chief!" I blurted without pausing to say hello. "Oh, man, listen, Chief, we picked up a new snitch last night, and we gotta sign him up!

This guy is the best, Chief. Solid gold. He's gonna be the greatest CI the DEA has ever seen. I promise you!"

Maltz was hunched over a stack of papers that seemed tiny in his massive hands. He didn't even look up at me over his reading glasses. "Get outta my office" was all he said.

"B-but, Chief," I stammered.

"You don't know what you're talking about," he added, making a note on one of the papers. "Take your buy-and-bust bullshit out of my face."

As if I still needed an exit cue, the cell phone in my pocket rang.

"Hold on a second, Chief," I said, taking the call. "This is my guy." Backing out of his office, phone to my ear, I could see Maltz scowling and shaking his head. I was impervious.

"Speziale here," I said.

"Hello, Jerry," said Paul in his cool, lightly accented voice. "I'm back at the office in Miami. Did you run into any walls about the blacklist?"

"Paul, you won't believe what I'm going through today! I've been on the phone with DC, talking to the DEA bigwigs. Hey, it's gonna be okay."

"That's good, Jerry, very good," Paul said, deadpan. "Once you're done with that, we go to the second part."

"Yeah, yeah," I said. "We gotta get to work right away, but this paperwork's takin' a little longer than I thought."

"Plenty of time for paperwork, my friend. It'll be quite a long time before you're ready to do any real work with me."

"What are you talkin' about, Paul?"

"Look, Jerry. I'm flying back up to New York in a couple days. Let's meet at Le Cirque for lunch and talk about clothes and a few other things."

"Le *what*?" I said.

"Le Cirque, it's a restaurant at Madison and Fiftieth. I'll meet you at 8 P.M, Wednesday. The table will be reserved in my name."

"Sure, sure," I said, glad to stall a few days to work on the blacklist.

"Oh, and, Jerry?" Paul said.

"Yeah, Paul?"

"Bring your credit card, my friend."

I returned to my desk to brainstorm a new strategy for dealing with Maltz. Obviously the BS approach wasn't working. Maybe, I thought, I should just lay it all out. I waited for Maltz to get back from lunch, and went back to his door. This time I knocked.

"Yeah?" snarled the voice behind the door. I opened it a crack and stuck my head through.

"Got a second, Chief?" I asked in a meek voice.

That got him. He actually invited me inside.

He let me take a seat and tell him about Paul, but interrupted me halfway through my spiel. "Why are you telling me this, Jerry? If you like him, sign him up. What the hell do I care?"

"Well, Chief. I need *you* to sign off on him. He got into some trouble down in Brazil, and he's on the DEA blacklist."

"Now we're getting to the point." Maltz said. "Gimme the sheet, asshole."

Maltz signed the reactivation request without even reading it. "It's probably just a load of crap anyway," he said. "Next time, Speziale, cut the theatrics, start with the important part, and see how much more I want to hear. Okay?"

"You got it, Chief," I said, standing up to leave before he changed his mind.

Two days later, I was eating snails at Le Cirque, one of New York's pricey five-star restaurants, and Paul was shaking his head "no!"

I looked around the restaurant, which was full of fat men in suits and ties and fancy women dripping jewelry. It took my eyes some time to focus. The restaurant was an explosion of lights and color, like being in some kind of crazy circus tent. I had scanned the right side of the menu; there was nothing for much less than twenty dollars, and the snails that Paul insisted I try were something like twenty-five.

"Tch, tch, tch, Jerry," he said. "You even eat escargots like a cop."

I exploded. "Jesus, Paul! *You* ordered these things for me—and you're eating tuna fish. I didn't want any goddamn snails! First you make me eat this funky shit and then you make fun of me for eating it wrong."

Paul sipped his Perrier with lemon while I gestured to the hovering waiter for another shot of Grey Goose. I had ordered it after Paul modified my initial request—Absolut—by barking, "Jerry, Absolut is cheap."

Paul folded his napkin on the meal and signaled the waiter for the $225 check, which I paid. He told me to keep my credit card ready.

Because we were going shopping.

"In this neighborhood?" I said. "Fegitaboutit. I'm not even sure how I'm going to expense the dinner."

"Look, Jerry," Paul said, "you smell like a cop. You act like a cop. And you look like a cop." He looked me up and down. "The off-duty cop outfit has to go," he said. "Look at how I'm dressed."

I had to admit Paul was immaculate. Every time I saw him, he was dressed like a successful investment banker. The three-thousand-dollar suit, the silk suspenders, the perfect tie, the finest Ferragamo shoes, and a pair of horn-rimmed glasses—for that intellectual look. (Did he need them? God only knows.) I think Paul slept in those clothes, standing up in the closet. You could go to his hotel room at four in the morning to debrief him, and he'd be wearing Armani.

"You think I care how much this stuff cost?" he asked me. "If you want to make a million bucks, you must look like a million bucks."

At the coat check he handed me his fancy black leather briefcase. "It's called a Bogotá bag," he said. "And you've got to have one if you're going to get inside the cartel. It's like a code with these people. Every respectable drug smuggler has a Bogotá bag. We'll have to get you one, Jerry, if you're going to meet with the right people. I'll get you one on my next trip to Bogotá."

I cracked up. "You act like I'm Julia Roberts and you're Richard Gere," I said.

"What are you talking about?" Paul asked as we stepped onto Madison Avenue.

"You know. In that movie *Pretty Woman*. You think you're the rich guy who picks up the cheap whore and makes her all fancy and presentable."

"Well, at least you've got the whore part right, Jerry," Paul said, checking the time on his gold Patek Phillippe Nautilus. He must have left his Rolex home that day. "But you are no Julia Roberts, my friend."

"Yeah, well, Julia Roberts didn't have to pay for her new outfit," I said.

We walked over to Fifth, and Paul ushered me down a block full of expensive boutiques.

We passed a snappy Euro-American number in a shop window. "Hey, now, this I like!" I said, stopping to admire it.

"Jerry, that suit is junk," Paul said with a grimace. "It's garbage. No self-respecting smuggler would be caught, even in a casket, in a suit like that."

Paul led me down the street a few doors, and into his favorite men's store. The salesmen gathered around as if he were a rock star.

"Don't lag behind, Jerry," Paul ordered. "Your suit must be either Ermenegildo Zegna, Brioni, or Armani. Do you notice a pattern here? All Italian. Think Italian, my friend, and maybe we can get rid of that cop smell that you're trailing behind you."

He led me through the racks of clothing, talking all the while. "Listen closely, Jerry," Paul said. "In shirts, like suits, you must always think Italian."

Before I knew it, I was in a Brioni suit (three thousand dollars), a Grupo Italiano shirt (five hundred), and Paul and his sales team were leading me into the shoe department.

"For shoes, always Bruno Magli or Salvatore Ferragamo," Paul said. He handed me a pair of buttery Ferragamo wing tips. I checked the price tag: $495.

I refused to make any purchases. There was no way I could afford anything he showed me. I knew I had no chance of getting the task force to pay for any of this stuff, but I figured it was at least worth a shot.

The next morning, I had a requisition sheet waiting on Maltz's desk. He almost spewed his coffee when he read it.

"Jesus, mother of God, Jerry!" he shrieked. "You want five hundred bucks for a pair of shoes, and three grand for a suit?" Not only did he say no, he posted my requisition sheet for the whole division to howl over.

———

Maltz did come through for me on one big-ticket item, one doozy of a car. The best thing about drug dealers is the cars they drive. They're the same cars we get to seize once we arrest them. When I went to pick up Paul at his hotel for our second shopping spree, I was driving a champagne-colored, V-12 BMW 750 IL with only three thousand miles on the odometer. Sticker price, $85,000.

When I pulled up to the Sheraton Center, I had a Lambada CD blaring full blast and the sunroof open.

"You're starting to get the idea, my friend," Paul said, smiling.

But when he directed me back to Fifth Avenue, I said, "No way."

He looked at me and raised an eyebrow.

"Look, Paul, I'll spend my retirement money on Italian clothes, but I'm not going to be buried in a three-thousand-dollar Brioni suit."

I drove him to a perfectly respectable discount shop, where I found an acceptable Armani for sixteen hundred, but it looked like a potato sack on me.

Paul laughed. "Well, of course, you must have it tailored, Jerry. You didn't think they fit this well off the rack, did you?" He gestured lovingly over his own tailored suit as an example. He was right. That suit didn't just fit him; it looked as if he were born to wear it.

Finally, embarrassment of embarrassments, I pulled into a deep discount men's shop. Paul ducked his head. "Please, Jerry, somebody might see me going in here," he said. But now it was my turn to lead.

"I am *not* going to pay seventy-five bucks for a pair of socks, damn it," I said.

Paul stood disapprovingly as I picked out a few nice ties, some suspenders, and dress socks—all for the Fifth Avenue price of a single silk tie. But when I started browsing the shirt racks, Paul stopped me cold.

"No, no, no, absolutely not, Jerry. No shirts here! The shirts are much too important. They're sure to notice a cheap shirt." I laughed, thinking back to the stained T-shirts I was wearing not too long ago as Crazy Jerry, and allowed Paul take me back uptown for a couple of four-hundred-dollar Zegnas.

We stayed uptown for the jewelry: David Yurman cuff links ("You gotta have good cuff links for the French cuffs"); gold tie pin by some foreign designer with an unpronounceable name; and finally, what Paul called the pièce de résistance, a fifteen-thousand-dollar Rolex Oyster Perpetual wristwatch with "a champagne-colored dial to match your new BMW."

"No, no, no, no," I said. "You do not understand. I know where to get a Rolex for much less." I drove Paul down to Canal Street, into a neighborhood I'm sure he'd never seen before, and found a guy selling fake Rolexes out of a cardboard box.

"Perfect!" I said strapping one on. "And only fifteen bucks!"

Paul just shook his head.

"You have a lot to learn, my friend," he said.

———

While our first deal was being set up, and before we began surveying airstrips in helicopters, Paul said over dinner one night, "Jerry, you must learn how to fly a plane."

"Yeah, sure, Paul." I laughed, looking up from the menu. "Anything you say."

"No, I'm serious, Jerry," Paul insisted. "You must be an authority on distance, aeronautics, runway surface, planes, fuel. You must know the difference between Avgas and jet A. You must know everything about latitude and longitude. You must know everything there is to know about flying."

The next day, I looked in the yellow pages and found a listing for McDan Aircraft School in Fairfield, New Jersey. I drove over and signed up for flying lessons. The plan was to take fifty-five hours of flight instruction, enough to learn the mechanics of flying, but not enough to take the final exam required to become a licensed pilot.

I don't care how tough you think you are, learning to fly is a nerve-racking experience. I went for my first flight lesson, and the instructor looked like he was about nineteen years old. I was immediately uncomfortable. I was expecting someone older. I would be the student of some punk at least ten years younger than me? This couldn't be happening. Worst of all, he called me "sir."

"Okay, sir, please buckle up," he said, as we put on our headphones and prepared for our first lesson aloft in a little plane after a few days of classroom instruction. The instructor took me through the preflight drill; then up we went over New Jersey.

It was March and it was cold in the cockpit. Through my headset, I heard the instructor say, "Okay, sir, it's all yours. I want you to do a forty-five degree turn to the left, then a ninety degree turn to the right; then I want you to go up and stall."

I started trembling uncontrollably. My teeth were chattering and my hands were shaking on the controls. I looked over at the instructor, pure panic written all over my face.

"Are you okay?" he asked.

"Well, it's really cold up here," I said.

"Are you sure you're okay?" he asked again.

I turned and said, "No, I'm not okay. Take the controls and put it on the ground. I'm not okay."

Safe on the ground, I laid off the flight lessons for a week or two. Then I returned to finish what I'd started.

———

After I got through the flight lessons, I met Paul for lunch at some Park Avenue clip joint to celebrate. I was feeling pretty proud of myself. I'd put together a serviceable drug-trafficker costume, managing to save a few thousand bucks in the process, and I'd learned the basics of flying.

"Okay, Paul, I did my part, now you do yours," I said. "It's time to set up some 'cred' with your guys."

Cred. Short for credibility. A street narc doesn't need much cred to bust a shooting gallery, which is how Crazy Jerry could get by on just a lunatic routine. But to move up in the drug trade, to enter the hallowed hallways of the Cali cartels, you've got to make yourself known as a major player. I wasn't looking to move up a few notches. I wanted to go all the way to the top.

Paul picked at his salad. "You're not ready yet, Jerry," he said.

"Whaddaya mean?" I exploded. "I bought the suit! Let's use it!"

"Best to wait awhile, my friend," he said.

"Wait for what, Paul?"

I could see him staring at my head.

"Well, to start with, there's the hair. You look like a hippie."

"Okay, I'll get a haircut."

"Not just any haircut, Jerry. I want you to go to the Frederick Fekkai Salon at Bergdorf's. Tomorrow. Tell Manny I sent you."

"Who the hell is Manny?"

"Only the master of men's hairstyling. Be careful what you say to Manny. He knows a lot of people."

"Okay, I got it. Haircut by Manny at Bergdorf's. Anything else?"

Paul looked me over, attempting to envision the final image.

"Well, even with the haircut and the clothes, you still reek of cop."

"Oh, for Chrissakes!"

"You need something else," he said. "Some edge."

He thought for a moment, flashed a little grin, and said two words. "Facial hair!"

"Okay, Paul, facial hair."

"But not a moustache, please, Jerry," he said.

"Fine. No moustache. So whaddya want? An Abe Lincoln beard?"

"Don't be stupid," he said. "A small, dignified goatee. Just stop shaving your chin, please. And one more thing . . ."

"Yes, Paul?"

He pointed to the little silver stud I wore in one ear, a remnant of my Crazy Jerry rigging.

"The earring must go, Jerry. Too eighties."

I popped the earring out and dropped it on the floor.

"Thank you so much, Jerry. Now, what you were saying about credibility?"

I told him I thought we should start flashing money around, maybe make a few buys, to establish a reputation with his guys.

"It doesn't work that easily, Jerry," Paul said. "So you show up as a buyer, pick up a few kilos here and there. You think that's going to make them trust you for transporting? No way. Don't you think they're gonna wonder why some guys calling themselves transporters are going around buying kilos at street prices? If you think that's going to give you credibility as a transporter, you're crazy. The fake Rolex will only get you so far."

"Okay, how about a more direct approach? What if we just show 'em a big stack of cash and say we want into the biz?"

"You want to beg these men?" Paul asked. He didn't hide his disgust.

"Not beg, Paul. Buy in."

"You'll leave that deal in a body bag," Paul said. "Cops chase, cops beg. Colombian drug traffickers do not chase, and they don't trust anyone who does."

I knew Paul was right about the begging. As Crazy Jerry, I'd be happy to stand on the corner with a sign on my head if that's what the dealers wanted. It was an acceptable strategy for a crazy, desperate junkie, but no way to act with the big boys.

"You have to be cocky, sure," Paul said, "But you must be able to back up the attitude. Don't forget you're getting ready to ask these dealers to trust you with forty or fifty million dollars worth of cocaine. That kind of credibility usually comes from a reference, preferably one from a Colombian. Which, of course, we don't have, since I've been out of transporting for a long time." He ordered coffee, and I pondered the problem.

"Screw it," I said. "Let's just flash 'em some coke."

That got Paul's attention.

"What coke?" he asked. "How much coke?"

"Well, how about a ton?" I asked.

"And how are you going to get a ton of coke, Jerry?"

"I'll sign it out from the evidence vault, and set it up in a van."

Paul dropped his coffee spoon. "Wait a minute. Say that again please?"

"We have an evidence vault down on Tenth Avenue. I can check out like a ton of coke, and then, when we're finished, I'll check it back in again."

Sinking back into his chair, Paul looked at me. "Keep talking, Jerry," he said, with a type of smile I'd never seen on his face before.

The plan was simple. When I finished laying it out, Paul jumped to his feet, letting his napkin fall to the floor. It was the first time I'd ever seen him lose his composure. Beaming, he grabbed my hand and pumped it as if I'd just won the lottery.

"Brilliant, Jerry. It's brilliant, and I think it will work!" From then on, he looked at me a little differently. The fact that I could put my hands on that much cocaine made me more respectable in Paul's eyes. He stopped talking about my cop look, my cop attitude, my cop smell. Paul was so excited, he wanted to go to work right away. He made me take him straight over to 108th Street and Roosevelt, in Jackson Heights, Queens, to a Tele-Paranda. He needed to make a call.

There are about three hundred Tele-Parandas in a three-mile area of Jackson Heights. Tele-Parandas are how South Americans drug dealers call home. A Tele-Paranda is a grimy little telephone shop, where you pay a clerk in a glass booth and then walk back to your assigned cubicle to make the call. It's a totally untraceable phone system with lines that are impossible to tap, which is why they're so popular with drug smugglers.

Paul led me into the cubicle, where I watched him make a few calls to Colombia. He was calling to get us some cred, he said. Sure, we had access to coke, but what good was coke without references? You can't just call up a Cali associate and say, "Come look at our load." To get some cred, we'd have to do some advertising.

"Avelino and Alonso," he said in the Tele-Paranda.

He knew them from his CI days. Avelino Devia Galvis was a hungry freelance broker who'd sell his mother for a nickel bag, and Alonso Tobon was an importer/exporter of fruit pulp, bananas, and cocaine out of Bogotá. They were fringe Cali operators, but close enough to help us lure bigger fish.

"All we have to do is suck them in," said Paul.

The bait would, of course, be money. Play to their greed, Paul said, and we'd have Avelino and Alonso in the palm of our hands. They'd swear to our authenticity, if we could hook them with cash.

"The trick is to make them part of our crew," Paul told me. "To get them involved in our success, because if we make money, then they make money, too. And once you get them thinking about the money, they'll lie through their teeth for us."

Paul called Avelino and Alonso from the Tele-Paranda and laid out the deal to the brokers. From the elementary Spanish I had picked up as a street cop, I could understand a little of what Paul was saying, but not much. But pretty soon, after a few trips to Central and South America, I'd be on my way to being halfway fluent in Spanish, learning the language as I learned the countries, hanging out in dives, mixing with locals, becoming one of them.

Paul told them that he'd found a new partner in transportation, one Geraldo Bartone, and that we'd transported a load for a group who couldn't come up with the transportation fee. That left us with four hundred kilos of grade-A coke on our hands.

"Do you know anyone who might want to take the load?" Paul asked. And by the way, he'd be willing to give them a finder's fee of, say, a thousand dollars a kilo, meaning that if they could find a buyer for the four hundred kilos they'd walk away with forty thousand dollars.

I could imagine Avelino and Alonso salivating all the way from Bogotá. They told Paul that they'd have a customer by the next morning. And I just knew those two hungry wolves frantically began calling every mook they knew, saying they'd found a dream load and swearing that they'd done business with us forever.

———

A few days later, Paul and I returned to the Tele-Paranda. Paul dialed a number, had a short conversation, and after a few minutes, put the phone down. "Next Tuesday," he said.

"What about next Tuesday?" I asked.

"That's when we do this. That's when we need the coke. They're sending Freddy Herrera to check out the shipment."

"Who's he?" I asked.

"Nephew of 'Don Pacho,' Helmer Herrera, a big player in the Cali cartel," he said. "Point by point, Jerry, remember, point by point. Number one, get the coke."

"Sure, no problem," I said. "So, uh, exactly how much do we need?"

"We need to make this totally real," Paul said. "So you'll need precisely the amount that will fit into your van, I mean the van that you're going to convince the task force to let us use. Not one ounce less. No one smuggling coke ever wastes transportation space—it's too valuable. And another thing. Freddy Herrera is no idiot. So this can't be coke from five years ago. Recent labels only—Rolex and La Reina."

I knew all about the brands. Jungle cocaine labs in Colombia use their own unique labels to distinguish one product from another. "Lewinsky" was a popular brand a while back, along with "Starr" and "Hillary." Labeling product was about the only part of the coke trade where a sense of humor was accepted. In the months when Paul and I were discussing this particular deal, "Rolex," "La Reina (the Queen)," and "Clinton" were the primo coke brands.

"I don't know what we've got, but it's fresh and it's great," I said.

"Remember, Jerry," Paul warned, "if we show up with a mix of too many different labels, we're dead. That would never happen in

Colombia—different product is kept separate. Transporters might have three or four different labels in one shipment, but that's it."

"Oh, no problem," I said. "We just had a few big busts recently. I'm sure we've got lots of fresh stuff."

I hoped I was right.

5

The Flash

After dropping Paul at his hotel, I headed straight for the bulk-storage vault to find out if anything I'd just told him was true. I'd made a few trips to evidence vaults in my time, but always to check stuff *in*. I knew the seized van would be easy to get—after all, I was driving a dealer's BMW—but I didn't really know if I could "borrow" evidence from the vault, and if I could I had no idea how much they'd let me walk away with.

First stop, the impound lot adjacent to the DEA headquarters on Fifty-seventh Street and Eleventh Avenue. The impound lot occupied an entire city block and had a twenty-foot fence with black slats so nobody could see the confiscated rigs that were parked inside. I did one better than a van; I got us a truck. It had the name ZOOM FURNI-TURE emblazoned on its side. The lot guards told me the truck had been confiscated by Matty Martuci in Group 76. Matty had stopped the driver, a Colombian, who was driving the truck to Mexico. "There was twenty-two mil hidden in the floorboard," the guard told me.

"That must be one hell of a floorboard," I said.

The guard shot me a sly smile. "Yeah, just wait," he said.

He climbed into the truck and pulled a lever. I heard a hydraulic whine, and the truck's floorboard, which turned out to have a special-built hidden compartment, rose up in my face like a billboard in Times Square. There was room in that hiding place for a fortune in coke, I thought, and flashing it to the Colombians would be like shining a klieg light in their faces.

Perfect to show off the stash.

Next, I headed to the vault, a massive warehouse where years of evidence is kept in storage, and I asked the custodian to let me look at a kilo block.

The custodian, who wore a crisp blue uniform and had a Boy Scout baby face, reluctantly tore his attention away from whatever was on daytime TV that day. "You want to what?"

"Look at a kilo block," I said.

"Which one?"

"The most recent seizure logged in," I said. "I need the most current dope available—and I need a lot of it."

The Boy Scout went to the back and returned with a kilo of coke compressed into a tight, heavy brick wrapped in heavy clear plastic. He dropped the block on the counter with a thud. I could see from the label pasted to the block that it was "Rolex."

"You got any more Rolex back there?" I asked.

He didn't know the name. "What're you talking about?"

I showed him the label with its Rolex crown logo, just like on the watches.

"It's the primo brand," I said.

"Oh, yeah, we got quite a bit of that," he said.

I took out my tape measure and a pad and pencil, trying to figure out how much I'd need to pack the hidden floor of the Zoom Furniture truck. A few minutes later, looking up from my calculations, I crossed my fingers and, trying to remain cool, asked, "Hey, would it be all right if I check out some of this stuff out for an undercover operation?"

The evidence custodian shook his head. "Buddy, you don't have a clue," he said. "You ain't removing a flake from here without the special agent in charge signing off on a twelve." He was referring to DEA Form 12, which was required to take evidence out for court. So that was my next step.

———

It was time for me to pay another visit to Maltz. His office was at DEA headquarters, and I walked in like I always did—not merely fearlessly, but a bit on the cocky side. It was the best way to play things with Maltz. Any hint of insecurity around the chief would immediately get me booted out of his office and my request would be forgotten.

"I wanna do a flash," I told Maltz. I explained that I had a dozen guys in Group 93, all slated to cover this make. "Here's the plan. We meet at the Moonstruck Diner over on Twenty-third Street," I said. "Three guys watching from the street, two more in the diner. We flash the scumbags the coke at a place called the Mendon Warehouse. That's a couple of blocks away, so the diner guys can cross-cover the warehouse if we need 'em. I'll have five of our guys around the warehouse. I'll have Joe Ayala in a van wearin' a wire. I'll be wearin' a wire, too, and I'll be with Paul every second. It's a great setup, Chief."

Maltz looked up from his paperwork. "Okay, whaddya need?" he asked, giving me "the stare." I knew I was on the right track.

"Four hundred kilos out of the evidence vault to show these Colombians," I said. "So we can gain some credibility."

Maltz shook his head. "Ain't no way Bryden's going for this."

I begged and pleaded, and finally Maltz relented. "Okay, let's go see Bryden," he said.

Now I knew I was out of luck. Robert Bryden, who did everything by the book, hated me, because I had pushed him with too many renegade requests far too many times. I wasn't too keen on him, either. As Special Agent in Charge of the New York Field Division, Bryden was everybody's boss—and he liked to think that he knew it all. I knew Bryden was no savvy street agent, just from his reputation and where he'd served in his previous assignments. But I also knew I had to suck up. Because I needed the twelve signed to get the dope out of the vault.

———

That same day Maltz and Eddie Beach and I went to see Bob Bryden.

Before being promoted to New York, Bryden was an associate SAC of the training division of the DEA academy in Washington—a glorified teacher. Before that, he was a group supervisor in the New Orleans field division. Before that, he was a group supervisor in Houston. I called him the Texas Weed Salesman, because he used to do a lot of grass cases in Texas. Because I was after bigger deals involving big loads of cocaine, I didn't put much stock in Bryden's usually nonsensical suggestions.

Bryden sat at his desk like he always did. I rarely saw him without that damned desk in front of him. He was the consummate police-issue bureaucrat—average height, thin, black hair parted meticulously to the side, clean-shaven, a stern all-American, no-BS type of guy. After I laid out my plan, and asked him for the four hundred kilos for the flash, Bryden started slowly shaking his head, like he always did.

We didn't need to do a real flash, he said. "Lemme tell you what I used to do, so you don't have to take any chances," he lectured us. Because he didn't want to gamble with real marijuana, he said he once took a photograph of a load of grass in the garage of the DEA building in New Orleans beside a newspaper showing the current date. All he had to was show the picture to the dealers, and a bust went down. "You can do the same with the coke!" he said.

I shot Eddie Beach a look that must've said, *This guy's got no clue!* But he was the boss, and he had the ultimate signature. So we were like, *Yeah, great idea, Mr. Bryden!*

"But, Mr. Bryden, I apologize," I said at last. "The CI already *committed* that they could see the stuff. So we need to do it with a real load. Otherwise, we would do it your way."

"Well, you shouldn't commit!" he said. "You never commit."

"Yessir, we know that now," Eddie Beach said. "If we'd known about your idea, we would have done it your way! But we've already committed and it's too late to go back now."

Bryden signed the twelve.

When we walked out, we got in the elevator and I slapped Eddie Beach five. "Yeah, let's take a picture of the coke and mail it in to the guys in Cali!" I said, and we both laughed.

Maltz looked at us, said, "You guys are crazy," and walked away.

———

Four days later, we were all set. I was a son of a bitch with the half dozen custodians at the evidence locker as they crawled around stacking kilos of coke in the Zoom truck's fake bottom. I insisted they stack it neatly in perfect rows, with each row organized by label. I refused to let them use anything but Rolex, La Reina, and Clinton. Paul's instructions were very specific, and I followed them to the letter.

Jimmy Makich, one of the vault cops, kept trying to needle me. "So, tell me, Jerry," he asked, "how come you need real coke for this make? I mean, looks to me like most of this load could be fake, you know? Just a few keys of the real stuff along the edge would do the trick."

"Just shut up and do your job," I snapped.

Jimmy didn't know it, but he'd just put his finger on a big, ugly detail I'd been trying to forget about. *Why couldn't we use fake coke?* Paul had told me, "Just a taste, Jerry," showing me how to flash the coke to our Colombians. "We're just going to give them a quick look—to make 'em hungry for it."

That was Paul's plan from the start: Flash the coke for a few seconds in a big show, don't let anybody touch it, smell it, or sample it. But one question kept kicking in the back of my mind. If we weren't even going to let Helmer Herrera's nephew, Freddy Herrera touch the stuff, then wouldn't a thousand pounds of carefully packaged chalk be just as convincing?

But Paul dismissed the notion with a wave of his hand. "You just can't fake it, Jerry," he said. "You've got to trust me about that."

I said okay, but, still, I didn't completely trust Paul Alexander.

———

So there we were, in a booth at the back of the Moonstruck Diner, Paul and I, or, our Cali names, Oscar Aguelo and Geraldo Bartone. I could hardly recognize myself. Gone were all traces of Crazy Jerry, street junkie. Now I was Geraldo, the suddenly sophisticated masquerader of the Cali cartels. I was dressed to deal, wearing Italian fashion from head to toe, finished off with a goatee, dark sunglasses, and that bogus Rolex.

As Paul had instructed, we were taking everything point by point, step by step. *First step, show 'em the coke.* Showing dealers an available load of coke is like throwing chum into shark-infested water.

While Paul and I waited for Freddy, my backup squad was in cars parked along the street, three agents watching and one listening to our conversation over the wire taped to my belly. There were more agents inside the diner, just in case anything went wrong. Paul sat facing the door, and I sat across from him. We ordered coffee and scanned the crowd, the ordinary New York City horde of locals and commuters, slugging down coffee and gobbling late lunches. We still had some time before the Cali representative was due to show up.

"So tell me about this guy," I said, drinking the dregs of my coffee and trying to stay cool. "What do you know about Freddy Herrera?"

"Okay, I'm sure you know about Don Pacho, Helmer Herrera, don't you?" Paul said, sipping his iced tea.

Paul seemed disappointed when I said, "Never heard of him."

He leaned in so close I could smell the mint on his breath. "Helmer Herrera is a very big man in the cartels," he whispered. "Second only to the main families themselves. And Freddy Herrera is his nephew. He runs a distribution cell from Long Island."

I stared at Paul in disbelief. I figured the cartel to be a bunch of thugs in the New York Mafia mold. "How come the big man's nephew has to do grunt work like distribution?" I asked. "How come he's not sitting by some swimming pool in Bogotá?"

Paul tried to explain how the cartel's hierarchy works. "It's not like the Mafia," he said. "I'm sure Helmer Herrera's sons are with him in Colombia, enjoying a multitude of privileges. But Freddy's father is not in the cartels. He keeps completely away from the trade. So Freddy doesn't have the status of his cousins."

"Has to work for a living, I guess," I said.

"Don't get me wrong," Paul continued. "I'm sure Helmer Herrera loves his nephew, and treats him very well. But, yes, Freddy must work to prove himself. Just like you, Jerry."

I ignored the last comment. "What's Freddy look like?" I asked.

"Well, you're about to find out," Paul said, sitting up and casually waving toward the diner's door. "They're here."

"They?" I said out loud. "What do you mean they? You said we were meeting just Freddy . . ."

All the doubt and fear I'd been ignoring for two weeks surfaced inside me. It was all I could do to keep myself from running out of that diner, calling the whole thing off. I was ready to face one Colombian drug dealer—but totally unprepared for a gang.

Paul's eyes followed the men as they walked up behind me. "Looks like he brought two friends," Paul said. "Just relax, Jerry. Same plan. We leave two of them here, that's all."

I had to trust Paul. I gritted my teeth and flashed a smile.

"Just keep your mouth shut," Paul said for about the hundredth time. "Don't say a word."

In a few seconds I was shaking hands with Freddy Herrera. He didn't look much like what I expected. His hair was long and naturally blond. His skin was light. Unlike Paul and me, with our go-to-hell suits and fancy shoes, you'd have to look real close at Freddy to notice that he was dressed in money. But the fine leather jacket gave him away. Obviously Freddy wasn't trying to prove anything with his clothes.

I was surprised at his long blond hair and Caucasian skin, but I tried not to show it. Freddy introduced us to his brother, "Javier," a short, pudgy dude in a black turtleneck, and another guy he called "Paolo," just some mope in a dirty T-shirt and jeans.

My mind was racing. What game were these guys playing? Why the extra horsepower? We all sat down and Paul began to speak in Spanish, which, since I was still a rank student in the language, I could only understand bits and pieces.

"I don't know how much you've heard about our operation from your bosses in the pueblo," he began.

My eyes scanned the diner, searching for the Group 93 agents who were supposed to be secretly watching us.

"As I told your broker, Alonso, we are not distributors, and have no wish to be," Paul continued. "We are transporters only."

I spotted Jack Higgins, dressed in his DJ getup: baggy nylon jumpsuit, headphones, and CD player, hunched over a bowl of *mondongo,* the spicy Spanish cow-gut stew. He was eavesdropping on our conversation—over my wire—and also monitoring the radio traffic outside. At the slightest warning from our boys watching the street, Jack was there to give me the signal—to get out fast.

So far, no signal.

I spotted Jerry Vetrano by the door, dressed like an off-duty janitor. Jerry had a standard-issue Glock 9mm folded into his newspaper, just in case he had to stop anybody from leaving early.

"So you see, we must find a buyer for this shipment, as soon as possible," Paul said. "Our vehicles and storage facilities are needed. They're bursting at the seams with new shipments on the way in."

Finally Freddy Herrera spoke. "Bueno," he said. "We are ready to see the product. Why don't we follow you in our car?"

Paul held up his hand. "No, my friend," he said. "You come with us, and your friends can wait here. We won't be long. You're going to like what you see."

———

Pretty soon, Freddy was climbing into the backseat of my new undercover champagne BMW 750 IL—alone. Before starting the car, Paul handed Freddy a blindfold.

"A necessary precaution," Paul said. "Surely you understand."

I steered the BMW around the corner of Nineteenth Street. I drove slowly around and around the block to make certain we weren't being followed, looking like any other slick, suave, immaculately dressed dope dealer talking on a cell phone. "Jose, please bring the truck around to Mendon," I said with authority.

Paul sat in the frontseat, watching Freddy Herrera's every move. Freddy was doubled over, hiding to make sure no one on the street would catch sight of him blindfolded, riding in the backseat of a new BMW.

The moment we parked at the Mendon Warehouse, the garage door rolled open and I drove the BMW inside. "Looks like the van's already here," Paul said. "It's okay, Freddy. You can sit up now."

We parked and removed his blindfold. Freddy Herrera blinked into the lights, looking relieved. Relieved to see again, and especially relieved to see no surprises—and no goons. Inside the otherwise empty Mendon Warehouse, there was an old, low-rent, twenty-five-foot panel van parked at the other end of the building, the words ZOOM FURNITURE in peeling paint on its side.

The truck's driver, Joe Ayala, was straight from central casting. We'd borrowed him from another group because we needed a Spanish guy for the flash. Joe was a tall, dapper Ricky Ricardo, who looked as if he were born to drive a drug truck. He climbed down from the cab and scurried up to greet us. "Boss!" Ayala blurted as he opened the door for Paul. "Hey, boss! I got the truck like you said."

"Thank you, Joe," Paul said.

Paul turned to me. "Geraldo, get the lights and unlock the truck," he ordered.

I did as told. In a few seconds, Paul, Freddy, and I were gazing into the truck's shadowy, yawning cargo bay. It was empty. Freddy Herrera stepped away from the van.

"What's going on here, *cabron?*" he said.

"Just wait, Freddy," Paul said, turning to me and giving me the signal.

I kneeled down and peered up beneath the van's chassis and reached carefully behind the bumper. I pulled a lever . . . and the show began.

An electric whine echoed into the warehouse. Two hydraulic pumps powered up, and the truck's tailgate lowered as the plywood floor began to rise. When it rose up fully in Freddy Herrera's face, exposing a truck bed packed with bricks, Freddy turned as white as the coke. He took a step closer, and the four-foot wall of solid coke must've given him a mental hard-on. Because he began to sweat. Big time.

He was staring at four hundred uniformly stacked kilo bricks of uncut "rock" cocaine, each brick labeled, and each of fifty rows organized by label. Rows of Rolex, La Reina, and Clinton, three Cali brands that Freddy knew to be fresh goods.

"Don Oscar," said Freddy, instantly addressing Paul with the ultrarespectful title "Don."

"Okay, that's a look, and a look is all you get," Paul said, cuing me to pull the lever and send the coke-packed truck bed back down.

"Vamanos," said Paul, and we hustled Freddy back into the BMW and the blindfold. In the rearview, I could see Freddy's big, wolfish, salivating grin, as he bent to duck his head between his legs.

The load of uncut coke he'd just seen had a street value of $40 million.

———

A few minutes later, the three of us were walking back into the Moonstruck Diner, where Freddy's compadres, Javier and Paolo, were nervously waiting. When they saw us, the men relaxed. The look on Freddy's face told them things were not only good . . . they were golden. I went to the counter for coffees, and once we all sat down, Freddy hit the speed dial on his cell phone.

"It's Freddy on behalf of Pepe," he said.

He was talking in code. "Pepe" was the code name for this particular deal.

"*Hola,* senor," he said. "*Sí, esta bien.*" In a few exchanges of rapid-fire Spanish, Freddy told his broker everything he needed to know about the deal—all without uttering a single incriminating syllable. "*Sí, senor, four hundred and fifty* pesos. Looks perfect. Thirteen (meaning thousand) for a peso, *sí.* Rolex, La Reina, Clinton. *Sí,* clean pesos. *Perfecto.*"

In the countersurveillance language of Colombian traffickers, "peso" can mean many different things. Sometimes, it means a hundred thousand American dollars. In this case it meant a kilo of coke. Freddy's broker would pass the information on to his boss, who would relay it upward through the Cali food chain until it reached Freddy's powerful uncle, Helmer Herrera.

"It's a very clean house, senor. *Esta muy bien.* They got a very nice bicycle."

"Bicycle" meant that Freddy was impressed by our truck.

Freddy handed the phone to Paul. "He wants to talk to Don Oscar," he said.

"*Bueno,*" Paul said into the phone. "Hello, Senor. Yes, this is Oscar Arguello. Yes, I spoke to your associate yesterday. I explained the situation to him. Yes."

"Senor" wanted Paul to repeat his history to him, for security's sake.

"As I said, senor, my partner and I are importers," said Paul. "We transported this shipment on behalf of some associates in Colombia who must remain nameless. You understand. Unfortunately our associates were not able to produce the necessary funds when the shipment arrived. They haven't told us what the problem is, but as you can imagine we are anxious to find a buyer for this shipment. That is why we are offering such an excellent discount. Thank you, senor."

Paul handed the phone to Freddy, who spoke to Senor for a moment, then turned to us with a deal.

"Don Oscar," he said to Paul, "I am sorry to say we cannot provide you with the cash at this moment. However, I am authorized to receive two hundred twenty-five pesos on consignment, and pick up the rest some time next week."

Paul shook his head no. "Have your boss give me a call when he is prepared to take the entire shipment—at the agreed-upon price—for cash, my friend, not credit," he said. "Good day to you."

Paul got up to leave.

"*Bueno,* senor," said Freddy. He wasn't surprised that Paul wouldn't take the credit deal. "You will hear from us soon."

And Freddy and his compadres walked out of the Moonstruck Diner.

———

I don't know how long we sat there after they left. Probably a long time, just to make sure they were really gone. When we finally drove off in the BMW, I couldn't stay quiet any longer.

"*YES!*" I screamed, Crazy Jerry once again. "All right, Don Oscar!"

I high-fived Paul all the way back to his hotel, buzzing from the insane thing we'd just done. We knew we had baited one big hook and the fish had it halfway swallowed. The look of greed on Freddy Herrera's face told us that his boss and his Cali partners would be calling us soon. Real soon.

To them, this was the break of a lifetime, the chance to make millions on a big shipment of coke without the risk or expense of transporting it. All they had to do was make one single, tidy buy and turn the load over to their distributors. No muss, no fuss, and no possible way to pass it up.

So what if the coke was NYDETF evidence from about four different busts? So what if the law required us to immediately return the stuff into the storage vault where it came from? "Don Oscar" and "Don Geraldo" knew something Freddy and his boys didn't: As soon as the big boys down in Bogotá were drooling to get their hands on this windfall shipment, the deal was going to fall through.

Somehow.

Someway.

If we did an actual deal, it would have to go wrong, and then we'd have to figure out a way to shift the blame away from us—and onto them. Because the first rule of Cali drug smuggling was whoever has the load when a bust happens or a deal goes bad is dead.

Paul and I knew that at the last minute our nameless "associates," on whose behalf we supposedly smuggled the load to New York in the first place, were going to come through with the money they owed us, and that big, beautiful white brick road would be nothing more than a sweet memory for the Bogotá brokers we'd just so successfully seduced.

But the load wouldn't be their only memory. They would also remember the dynamic smuggling duo responsible for the whole thing. They'd remember Freddy's stories of a top-secret rendezvous, a yawning warehouse, and a magical truck with a dramatic hydraulic mechanism. And soon, the brokers would learn from "Don Oscar" about a string of nonexistent airstrips down in Central America, and a fleet of phantom cargo planes. They'd remember the whole perfect operation, and with any luck they'd want to use it.

Then we'd have them in the palms of our hands.

———

For six days after seeing our stash, Freddy Herrera worked frantically to buy it. He spent hours on the phone with his Colombian bosses, and met several times with Paul. The meetings were mostly fact-finding missions in diners, cheap restaurants, and outside of bodegas. The *jefes* in Bogotá wanted to learn more about the mysterious smuggling operation they stumbled into. Paul made sure that everything they learned, *they liked.*

Freddy had lots of questions from his bosses. So we had a fleet of panel trucks with ingenious false floors. *"Cuanto?"* they wanted to know. How many? "Enough" was all that Paul would reveal. We had warehouse space in the heart of New York City and other locales, he said. Airstrips and cargo planes in Costa Rica and Guatemala. *"Es un operación perfecto,"* Paul assured the Cali *jefes.*

At last, the Colombians were ready to deal. Freddy had been given the beeper number of a "banker," a Cali moneyman, somewhere in New York, along with a special code. The banker was ready to deliver the cash, and it was up to Freddy to arrange the details for the exchange. Excited, he called Paul.

We were sitting at the mezzanine bar at the Holiday Inn Crown Plaza Hotel in Times Square when Paul's cell phone rang. I could hear Freddy's excited voice booming from the phone's earpiece. He was ready to do the deal, immediately. A look of resignation washed over Paul's face.

"I'm so sorry, my friend," he told Freddy. "The shipment has been sold, to the original buyers. They finally got the money."

I heard Freddy speaking rapid Spanish, but Paul cut him off at the first *"Que pasa,* hombre?"

"I hope you understand our position," said Paul. "We could hardly say no to these men. But, Freddy, I feel we owe you something for all your trouble."

After preparing the garden for a month, Paul planted the golden seed. "You must call me if our organization can ever be of service," he said.

When Paul hung up the phone, he turned to me.

"What did he say?" I asked.

He imitated Freddy Herrera's voice. "Those old men in Bogotá are too slow." Paul smiled. "He said he'd be back in touch with a new deal. Soon, Jerry, he'll be back in touch very soon."

━━━━

The next weekend I was hanging around my living room with Maggie, just happy to have some time to relax.

What can I say about my wife, Maggie? She's not only my heart; she gave me my spine. Whatever balls I've grown I owe to her. To anyone but her family and friends, Maggie seems like a shy woman. But she's the strongest person I've ever known. Tall, thin, blond and pretty, she's always been my Steel Magnolia, rising up in the soil of New Jersey.

I never looked to Maggie for sympathy. None of that "It's gonna be okay, poor Jerry" from her. She refrained from telling me "I told you so" about my big-city cop's job, which she had tried to talk me out of doing, but she'd bust my chops at any sign of weakness. "You got yourself into this," she'd say. "Now you get yourself out. Don't be a wimp, Jerry!"

She made me prove to the world that I could be as good as she thought I could be. She didn't want to know the minutiae of my job—after all, why should both of us worry about the armies of Colombian coke dealers who could, at any minute, bust down our door? All she asked was that I keep my business away from our home. She wanted to keep our home a haven—and she refused to allow my job to make her crazy.

At the time, our home was a haven, but it was hardly a castle. It was just a modest and cramped two-bedroom town house, in the middle of a mountain of town houses, whose major piece of furniture was a big stand-alone TV. We were sitting on our white leather couch and staring out at our little deck, which today seems a little too accessible to climbers. That night, after a couple of glasses of cheap red wine, Maggie did something unusual. She asked me about my work.

"Well, I'm curious!" she said. "I was just getting used to life with Crazy Jerry, the junkie. The stink, the beard, the disgusting hair. Now you're so clean that I feel like I'm living with Rico Suave himself. I don't know. You just seem so happy, so normal. It's weird. And you sure smell better."

I laughed. "I guess I am happier!" I said.

"So it's going okay?" she asked.

"Oh, yeah, this new informant I'm working with is turning out great. We get along beautifully. Any day now we'll be meeting up with the big boys from Bogotá."

I could tell the whole thing sounded crazy to Maggie. Foreign and dangerous. Things got weird for Crazy Jerry now and then, but at least he moved in a world Maggie knew something about. These cartel guys were a whole new ball game, and she didn't know what to expect. Truth is, I didn't either.

"Where's all this going to lead, Jerry?" she asked me.

Before I could answer, the phone rang. It was Paul.

"Guatemala, my friend" was all he said.

"What?" I said. "Paul? Whaddaya mean?"

"We're going to Guatemala," he said. "We got to build an airstrip."

6

Shopping for a Country

In his nonstop tutorial about drug smuggling, Paul told me, "Everything comes down to the guarantee."

"So?" I asked. "What kind of guarantee?"

We were sitting in Paul's house in Miami, just before heading down to Guatemala. The house sat in a cul-de-sac that could have been called Alexander Acres. Next door were two smaller, yet similarly designed houses, one that Paul had built for his brother-in-law, and next to it the house that Paul had built for his mother-in-law. All three houses were big Colonials decorated in a modern style. They were filled with sleek leather furniture and expensive art and marble statues.

Paul and I were alone in the living room, but Paul Lir Alexander was never truly alone, anywhere. He always surrounded himself with an entourage, which included his wife, Erica de Sousa, and her sister, Marjorie, both knockout Brazilian beauties, real girls from Ipanema, their hometown. Then there was Antonio Calderon, a former Nicaraguan contra general, whose dark pockmarked face and penchant for open military shirts made him a dead ringer for General Manuel Noriega. Antonio rarely spoke—and never smiled.

Paul's all-purpose mail boy and gofer, Nielsen, a six-foot-tall hippie with his long hair parted to the side, was doing busy work in the kitchen. Finally, there was Mary Lola, a Cuban-American whose sole job was to serve as Paul's switchboard operator. It was a big job. Paul

had an elaborate phone system, which allowed him to have calls relayed via forty different cell and landlines.

Nielsen scurried out and offered me a drink. I ordered a vodka and
was taking a deep sip when Paul grabbed me by the suit sleeve.

"Come with me, Jerry, let me show you something," he said, leading me upstairs and into a little room off of his master bedroom. I
walked in and found myself in a command center containing about six
TV screens and lots of audiotape recording equipment. Paul flipped a
switch. I could see his wife Erica in the baby's room on a TV screen.
He flipped another switch. There was his mother-in-law in her living
room on another screen.

"You don't trust anybody, do you?" I said.

"It's not that I don't trust them," Paul said. "But it's very important to always know what everybody is thinking and, even more importantly, what anybody is saying. I know everything that's going on
around me, and you should, too, Jerry."

Oh, yeah, right, I thought. If I put a surveillance camera on Maggie, if I dared try to bring any sense of drug cop paranoia BS into our
home, she'd butcher me for breakfast ham. I could hear her yelling in
my ear just for thinking about it, "How dare you not trust anybody
here? While you're bouncing around from country to country, playing
drug smuggler, you have the balls to come here and not trust anybody
in your own home?"

We returned to the living room, where Paul had a wall of TV
screens hooked up to three big satellite dishes in his backyard. He
picked up a remote control, pushed a button, and the satellite dishes
began swiveling and the TV screens began showing the news in several different countries. One minute we were watching the news about
a cartel guy getting busted in Bogotá. The next, we were catching up
on the latest news from Guatemala.

"It's critical to know what's going on in a country before you start
an operation there," Paul said. "You wouldn't propose an operation in
Central America during the rainy season when they're having floods.
You need to do your homework."

Neilsen returned to freshen up my drink, which I warmly wel-
comed. He brought Paul another iced tea.

Paul took a sip, then resumed his tutorial on the "guarantee."

"They're always going to ask you, 'What's the guarantee?' And the answer, the guarantee, is always the same thing." Paul set down his tea and drew his finger across his throat. "That's what you would do in a meeting. If you're transporting someone's drugs, someone's load, they're going to ask you, 'What is my guarantee?' And you draw your finger across your throat and say, 'I put my neck,' so they know that you mean, 'You have the right to kill me if the deal goes bad.'"

I took a stiff belt and thought about how Maggie would react if I went down in the line of dope dealer fire. I could imagine the uniformed notice-of-death crew from the DEA, wearing their dour funereal faces, and knocking on our town house door. I could imagine Maggie opening the door and, without a word from the cops, cursing me to hell for dying in a job she never wanted me to take. Just the thought made me squirm in Paul's white go-go boot-leather chair.

"Okay, fine," I said, knowing full well that if it came down to me or them—it would be their neck, not mine, being sliced.

"Number two," Paul said. "You have to learn about prices. You can't just offer to transport coke. You have to know the current rates. You have to understand, if we transport the load from Colombia to Central America and then into the United States, and their cost is five hundred to a thousand dollars per kilo from the coke labs in Colombia, then our transportation price would be twenty-five hundred per kilo to the United States from Central America."

"Five time as much as the cost?" I said, almost choking on my drink.

Paul nodded. "If you pick up in Colombia, the price rises, as high as five thousand a kilo. It's a rule among smugglers—the closer the coke is to the States, the lower the transportation fee. If you transport a load out of Colombia to the U.S., the transportation fee is the most expensive because the journey is farther—and more dangerous. But once it gets closer to the U.S., say, Central America, the fee is lower, anywhere between two thousand and twenty-five hundred per kilo."

Paul switched channels, from Brazil to Colombia, where, as always, the news was round-the-clock murder and mayhem.

"Do you understand?" he continued. "You don't just go in and say, 'Hey, I'm going to transport ten tons for you. I'll charge you fifty million.' It doesn't work that way. And you wouldn't say, 'I'll charge you a thousand,' because they would say, 'You don't know this business.' Once you learn about the market price and about the fees for transportation, next you have to learn about how much to ask for up front. Would you be a partner in the load? Or just a transporter? There are different categories." He got up from his chair and paced the room, letting a few seconds tick by, before sitting down and glowering over me.

"Finally," Paul told me, "you have to learn about high-frequency radios, which the government listens to. You have to know that the cops listen to frequencies going up to fourteen thousand five hundred megahertz, so you have to know how to kick the radio up in the fifteen thousand range, which nobody listens to."

"Then, of course, you have to know all about airplanes," he said.

"Yeah, Paul, I know all about flying," I lied, thinking back on my white-knuckle flight instruction. Just the thought of flying a plane on my own still gave me the shakes.

Paul didn't even stop to respond. He was rolling, loving his own dialogue, insights, wisdom. I was, as always with Paul, the ever-eager student, doing more listening than talking for the first time in my life.

"You can't just say, 'Hey, pal, I'm ready to transport your drugs.' Questions are going to be asked, Jerry, and you must know *everything*. You can't just bluff your way through."

He leaned back in his chair, and stared at me hard. "We're getting ready to travel to Guatemala, Jerry. I will teach you all of the fine-line mechanics about dealing and negotiating and transporting. But there is one thing you're going to have to learn for yourself—patience. You have to cool that red-hot head of yours. Never be anxious. Always remember, we don't chase."

I stood up, pacing again, trying to imitate his cockiness. "I know, I know, Paul," I said. "You've told me a million times. Cops chase. We don't. We bait—and wait."

He nodded for me to sit down and listen, really listen. Then, once I was seated, he leaned toward me and spoke as if I were a Cali associate he was addressing. "You want the deal? Okay, it's two hundred and fifty thousand up front. These are our terms, and our terms are final. We've got the facilities, the contacts, the airstrips to back it up."

He sat back. "You have to be extremely cocky, Jerry," he said.

"But you can't just be cocky and not know what you're talking about."

———

Pretty soon our two bait fish, Avelino and Alonso, and the bigmouthed Freddy Herrera had lured a major shark to our operation. It was early April 1991, and New York was thawing out from winter into spring. I'd only been working with Paul for a couple of months, but it seemed like years. One day that April, Paul told me he was going to fly down to Colombia to meet Dr. Jose Lizardo Losada, a major Cali cocaine associate who had told Avelino and Alonso that he wanted to move a major load after being assured by Freddy Herrera that we were for real.

"Okay, whaddya want me to do?" I asked.

"Before I go to the meeting, I need to know where we can do an operation. Please start calling the different embassies to see where they will allow us to do a 'control.'"

Meaning a controlled-delivery undercover operation.

"Try for Guatemala," he added. "I understand they'll let you do a controlled delivery there."

———

I started shopping for a country. I knew where "controls" were prohibited. In Brazil, controlled deliveries were illegal. In Mexico and Colombia, you couldn't trust the government. They'd sell you out in a heartbeat. That had happened to Kiki Camerena, a DEA agent working undercover in Mexico until the local cops caught, tortured, and killed him. The list of prohibited countries goes on and on. But Guatemala, well, I'd heard things could happen down there.

I called Sheldon "Shelly" Katz, the assistant U.S. embassy attaché in Guatemala, a big Texan whose tough demeanor befitted his name. I told Shelly that I was a DEA task force agent from New York, and we wanted to do a controlled. Would his country allow it?

"Yeah, there's certain things we let go down," Shelly replied.

Within five minutes I had Shelly Katz giving me the okeydoky for controlled deliveries in Guatemala. I called Paul and told him to tell Lizardo that we could do a load there.

I was only half lying. I didn't have formal authorization yet. I just had the simple phone call with Shelly Katz.

Paul flew down to Colombia and met with Dr. Jose Lizardo Losada, whom we called simply Lizardo. Paul told Lizardo that he had this exceptional partner, Geraldo Bartone, whom Paul always referred to as "the senator," though I never knew why. I guess Paul was so accustomed to South American corruption that he wanted to create the appearance that he was in business with some political official gone bad.

Paul told Lizardo that we had an import/export company called Genesis in Guatemala City. He said we had facilities to land planes in the Guatemalan jungle, that we could off-load the planes, refuel them, and then ship the coke in our containers with our import/export business back to New York to the distributors.

Lizardo liked what he heard.

The next step: Paul negotiated the transportation fee, $2,500 a kilo for 767 kilos of coke. The plan was to offer Avelino and Alonso a percentage in the load. If the number of kilos transported was up to Paul's estimate, Avelino and Alonso would pocket $175,000. That was the side deal we made with them.

With Avelino and Alonso as our credibility, Paul's life and the mysterious "senator's" life as a guarantee, Lizardo was ready to do business. He told Paul that he wanted to send one of his pilots with Avelino and Alonso over to Guatemala to view our airstrip and inspect our business operation.

"I'll make all of the arrangements within the next month," Paul said, "and I'll meet with your pilot, as well as Avelino and Alonso, over in Guatemala City. We'll show you our airstrip, our business, and we'll begin the operation."

One big problem. We didn't have an airstrip—yet.

Paul called me from Colombia and said the deal was cooking, but that we needed cash, fast, specifically $175,000, up front to give to Avelino and Alonso to lie through their teeth for us. We were going back and forth on the phone about how we were ever going to get $175,000 in cash, until Paul finally said, "Jerry, I'm going to force Lizardo to drop us some money in New York."

"Great idea," I said. "Brilliant."

"Okay, see you in New York next week," he said.

Paul went back to the meeting and said, "I spoke to the senator, and with all due respect, sir, he says to put your money where your mouth is. You've seen our operation because Freddy Herrera has seen it and Avelino and Alonso vouch for us. You want to use us as your transporters? No problem. But we want one hundred and seventy-five thousand dollars, U.S., as good-faith money dropped in New York City before we go forward. Once we have the cash, we will show you our airstrips, our import/export business . . . everything."

Lizardo agreed and they set up the drop for two weeks away in New York.

———

"Jerry, we're in business," Paul told me when he got back to Manhattan.

We were in the back in the lobby bar of the Holiday Crown Plaza in Times Square. To the other patrons in the bar, we must've looked like two typical goombahs after a hard day's crime.

"The one seventy-five will be dropped in two weeks," Paul went on, "and then we'll show them our operation. I can handle setting up the import/export business in Guatemala City. I'll hire a secretary, get the phones, the stationery . . . Naturally, we'll need a helicopter so we can show them our airstrip where we're going to land the planes filled with their cocaine."

My head was spinning. I felt as if I'd just slipped on a banana peel and landed on a roller coaster, which was going faster and faster. I ordered a drink to steel my nerves and gulped it down almost before the waitress could put it on the table.

Paul looked at me warily, then grabbed my arm and told me to calm down.

"Point by point, Jerry, point by point," he said. "Here's what we're going to do." First, he told me that *I* had to arrange for the cash pickup. Then I had to give the $175,000 to Paul so he could fly to Miami and give it to Avelino, who needed a visa to come to the U.S., which I also had to arrange.

That made me call for another drink. Once again, Paul put his hand on my arm and told me to calm down. But I wouldn't calm down, couldn't calm down.

"I don't know if it's legal for me to pick up that kind of cash," I said. "I don't want to go to jail, Paul."

The businessmen at the next table shot me a glance when they overheard the word "jail." But Paul merely started shaking his head, and I knew what he was thinking, that I was thinking like a cop, instead of a smuggler, again.

"You have to get the authority to do the pickup," Paul insisted.

I stood up to leave. "Let me go back and research it," I said.

I went back to the office and sat down with Danny Brown, another one my supervisors, and told him what Paul was asking me to do. Danny always reminded me of Andy Griffith, a nice, wholesome, honest, hardworking, all-American cop. We started flipping through the DEA manual and couldn't find anything about giving money to one bad guy and letting him give it to another bad guy.

"That's called trafficker-directed funds," Danny said at last. I found the chapter and verse regarding trafficker-directed funds. Basically, it said that I could do what Paul was asking me to do, but I had to get it signed off on by all of my supervisors, which meant Maltz, as well as Bob Bryden and a higher-up in DEA headquarters in Washington, D.C.

First, I had to put the whole proposal down on paper, so I plopped myself down in front of a word processor and started typing. Thirty pages later I had it written—Paul's meeting with Lizardo, our baiting Avelino and Alonso, our plan to do a controlled delivery through Guatemala, the reasons why Paul and I and the rest of Group 93 were going to pick up "trafficker-directed funds" to give to Avelino and Alonso, and how we were then going to elaborately flash Lizardo our bogus operation in Guatemala. The memo read like a dimestore novel.

I sent it out over the telex machine, and lo and behold, I got the approval.

I called Paul with the good news. Paul called Lizardo, who gave him a beeper number and code—"Paulo on behalf of Lizardo"—and set the date for the drop of the cash.

It was early summer when we did the drop. All twelve members of Group 93 met in our evidence locker of an office at DEA headquarters, and our sense of anticipation threatened to blow the flimsy walls down. All of us were dressed to blend in with the drop site, which would be in front of a pay phone on Second Avenue on Thirtieth Street near a CitiBank. That meant some of the guys were in banker suits and ties, others were dressed like delivery boys, others like street people, and, of course, Paul and I like the consummate drug smugglers in our fancy suits and dark sunglasses.

Before we left headquarters, Paul called the number Lizardo had given him from his cell phone. Within a minute, the phone rang back and I heard Paul say, "This is Oscar on behalf of Lizardo." The guy on the other end must have asked Paul when he wanted to do the drop, because I heard Paul set the time for 4:00 P.M.

At four, Paul and I were standing on Second Avenue with the rest of Group 93 in character all around us. Some of them were strutting down the street with briefcases, others delivering pizza and packages, others begging for spare change, and some just standing around looking like they were loafing. An old dark blue Bonneville rounded the corner with a mule, or low-level transporter, at the wheel.

Paul had told me that mules drive basic cars to avoid bringing attention to themselves. This was a money mule. He cruised to a stop, rolled down his window, and said to us, "I've got something for you." Then he parked, got out of the car, and the three of us walked into a Chinese restaurant and shook hands.

"I understand you have checks for us," Paul said.

The Colombian nodded. "Yes."

"Okay, we're going to walk one block up," Paul said. "We'll be standing on the corner."

The guy nodded. Paul and I walked up to the next block. The car rounded the corner and stopped. The mule got out and opened the trunk, where a big black duffel bag was waiting. Paul took it out and we walked away. I was carrying the bag and my heart was pumping. I was wondering if the mule was following us. I was wondering if we were going to get killed.

This was my first big deal. We had gone from a flash to serious drug money, and I was flying.

Back at the Group 93 office, the former evidence room at 555 West Fifty-seventh, Paul and I set the duffel on a desk and the whole group gathered around. I opened the bag and we all looked inside.

"Look at the greenbacks!" I screamed.

There were solid bricks of cash—fives, tens, and twenties, bundled in two-thousand-dollar increments, then rubber-banded together in stacks of ten worth twenty thousand each.

From that point forward, I was psyched. The money had made me a believer, just as it had Avelino and Alonso. Everybody was whooping it up, slapping five, screaming. This was the best thing that had happened to the group, our first major score.

We called Maltz and told him to get over quick. Maltz came in, all six feet, four inches of him, with his Hulk Hogan hairdo and long mustache that flared out into muttonchops, snaking down the sides of his face. He looked at the cash and gave me a big grin.

We counted the cash and did our report, and we were on our way in the drug business. Paul and I retired to Le Cirque for dinner.

"Okay, this is the beginning," Paul said. "Now, once again, we go point by point, Jerry."

———

After we picked up the money, Avelino started pressuring Paul to arrange for him to come to Miami and pick up his share. Avelino felt that it was as corrupt in the U.S. as it was in South America, and since Paul kept referring to his partner as "the senator," surely pressure could be applied to get him an instant visa.

"Your senator must have connections," Avelino told Paul.

Paul said sure, then called me and said, "We've got to get Avelino a visa to pick up the money and stay for a week; otherwise the deal won't go."

We were back at headquarters, Paul and me sitting in our little office with a few of the other group members milling around. When Paul told me what he expected me to do based on his big, grand promises, which he hadn't checked out with me first, I felt the blood rise from every inch of my body into my brain. I shot up from my sorry excuse for a desk straight up into Paul's face.

"How could you commit to that?" I screamed. "What are you,

nuts? I don't know if I even can do anything close to what you're promising, Paul. You could have asked me first."

"Jerry, you don't understand," Paul said. "We're being tested for credibility every minute. These people think that the United States is like their country."

I calmed down enough to make a few calls and I discovered that there's a nine-month wait at the American embassy in Bogotá, the channel someone like Avelino would be forced to take. Of course, Avelino, being involved in the coke trade, was petrified even to go near the U.S. embassy.

I started trying to pull strings and found a woman in the State Department in Washington. I tried being charming and talking nice and going down and visiting, and before you know it I had got her word for a visa.

We told Avelino to express-mail his passport, and after it arrived I drove to the State Department in Washington. My new friend stamped the passport with a six-month visa, allowing Avelino multiple entries. The whole turnaround was three days.

When I took the visa back to Paul, he flashed me a rare smile. "This is tremendous, Jerry," he said. "You're really starting to learn. You don't realize how much credibility we gain with this."

We sent Avelino's passport back to him, and from that moment forward he thought we walked on water—of course, he didn't realize that some savvy customs officer might look closely at a swarthy Colombian with a visa stamped out of DC. Nonetheless, Avelino flew into Miami.

Paul flew down with the $175,000, and I met him down there, staying in the background. Avelino and Paul spent a couple of days together. Paul gave him the $175,000 cash—and I tried my best to keep him from being busted on his way home. My concern was that he was going to get on a plane and get pinched for having more than the ten thousand dollars cash maximum.

I had Paul ask Avelino to give us his return flight itinerary. Then I went to the U.S. customs agents in Miami. They're called the Rover Team because they work the airport searching for people smuggling money out and smuggling dope in. I had a telex substantiating that Avelino's $175,000 was trafficker-directed funds.

I told the Rover Team's supervisor all about our undercover case and that it was imperative that Avelino get through without a hitch. So Avelino flew back to Bogotá, his bag packed with $175,000 cash and his mind full of admiration for his new associates.

He didn't dare tell Lizardo about the $175,000, which he and his partner had taken behind Lizardo's back.

All he told Lizardo was that we were the greatest coke smugglers in the world.

———

"Next point," said Paul. "We have to go to Guatemala and set up our operation."

"Okay, Paul, let me get the authority to go."

Eddie Beach, Danny Brown, and I sat down with Maltz.

"Listen, Chief, we have to go to Guatemala," I said. "We have to start making the arrangements to build an airstrip, set up a business, do what we got to do, and we need ten thousand dollars for travel and miscellaneous."

"All right," Maltz said. No hemming and hawing this time. After seeing the $175,000, he too was a believer. "Good luck, be careful, and get the State Department's warnings."

I felt that roller-coaster ride ratcheting up another level.

7

Welcome to the Third World

I knew I was in way over my head before the plane even landed in Guatemala City. I'd barely been out of the New York area, and this was my first time to a foreign country.

Before I left New York, I'd read the State Department's warnings about Guatemala and . . . *Holy Jesus!* The place was a riot, a country that had suffered under every variety of military and civilian government as well as a thirty-six-year guerrilla war. Until the government signed a peace agreement formally ending the war in 1996, more than a hundred thousand people would die in Guatemala and a million refugees would be homeless.

In the summer of 1991, Secretary of State James Baker had cut economic aid to the country because of human rights violations. People were being strung up and hanged by the government for seemingly minor infractions. There was an epidemic of amoebic dysentery. There were guerillas. And that was on a quiet day.

I was reading these warnings and thinking, *What am I heading into?* The one good thing about Guatemala City was that it's known as the "City of Eternal Spring" because of its twelve months of sunny weather. Well, I thought, at least I could wear short sleeves.

Danny Brown and I flew to Miami, where we met up with Paul for the flight to Guatemala City. Before we left, one of our DEA supervisors said to us, while looking straight at me, "We don't want any international incidents."

I was like, "Yeah, yeah, I understand, I understand."

As I walked out of that meeting I looked over at Danny Brown and said, "Let me tell you something about that international incident. I'm coming home, and I'm coming home alive. I don't know about you, but I'll take a 747 out of the sky to get home, if I have to. I want a room on the first floor, so I can back a Jeep up against the window. That way, God forbid, if something goes wrong we'll jump out the window, hop into the Jeep, and ride to the airport."

Danny said, "Calm down, pal, calm down."

On the flight to Guatemala, Paul was telling me everything we needed to do, "Point by point." A million points, from creating our bogus business to building our landing strip, until my mind was spinning.

"Just do your part, Jerry," Paul kept saying. Always those famous words, "Point by point, Jerry." I could ask a zillion questions, but Paul would always stop me with, "Point by point. You're getting way ahead of yourself."

As the plane banked for a landing, I looked down at the city of my first major drug deal. It looked more like a movie set of a foreign country than a real big city. As we got closer, I could see endless green fields, then miles of aluminum-roofed shanties with livestock in the yards, linked by archaic roads flanked by overgrown bush. When I got off the plane, I walked into what seemed like a military base. The airport was filled with uniformed officers toting machine guns. *Welcome to the third world,* I thought.

But even there, my roll was raging. Guatemala City! Population— two million—and now one Crazy Jerry, who had morphed into Geraldo Bartone. I was too wired for sleep and itching for indoctrination into my first foreign land. This being a military-ruled country, there were armed soldiers all over the streets. Machine guns, shotguns, every kind of gun everywhere you looked. I leased a Nissan Forerunner, and Danny Brown, Paul, and I drove over to the Camino Real Hotel.

"Hey, bud, you just slow down, because you're in a foreign country now," Danny Brown told me as we were driving from the airport to Guatemala City. "Straight to your room and go to bed."

"Okay, Danny, but remember, I want a room on the first floor!" I said.

Once we got to the Camino Real, the Paul Lir Alexander Show kicked into high gear. With his jacket draped over his shoulders, Paul roamed the lobby as if he owned all of Central America. He knew everybody. He spoke to his far-flung friends—everyone from diplomats to dopers, socialites to hookers, politicians to pimps—in four fluent languages. Snapping his fingers and ordering people— bartenders, waiters, cigarette girls, etc.—around. He wanted everyone to know he had money, and he knew how to flash it. The quetzal is the Guatemalan currency, and Paul always had a stack of quetzals, throwing the greenbacks around in his twenty-four-hour-a-day masquerade as the biggest, baddest coke transporter in all of South America.

Always in control, his drink of choice was, of course, fruit juice. Meanwhile, I was Paul's polar opposite, running at 150 miles an hour, and getting increasingly fired up.

"Hey, bud, to bed," Danny Brown kept telling me as I got wilder by the hour. "To bed, Jerry! You're in a foreign country. I don't want any international incidents. You get to bed."

"Got it, Danny, no problem," I lied. "I'm going to bed."

I did go straight to my room, dropped my suitcase, looked out the window, and saw Guatemala City, that city of aluminum-roofed shanties, front-yard chickens, machine-gun-toting cops, and murder and mayhem, awaiting me.

"I'm outta here," I said to myself, heading downstairs to greet the midnight hour alone.

That's when the weirdness started. I was outside the hotel, all dressed up, buzzing with excitement and eager to share it. I looked over at the first guy I saw standing outside and said, all friendly, "Hey, how are you, pal?"

"Good, good," he said.

"Oh, you speak English, huh?" I said. "Where are you from?"

"Louisiana," he said. "Where are you from?"

"New York."

"No kidding. You here alone?"

"Yeah, yeah, I'm here alone."

"Yeah, I'm here alone, too."

"That's cool. What's there to do around here?"

Out of the blue he said, "Why don't we go up to my room and have a good time?"

I didn't think I heard him correctly at first. "Huh?" I asked.

"Yeah, why don't we go upstairs to my room and have a good time?"

"How about I knock your teeth out?" I said.

"Well, do you want to just go downtown and hang out?"

"Get the hell away from me!" I said, ready to belt him.

All of the guards overheard the conversation and understood enough English to know I'd been hit on. They gathered in a circle around us, laughing at me for making a jackass out of myself. I said, "Fuck you!" to all of them and jumped into a cab.

"Take me to the wildest place in town!" I ordered the cabbie. He took me to a street lined with restaurants and bars. I was out of my mind, like a kid who had just been let loose.

When I got back into the lobby, Paul was there, surrounded by women, beautiful Nicaraguans dressed in flowing fabrics straight out of *I Dream of Jeannie*. I had a drink with Paul and his harem. Paul drank his juice, I drank my vodka.

Finally, I called it a night and went upstairs to my room. I hadn't been there two minutes when there was a knock on the door. Two Nicaraguan girls were peeking through the peephole. I cracked open the door. "Don Oscar, Don Oscar," they cooed, meaning my "partner" had sent them there to service me. I opened the door and in an instant they were buck-ass naked and doing a hoochie-coochie dance.

Every rookie cop knows you don't ever give anybody anything that they could use against you.

Especially women.

Especially in a foreign country.

Especially on your first night!

I was thinking, *You're drunk. You've got two beautiful naked girls in your room. You've got Danny Brown in the room next door. You've got a wife, a daughter, and about a hundred supervisors all hungry to bust your ass for the slightest indiscretion. You've also got a partner who obviously didn't just send these babes to your room out of the goodness of his heart. You tap these women and Don Oscar will tap you big time.*

They were obviously very high priced whores.

They were also obviously drop-dead gorgeous.

One was lying spread-eagled on the bed and the other was dancing around me as if I were some billionaire with a pocketful of quetzels all earmarked for lap dances. I shook myself awake from what seemed like a dream and said, "Excuse me, ladies. I'll be right back." Drunk enough to doubt my effectiveness as a bouncer—or my restraint as a man—I went next door and pounded on Danny Brown's door.

When he opened it I launched into a full confession. "Hey, Danny, hey, Danny, hey, Danny! Listen, I broke all the rules. First, a guy hit on me; then I jumped in a cab and I went downtown. I got drunk and hopped through Guatemala City like the Budweiser frog. Then I was drinking with Paul in the bar. And now he's sent two whores to my room. They're dancing around naked and I can't get rid of them. You've got to help me!"

"Bud, I told you to go to bed!" Danny roared.

"Okay, Danny, never again, but please just help me now."

Big, burly Danny walked into the room where the naked dancing girls were smiling and thinking Danny was going to orchestrate a four-some. "Ma'am, we cannot have this kind of conduct!" he screamed. When that order failed since the women didn't speak English, Danny barked out in Spanish, "*Salgan ahora!* Leave now!"

But they kept right on dancing, thinking Danny was cheering them on. Then Danny barked like a drill sergeant, "You must leave, ma'am. Leave! We can't have this. I am the supervisor."

They kept dancing.

Finally, Danny got the message. *"Vamanos! Vamanos!"* he yelled, throwing them their clothes and pushing them out into the hallway naked. He slammed the door behind them and then turned his rage on me.

"Now, Bud, you go to bed—and stay in bed. I don't want to see or hear any more of you tonight!" And he stormed out and slammed the door behind him.

━━━━━

The next day got worse. I called the American embassy and said, "Jerry Speziale, New York Drug Enforcement Task Force, Group Ninety-three. I'd like to check out a weapon for use while I'm here.

Bring me a few guns. Nothing excessive, just two big nine-milli-meter *pistoleros*."

Of course I wanted guns. Who wouldn't in Guatemala? It was my first trip out of the country and no way I could bring a gun there. So within the hour some guy was knocking on my door holding a paper bag with two big pistols inside. Easy as calling Domino's for pizza.

I had the guns on me while driving with Ray Manzillo, a DEA agent who was assigned to the Guatemalan Cadence Unit for the American embassy. We were just outside the city when the Guatema-lan police, Guardia Hacienda, pulled us over. I thought, *This is the end. We're going to go to jail. They're going to kill us when they figure out who we are.*

"Just keep your mouth shut, Jerry, and let me handle this," Ray said as the cop pulled us over. "Let me show you how things work here."

He took twenty quetzals out of his pocket and when the cop said, "You were speeding," Ray just slipped him the twenty. "Ah, *sí, sí,* no problemo," the cop said with a grin, and before you know it, we were back on the road.

Next, I met with Sheldon "Shelly" Katz, the big, burly, redheaded Texan who served as assistant DEA country attaché for Guatemala. I wanted his help with barrels of gas and miscellaneous equipment to refuel the Colombians' plane for their return trip to Bogotá after we off-loaded the dope.

"Okay, I'll do it," Shelly told me during the meeting. "Gimme fifteen grand." The figure wasn't unreasonable. Two thousand for fuel, a grand or two for barrels, pumps, and miscellaneous equipment, and the remainder to grease the palms of the Guatemalan cops. I agreed and left Shelly with fifteen thousand in DEA funds.

Next, we needed to find an airstrip—or land to build one. It's not a major thing to build a landing strip. You don't need a bulldozer. All you need is length, surface, and width. On our first deal, Paul told me we'd need to land a twin-engine Turbo-Commander or a Queen Air. "So we'll require fifteen hundred meters of runway," he said. "Hard surface. The grass cannot be soft, or the plane will sink."

I would supervise both finding the location and building the air-strip. Finding it was easy. I just used the local Guatemalan police. They make about fifteen dollars a month for being cops; for a few quetzals they would do anything. One of the officers knew a farmer in San Jose, and he said we could take a look.

Wearing my army fatigues, which had become my uniform, I arrived with the officers at a farm in the jungle of San Jose, and there was almost exactly what Paul said we needed. It was the perfect location for a landing strip—a hard, flat field, about fifteen hundred meters long, covered about three feet high in grass. The farmer said he'd rent it to us for a few months for five hundred dollars and he gave us a stack of machetes. The cops who tagged along with me began hacking down the grass like a bunch of human weed whackers.

Next, we needed to meet the coke smugglers.

———

We couldn't just tell our new Colombian coke associates that we had a business, Paul informed me. We had to show them, flash them the proof, just like we'd flashed Freddy Herrera the truckload of coke.

While I was building the airstrip, Paul was putting together our offices—a secretary, multiple phone lines, our names on the door. Genesis Import and Export was soon open for business. Of course, the company was a sham, a shell that had been used by another confidential informant in another dope deal that Shelly Katz had found for us. But Paul handled the setup so well that I felt as if we really had a business.

Our rented office was in a brand-new building. We even held a ribbon-cutting ceremony, with me in dark blue glasses and Paul dressed in head-to-toe Armani. The next day, our mugs were grinning from the Guatemala City newspapers. We were the city's newest import/export entrepreneurs.

Once we had our infrastructure set, we were ready to flash the Colombians our bogus business and our landing strip. Everything had happened at warp speed, as, I would soon learn, it always did with Paul. We had only been working together for a few months, but now it was summer and we were doing another flash. Two months of negotiation and on-site arrangements had come down to a single pivotal moment—the grand tour.

I called Shelly Katz. "Everything is a go," I said. "The crooks are in place, and we're ready to show 'em everything."

"Hold on, time out, we got a problem," said Shelly.

He said the shell business he had provided us was involved in another DEA operation in Cali and might already be burnt, meaning exposed.

My face turned red. "What the hell are we going to tell the Colombians?" I asked.

"Just tell them you can't show the business for security reasons," he said.

When I told Paul, he hit the ceiling, ranting and raging about the ineptitude of the DEA. He called Lizardo and they argued for days. Finally, it was agreed. Lizardo would send his pilot; then Paul would fly to Bogotá to present himself before Lizardo, who would decide whether the deal was on or off.

———

We borrowed a brand-new DEA informant's chopper for the site inspection.

Lizardo's inspection committee consisted of our money-hungry stooge, Avelino, a pilot called Juancho, and Lizardo's "gopher," a smuggler named Louis Perlaza. Paul and I laid it all out for them with the orchestration of a Broadway show opening. We took them over to the La Aurora International Airport in Guatemala City, where we got into a copter and flew up over the Pacific Coast to San Jose. There in a clearing our fifteen-hundred-meter runway was just begging for a coke load.

"There's our airstrip," Paul said proudly.

"Oh, senor. Very nice. Very nice! *Que bueno!*" the Colombians said. They complimented us on the site and the way it was set up in the jungle and how they could reach it so easily and unobtrusively from the Pacific.

Once we landed, the pilot measured the coordinates and Paul asked a hundred questions. What kind of plane were they going to land? How many gallons of fuel would they require to return to Colombia? What was the proposed date for the operation? What radio frequencies were we going to operate on? They were getting a dose of Paul's point-by-point approach.

When the trio left for Colombia to regale Lizardo with the specifics of our operation, we were left with a million details to handle. "Point by point," Paul said, once, twice, a million times, while I was ready to break out the vodka to celebrate the success of the flash.

———

The next day, Paul was on a plane to meet Lizardo. They met in Lizardo's hotel, and the Cali kingpin was steamed, demanding to see our business, his best proof that we were who we claimed to be.

"With all respect, this is our first deal," Paul said. "After this first one, we'll be happy to show you everything. But by the same token, you're not showing us where you store the loads."

Lizardo demanded leverage. "Okay, Don Oscar," he said at last. "We'll proceed, if you give us a family member as a guarantee."

Meaning a hostage. To ensure that things didn't go south. Paul didn't tell me about this, because he knew that I couldn't go along with it. Giving up a hostage is not only against every rule in the DEA book; it's also tantamount to murder. We knew the load was going down, so the hostage would be as good as dead.

"Okay," Paul said.

He called his sister-in-law, Marjorie de Sousa, his wife Erica's sister. Marjorie was, of course, a brilliant choice. A black-haired Brazilian beauty, she was about five-seven with the longest legs I'd ever seen. She wore skintight, bright, fire-engine-red dresses and stiletto heels. She had a taste for the good life, for Cristal champagne and men with the kind of flashy money that only coke dealing can buy.

Like her sister, Marjorie was from a dirt-poor family in Ipanema, Brazil. She saw her baby sister traveling the world with Paul Lir Alexander, riding in expensive cars, living in Rio mansions, and she frequently tagged along in Paul's entourage. Paul had unbelievable power over friends and relatives like Marjorie, who were in poverty until Paul broke them out. They would kill for him.

Paul called Marjorie and said, "I need you to go over and spend a couple of weeks with some friends of mine in Bogotá. Erica and I will meet you there as soon as we can."

Marjorie said, "No problem."

He didn't tell her that she would be a hostage. She just thought she was doing some reconnaissance work for good old Paul.

Marjorie de Sousa checked into the Hotel Intercontinental in Bogotá, where she was accommodated royally in the big drug-dealer suite, all expenses paid. She had round-the-clock bodyguards to take her shopping, dancing, dining. Her every wish was granted. This poor girl from Brazil had no idea that, should the deal go bad and should we be blamed, she would be dead.

Paul called me late that night after his meeting with Lizardo and said everything was set to go.

"What did you tell him?" I asked

"Don't worry about that," he said. "I did what I had to do."

I flew home for a weekend to be with Maggie. She hadn't asked me to, but it was something that I knew both of us needed. She was concerned about my welfare, and I knew that one face-to-face means more than a thousand telephone calls. So I flew home from Guatemala in the summer of 1991 to take Maggie to a Yankees game and then to dinner at our favorite restaurant, Little Charlie's Clam Bar in lower Manhattan.

Sitting there over a tableful of seafood, I looked over at my wife and thought, *Jerry, you're one hell of a lucky guy.* Maybe it was a defense mechanism, but Maggie didn't ask me a single question about my drug-smuggling escapades in Guatemala. She couldn't care less about Geraldo Bartone. To her, I was and always would be Crazy Jerry.

We talked about our daughter, Franki, who was five and growing up to be as beautiful as her mother. And we talked about returning to normalcy as a family, which I knew wouldn't happen for a long time.

"Well, Jerry, when are you going to be home again for good?" Maggie asked me.

"Not long, Maggie, I hope it's not long," I said, hoping it was true.

For the next couple of weeks, I set up a command center in the basement of our home, into which Maggie never ventured. I had one of those shortwave radios with a big die-pole antenna, two big ninety-foot copper wires that I strung up on a tree beside the house. My house looked as if Martians had landed. The radio's power was so immense, I was blowing television sets out in my neighborhood. It was yet another point in Paul's plan.

For a week before the planeload of coke was to leave Colombia, we had to test the radio frequencies that we would use. Every night at seven o'clock, I would go downstairs and dial up the frequency. "Omega, omega, omega," I would say, through the static, and I would hear a whistling signal back from the Colombians on the other end. Their guy would whistle and I would whistle back until we were whistling back and forth like two songbirds. Then I'd say, "Omega, omega, omega, uno, uno, dos, dos, tres, tres," and keep counting. Then they would do the same thing. "Omega, omega, omega . . ." It went on like this night after night, every hour on the hour.

These are the sounds of a major drug deal about to go down.

8

The First Deal

Finally, I got the call from Paul. Our first deal was going down on August 12, 1991.

Everything was ready. Our bogus personas. Our bogus business. Our landing strip. All we needed was fuel, specifically two hundred gallons of jet-A fuel, for the Colombians to return to Bogotá, once we loaded their coke onto our airstrip.

The fuel was my responsibility. I called Shelly Katz from the States and said, "We're on the next flight out. We need the fuel."

"Well, you can start heading down, but I think we're going to have problems," said Shelly. "You've got to tell them that it's got to be in a couple of days. It's the weekend and we're in Guatemala; it's tough to get fuel."

That's the way the bureaucracy worked. Shelly was just a typical government bureaucrat and I was ruining his weekend. I lost it. "Listen, Shelly, we were there for three weeks, we set this all up, we left you money. Now you get the fuel!"

I slammed down the phone.

Paul and I each headed back to Guatemala, Paul from his home in Miami and me from New York. When we got in that night, we met with Shelly at the Camino Real Hotel. Paul was wearing his usual suit, and big six-foot-three, stocky Shelly was dressed as always—Texas style with a bolo tie and cowboy boots. I was dressed in army fatigues, which was apropos, because we were going to war. With our own guy, Shelly Katz, who would turn out to be more trouble than a boatload of Colombian drug smugglers. He sat there in the crowded bar, two hundred-plus pounds of roadblock, sipping a drink and spouting negatives, while half of Guatemala partied riotously around us.

"Listen, Jerry, you just can't do the shipment this weekend. You've got to tell them to turn the plane around and delay it a couple of days."

Paul wouldn't hear of it. "We made a commitment," he said. "If we tell them to turn around, the deal is off and our cover could be blown."

I took a deep drink of vodka. Everything was on the line. My credibility with my division chief, Jimmy Wood, who had vouched for me, supported me, and pushed my case with the higher brass. All the work in the jungle building that landing strip. The endless weeks away from Maggie and Francesca. Everything Paul and I had done and all the money we'd spent and all the travel . . . everything was on the line because of this fat slug, who had made a promise, taken our money for payment, and now, out of either fear or laziness, was stalling.

I interrupted Paul's logical, calm conversation, ranting, "Just find the fuel, just find the fuel!"

"Well, we can't do it this weekend, Jerry," said Shelly. "You're going to have to call it off."

I took another slug of vodka. "Okay, Shelly, no problem," I said. "I've got everything solved. We're going out to the landing strip in San Jose, as planned. We'll off-load the plane, as planned. We'll do everything, as planned. But once they're ready to take off . . ."

I paused for emphasis, and Shelly said, "Yeah? What are you going to do then, Jerry?"

"Since you won't get us the fuel like you promised, I'm going to load the fuel barrels up with water," I said.

"What do you mean?" asked Shelly.

"I'll load them up with water, the Colombians will fill up their plane, and they'll get over the ocean and they'll crash."

Shelly looked at me and said, "That's murder."

"No, that's life in the drug business, pal," I said. "You either get me fuel, or we're going to go into plan B."

The next day, Paul and I were standing at our airstrip in the jungle at San Jose. I was wearing my usual fatigues and Paul was in his expensive, elaborate, perfectly ironed Adidas jogging togs and silk running shoes. We were going over the details, point by point, and trying to figure out how to buy or borrow enough jet fuel to get the plane back to Colombia.

Suddenly, down the bumpy dirt road came a caravan of Nissan SUVs, bringing in our six-member Guatemalan cop off-loading crew and a couple of agents from the U.S. embassy. And there in the back of the caravan, like a gift from God, was a fuel truck. Turned out Shelly convinced the Guatemalan police to "borrow" a fuel truck from the international airport.

We were back in business.

We had a radio set up in a shack near the landing strip, and the calls and radio communication began. All day and night long, the Colombians were testing the airwaves, the connection, the situation. Every moment, they were on the lookout for a hiccup, a screwup, a sign, or even a hint that there could be lurking, in the air or on the ground, a cop. "Omega, omega, omega . . . Uno, dos, tres . . ." and all of the whistling back and forth. Then came the phone calls from Lizardo, which Paul would always answer softly, *"Tranquillo, tranquillo.* Everything is on, everything is perfecto."

The plane loaded with 767 kilos of coke would take off from the point where most Cali coke loads began, the area of La Guajira in the mountains near Cartagena, home to the Guajirians, the Colombian Indians. La Guajira is on the mountainous coastline, and here the Colombians would pay the Guajirians to allow the planes to land in a clandestine strip on their land. The coke would come in from the village of Leticia or points beyond by land and the planes would fly in from major airports. The Guajirians would refuel planes and load the coke. The smuggler pilots would lay in overnight, then take off at three or four in the morning. La Guajira became such a popular point of embarkation that, in the height of the coke trade, dozens of planes would take off daily, just like at Newark International Airport.

Once the $1-million, twin-engine Turbo-Commander Queen Air, filled with 767 kilos of coke, with a street value of $59 million, took off from La Guajira on the morning of August 12, our radio and cell phones went crazy. The Colombians were talking and whistling like magpies, every second focused on making sure we, their new transporters, were ready to accept the load. If we were not ready, or if, God forbid, we were not there waiting to off-load the coke in a millisecond, their pilot, their plane, and their coke would be history, prey to cops or, worse yet, thieves . . . and $59 million in coke, plus $1 million in plane and a priceless smuggler pilot could vanish like smoke.

"Tranquillo, senor, *tranquillo,"* Paul kept telling Lizardo. "Everything is perfecto."

Then, Paul, standing there in his Nike jogging suit with a walkie-talkie in one hand and a cell phone in the other, turned to reassure me. By early the next morning, we were hiding in the woods with our off-loading crew, awaiting the plane's arrival, and my heart was banging away like a bass drum. I was thinking the worst, that our cover was somehow blown and the pilot, and God knows who else, would come out firing.

"Everything's going fine, Jerry, just relax," Paul said a million times. "Point by point, Jerry, point by point."

At about 5:00 A.M., just as the sun was streaking the night with wisps of light, this majestic bird floated down out of the sky. It made a perfect landing on the grassy strip, nosing down at the end of the short runway. Paul, shouted out, *"Rapido, rapido, rapido!"* to our off-loading crew. Our half dozen Guatemalan rent-a-cops ran toward the plane like cargo crews run toward planes at airports everywhere.

I watched the plane's door crack open and the round-faced, pudgy Colombian pilot with straight black hair peeked out. Wearing a Guaya-bera shirt, as if he'd just flown in for a vacation, he looked like a guy thirsty for a *mai tai*. There were no greetings. The pilot just started heaving big white burlap bags out of the plane. Each bag was marked with a handwritten number indicating how many kilos were in it. Within six, seven minutes at the most, the pilot had heaved sixteen or seventeen big three-foot-high bags onto the runway, leaving a big mountain of burlap containing 767 kilos, or sixteen hundred pounds, of grade-A pure cocaine.

While the pilot was hurling bags out of the plane, our refueling crew was pumping fuel into the tank. Within five minutes, it was all over. The coke was off-loaded, the fuel was on-loaded, and the plane was taking off for Colombia, leaving a mountain of coke on the runway.

Party time.

Paul and I and the agents from the embassy and the Guatemalan cops all started slapping fives and cracking open the cervezas. There were photographs of us around our trophy, our mountain-high pile of coke. We tore open a bag and pulled out a kilo brick, which had been wrapped as tightly as a diamond wedding case at Tiffany's.

The white paper was labeled with the big red, white, and blue circular brand and stamped with the word *Gordos*. Paul had already told me what that meant. At that time, Gordo was primo, fresh coke from the house of Gilberto Rodriguez-Orejuela, a mean, stone-cold killer and one of the main families of the Cali cartel. I imagined him on that morning, lounging in some white mansion, a harem of hookers at his side, with absolutely no idea that his associates had just transported 767 kilos, sixteen hundred pounds, of his purest cocaine to a gang of cops in the jungle.

"Point by point, Jerry!" Paul exclaimed, slapping me on the back. "Next point, we load the truck and get the hell out of here."

"Vamanos!" he yelled to the crew. And everybody loaded the bags of coke into the trucks. We bounded into the SUVs, and the caravan of coke and cops were headed back to Guatemala City. It was about 8:30 A.M.

We were back in Guatemala City by noon, all of us exhausted. The coke went into a storage room, basically a closet with a lock on the door, in the U.S. embassy downtown.

———

The next morning we were all rested and eager for work. Paul and Danny Brown got a truckload of *mudanza* (Spanish for moving) boxes and started packing them with inventoried kilos, labeling each one: *1 of 20, 2 of 20, 3 of 20.* Then everybody—Paul, Danny, the agents, the Guatemalan cop off-loading crew, and I—loaded the boxes into three trucks and headed to the Guatemala City Airport. One of Pam Am's security directors had been contacted in advance to reserve us a container that could hold our sixty labeled boxes, whose contents were confidential.

By the time we arrived, the container was waiting. We loaded the boxes of coke inside, then hefted the container onto the Pan Am plane. Just to make sure there were no screwups, I planted an agent from the Guatemalan CIA, the D-2, in the airport when we arrived and on the plane when we loaded and locked it up. And there, in a container surrounded by boxes and luggage, $59 million worth of Cali father Gilberto Rodriguez-Orejeula's coke was headed to DEA headquarters in New York.

I changed from my fatigues into my suit in a spare room. Dressed all spiffy, I was once again Geraldo Bartone—and nothing could make me break character. I boarded the plane, sat down in my first-class seat, and thought, *If these people only knew what was in the belly of this plane!*

Next to me was a beautiful blonde, who shot me a welcome-aboard smile. "How you doing?" she asked.

"Good, great," I said.

"Heading back to New York?"

"Yes," I said.

"And what do you do?"

"Import/export, just sent out a load of *chayotes,* green squash. Ever tried one? Wow, they're good, just great to eat. We think it's going to be the next big food craze in New York, maybe the next pasta, and we'll be on the front end of a fortune."

I never broke character. Because you never know who you're talking to. Yes, she was a beautiful blonde, but she could also have been a Cali plant.

I opened up a copy of the *Wall Street Journal* and fell asleep.

We flew first to Miami, where we had agents watching the plane from the moment it touched down until it took off again. Then it was on to La Guardia in New York. Once the plane landed, I let all of the other passengers disembark first. A tug pulled the plane to a hangar where everybody was waiting. I put on my big, broad straw Guatemalan hat and headed for the little door on the jet-way, which led directly onto the tarmac. I was physically and mentally exhausted, but I was walking on air.

When I opened the door, a cheer went up. I could see the members of Group 93, smiling, hugging, slapping five, all yelling, "Jerry, you did it! You did it! You did it." I climbed down the stairway and was enveloped in hugs, handshakes, and high fives.

"I knew you could do it, Jerry, I knew you could do it," division chief Jimmy Wood kept repeating. Jimmy was one of the NYPD's original undercover agents, and he really believed in me.

Finally, it was time to crack open our prize. We stationed a Pan Am security officer inside the belly of the plane and made a human chain, every member of Group 93 passing the boxes back from the container into a waiting DEA cargo van. When we were done, 767 kilos of coke had been off-loaded and everybody had to blink twice to believe their eyes. Then everybody followed the truck down to the evidence vault at DEA headquarters, where each box was registered and stacked up as pretty as presents on Christmas morning.

A week later, Paul arrived.

It was time for the delivery to go bad.

Point by point, Jerry, I could hear Paul saying, even when he wasn't around. For weeks, he had made the next step clear: Now that we had Cali's coke, we had their confidence. It was time to locate a ship leaving from Guatemala City so we could create a dummy bill of lading and convince Lizardo that the container with *chayotes* from Genesis Import and Export had left on schedule and was headed to New York. We also needed the seal number that goes on the container receipt as additional proof.

With the help of a customs agent, I had forgeries squared away and faxed to Colombia within a day, and Paul was on the phone to Lizardo, saying, "Perfecto, my friend, everything went perfecto. The shipment will arrive in New York in thirty days."

The clock started ticking. In thirty days, we would have to figure a way *not* to deliver the coke, some way for our perfectly constructed deal to fall apart, for somebody—not Paul and me—to screw up and have the 767 kilos of coke land in the hot hands of the New York authorities.

Near the end of the thirty days, Paul called Lizardo. "The shirts are here, my friend, and they are very nice, neatly pressed," I heard him saying on the phone in the Tele-Paranda.

Then I saw Paul's face turn dark.

"No, senor, we cannot make three deliveries, my friend," I heard him say. "Only one delivery, only one. Any more is too dangerous, too risky."

When Paul hung up the phone, I got hot. "Why can't we do three deliveries?" I asked. "Let's just deliver the stuff and bust three different customers!"

Paul held up a hand. "Remember about the responsibility, Jerry," he said. "Whoever is holding the coke when this load goes down is the guy who is responsible, the guy who is dead."

He explained Lizardo's strategy with the three deliveries. "He's testing us again," Paul said. Lizardo wanted proof from the first deal out of the box that we weren't cops—and three successful deliveries would prove it. Three deliveries meant three different exposures. If we did three deliveries to three customers who didn't know each other and all three failed, well, Lizardo would immediately know the problem—us. If all three deliveries go bad, guess who would be dead? Me and Paul!

If we did one delivery of the entire 767 kilos and the deal went bad, who could ever say who was really responsible? We could argue, "Sorry, senor, it was you, not me." We could find a way to make them think *they* were responsible for the failure. "We've got to pin it back, Jerry, pin the blame back on them," Paul said.

A day or two later, Paul and I were back in the Tele-Paranda, and Paul was back on the phone with Lizardo. I could see him nodding his head and saying, *"Sí, sí, sí,* okay, my friend, we'll do it your way."

Paul hung up the phone. "Three deliveries," he said. "We've got to figure out how to do three deliveries."

He thought about it a minute. Then he looked me square in the eye with an expression that I hadn't seen much of before. He almost seemed to be pleading. "Listen, Jerry, all we have to do is let one of the deliveries go through," he said. "We'll make it a small one, forty kilos. If we let the first load go through, then we'll gain a lot of credibility. We'll be able to seize tons from then on. We'll still seize the other 727, but we'll let forty out on the street right out of the box."

"Paul, I don't know if that's possible," I said. "But I'll see what I can do."

———

Paul's idea didn't seem that implausible. I immediately thought about Ronnie Foti.

I had recently helped another DEA group bust Foti, a corrupt department of transportation official in the city of Yonkers. As my fame in the DEA grew, the other group "borrowed" me to bait Ronnie Foti with five pounds of pot. I drove up to Yonkers in my BMW and sold Foti the pot. Foti was busted, but not until after the pot was actually allowed to go on the streets.

When I took Paul's idea to my supervisors, I was talking Ronnie Foti all the way. First, I took the proposal to Jimmy Wood, selling it as an opportunity to seize tons. "And don't forget about Ronnie Foti and the five pounds of pot," I said. "We were allowed to let that get out, and this time we're talking about *a ton of coke!*"

"Okay, let's take it to Maltz," said Wood. "I think he's going to blow a gasket, but let's see."

I pulled the same Ronnie Foti sales job on Maltz.

"I don't think it's going to happen, but let's take it to the next level," he said.

Robert Bryden gave us the okay to communicate with the next level, the U.S. Attorney's office. Someone there called down to Department of Justice headquarters in Washington, and our request rolled back to us like a rotten egg. "Who the hell thought of this?" they asked each of my supervisors, until the blame finally rolled back on me. We were not allowed to let one gram of coke out on the street.

I called Paul in Miami. "I got bad news," I said. "We can't do it. We gotta come up with plan B."

"These idiot cops!" he said. "They don't understand! We could seize tons!"

"I don't care, Paul, it's not my decision, and I don't want to go to jail."

———

We hatched a new plan, going back and forth on the phone. There was no way to do three failed deliveries, so we came up with a way to get all of the coke busted in the first one. Paul returned to New York and we went to work.

Point number one: Lizardo wanted us to deliver the first two hundred-kilo shipments to a Colombian named Mario and a woman from Cali named Delphin. He gave us two beeper numbers and told us to beep the buyers and arrange for them to pick up the loads.

Mario called back first. He dispatched his mule, Julio Mendez Yepez, to accept the load. Because you never send your best man for the first deal with untested transporters, Julio was a nobody, a sacrificial lamb.

Julio met Paul at a Wendy's near Sixty-ninth and Northern Boulevard in Jackson Heights, Queens. He was a short, dark guy driving a blue van. Paul told Julio that his aide-de-camp, Alexander Calderone would drive the blue van to our warehouse, pick up the hundred kilos out of our stash, load it up, and deliver to a location on Northern Boulevard that day at 4:00 P.M. Paul said he would beep him with the cross street.

The code we used was 400-6969, so he knew to go to Sixty-ninth and Northern and look for the blue van at four. There would be no more telephones, beepers only at this point. That's how they always insisted we do it. Telephones were too dangerous when the deal was about to go down.

Point number two: When we got the blue van, we had two hours to load it and deliver it to Julio. We ran all the checks on it and discovered, lo and behold, the van had a suspended registration and expired license plates. That was a tremendous gift. An idea immediately bubbled up in my brain. I turned to Paul.

"I've got it!" I exclaimed. "We'll lie to the press and say that we followed the van because it had suspended plates. We'll say, we followed it back to the warehouse where it was loaded with the other 667 kilos. We'll be clear and we'll have the reporters write articles that the suspended license and registration led to this cocaine seizure."

Paul flashed a rare smile. "It's brilliant, Jerry," he said. "Let's do it."

———

To make sure Julio Mendez Yepez wouldn't have any problems stopping for police, we installed a remote kill switch in the van.

Just before 4:00 P.M., we loaded the blue van with the hundred real kilos and parked it at a Dunkin' Doughnuts at Sixty-ninth and Northern Boulevard. We beeped Julio with the 400-6969, and right on time, he showed up, climbed into the van, started it up, and made his getaway. He pulled out of the parking lot and was driving down Northern Boulevard when we flipped the remote that triggered the kill switch. When the van went dead, a car driven by one of the members of Group 93 banged into the back of Julio's van, and almost immediately Julio Mendez Yepez was surrounded by cops. Not real patrol officers, but the members of Group 93 in patrol uniforms.

From where I was watching, I could see Julio sweating, just soaking wet. He didn't say a single word. Not when he was yanked out of the car. Not when he was taken down to headquarters where he was booked for possession of narcotics, along with the traffic violation. Not one word. We would do his talking for him.

Paul called Mario in a rage. "Look, something is going on because the police just hit my warehouse."

"Yes, something is going on all right!" Mario replied. "You guys are snitches! The police just took my driver."

Then the Blame Game began. Paul, knowing that we couldn't risk busting a second delivery, had to pin the blame back on Mario. We had to convince Lizardo that Mario not only was dumb enough to deliver a stolen van with expired license plates for us to load the stash, but had also brought police surveillance on the van, causing the seizure of both the one hundred kilos of coke in the van and the additional 667 kilos in our warehouse.

Next point: Paul and I went back to the DEA, and I wrote a phony press release that told the whole story the way we wanted it told—we followed a blue van with expired plates to a warehouse and busted its driver after watching him load 100 kilos of a total stash of 767. I took the press release to all of my superiors, including Chief Maltz. This time the snowball didn't roll uphill, only down. "You ain't lying to the press," everyone told me.

"What do you mean we ain't lying to the press?" I said. "We'll be dead. They'll kill me and Paul once they find out what happened."

"Figure something out," said Maltz.

I ranted and raged. "You can't do this to us! We're gonna be history with the cartel when we're just getting started."

"Absolutely, positively, you're not lying to the press," said Maltz. "Pay the informant and that's it. Operation over."

That was always their way out: "Give the informant extra money. Pay him and let him explain things to the cartel." That type of mentality was why we were losing the drug war in New York. Paul didn't care about a couple of extra thousand dollars; he cared about keeping his credibility.

———

It was the summer of 1991. I had been working with Paul for about six months, and had learned to think outside of the box. I thought of what Paul always told me: "You've got to lay the foundation." Meaning the foundation for whatever scam you're going to pull. I had to come up with something great.

It hit me when I was walking out of Maltz's office, *Okay, so we can't get the press to lie for us,* I thought. *But why can't we print our own paper and write our own story, the way we want it written?* With my heart pounding over the perfect beauty of the ruse, I ran down the stairs into Group 93 headquarters and called my best friend, Bernie Kerik. We had been buddies since he served as warden at the Passaic County Jail. I had been introduced to him while I was still working as a narc by Maggie's brother's friend, Jeff Breckenridge, who worked for Bernie as a corrections officer. Bernie would call me all the time, and I would tell him war stories about my escapades in the NYPD. On the day after I got shot, Bernie read the news of the gunbattle in the newspaper. He called the hospital where I was recuperating and instead of talking about the danger of the gun battle or the bullet in my arm, I rambled on about how much I loved police work and how it was a "great fuckin' job!"

And the funny thing was he may have sounded crazy to most people, but for one of the few times since I've known Jerry Speziale, he made perfect sense to me, Kerik would later write.

Bernie and I continued to talk frequently and soon we were the best of friends. In 1986, I convinced Bernie to join the NYPD and helped him get on to the narco squad as an undercover. Bernie worked a foot post on 42nd Street known as The Deuce. Because I was in the

Street Enforcement Unit, I would occasionally work The Duece as Jerry the Junkie, buying dope and crack. When I was working The Deuce, I would hook up with Bernie after our respective tours of duty and we would BS. I was making a name for myself as an undercover, so I called Joe Lisi, the lieutenant who ran the Ninety Day Wonder program, and asked Joe and his assistant, Richie Platzer, to get Bernie into the program. Lisi and Platzer liked me. They gave Bernie an interview and he became a Ninety Day Wonder.

He would eventually go on to become NYPD Police Commissioner. But before that, he and I were inseparable in Group 93. We worked together, hung out after work together, and shared holidays with our families together. When I was abroad, Bernie checked in constantly with Maggie and Franki. He made sure that my family was okay. I trusted Bernie with my life, my family and every secret I had, even things I couldn't tell Maggie, like where the life insurance policies were kept and what I wanted done for Maggie and the kids if I didn't make it back. We were tighter than tight.

With Bernie's skills as a manager and his talent in writing affidavits for what would soon total 450 eavesdropping warrants, and our combined knowledge of wiretaps and our intense, take-no-prisoners style, we would become the perfect team. But when I called Bernie for help in August, 1991, I was calling for a specific contact—his girlfriend, Dee, who I knew worked at Buddha Graphics and could, of course, print the dummy newspapers.

Bernie agreed to enlist Dee's services at Buddha. He then called Kevin Gibson at the *Bergen Record.* He knew Kevin from when he had been a warden, and Kevin wrote stories about him. Bernie arranged everything. Kevin agreed to write the story. I bought three *New York Posts*, three *New York Newsdays*, and brought them back and took out page 2 from each of them. Kevin Gibson wrote us an article according to our specifications.

The headline was SUSPENDED LICENSE PLATE LEADS TO COKE SEIZURE, and it was beautiful. The article reported the bust exactly as we wanted it to go down: This dumb schmuck Julio Mendez Yepez blew the deal because of expired plates. Once the police had the van under surveillance, the cops later hit another location, a warehouse in the Bronx, where they found another 667 kilos of cocaine. We sent a set of the papers to Lizardo in Bogotá, then set up a meeting with Mario in a diner in Queens.

We showed him the fake newspaper articles, and you should have seen his face. He blanched pale white and beads of sweat dotted his upper lip. He could argue with us, but he couldn't argue with the *New York Post*. If he or his mule was dumb enough to do a dope deal with expired plates, well, Mario knew, he might as well be reading his own obituary. He was the one holding the bag when the deal went bad, and he knew what that meant.

"What kind of operation are you running, pal?" Paul asked. "Expired plates? We thought we were dealing with professionals."

━━━

Next point: Paul and I left Mario and returned to the Tele-Paranda. Paul called Lizardo in Colombia, just to report in, to show that we weren't ducking him. "Yessir, we've sent the newspapers," I could hear Paul saying. "We'd be happy to come down and explain everything."

Meanwhile, Mario began ducking the *jefes* down south. So the cartel associates began looking at us like, *Hey, these guys aren't afraid of anything, and Mario has disappeared.*

Which meant Mario would soon be dead.

And we were ready to move up in the organization.

On Lizardo's invitation, or demand, Paul flew down to Bogotá and met with Lizardo and all his people, and another flash was about to begin.

9

The Trial

"**W**e're going to turn it around, Jerry," said Paul, calling me from the airport. "We're going to pin it back on them." Although I stayed behind in Miami, he told me everything about the meeting, point by point.

Paul was flying down to Bogotá to meet Lizardo and his associates to prove, once and for all, that we were not responsible for the loss of their 767 kilos of coke.

"We're going to pin it back on them, Jerry, that's the key," Paul told me again.

That was always Paul's strategy, shift the blame and be aggressive about it. There is no room for timidity with the Cali cartel. "If you go down there and tap-dance, you'll never leave the meeting, except in a body bag," Paul said. "They'll blow your brains out right there at the conference table."

Arriving in Bogotá, Paul descended from the glories of first class into a police state. Green-uniformed, stern-faced military were everywhere, toting machine guns that they looked eager to use. The smell of rotting food and back-alley urine assaulted Paul's nose, while the cacophony of the bustling city blasted his eardrums.

A black town car and a driver in a blue suit were waiting at the gate, because Paul never took taxis, especially not in Bogotá, where you never know who could be at the wheel. The driver greeted Paul like family and whisked him off to one of the best hotels in the center of the city. The location was convenient for Lizardo, since he owned the place.

As soon as he walked into the conference room, he knew that this was no mere meeting.

It was a trial.

Paul opened what seemed like an ordinary door. Behind it was a wall of steel bars. The wall of bars opened and there stood the biggest guard he'd ever seen in his life. He walked inside and the bars clanged shut behind him.

The conference room had bars on all the windows. His eyes took in the scene and he knew he was trapped. There was no escape route.

A big, long black oval conference table dominated the room. Under it was a thick blue carpet, and around it were maybe twenty men in business attire sitting in big leather chairs. The room was smoke filled and the men could have been representatives of IBM, Colombian Division. They were all wealthy, with homes in various countries, and they sent their children to Ivy League American colleges. Their wives shopped at Bergdorf Goodman and ate lunch in the same restaurants as the wives of American business titans and movie stars. But their outward appearances were as bogus as Paul's and mine, because these men were gangsters. Each had risen to the pinnacle of his profession. These were stone-cold killers, the Mafia of dope dealers.

When Paul entered the room, there were no handshakes, just a roomful of pissed-off, thirty-something businessmen in suits and ties. This was the highest echelon of the Gilberto Rodriguez-Orejuela Organization, which in the early 1990s was responsible for importing and distributing more than five thousand kilos of coke to the U.S. a month. With cells in New York, Houston, Chicago, Miami, and LA, it was a global network of smugglers and foot soldiers, but the men in this room were its heart. There were a half dozen leaders, and the rest were high-level associates.

The enforcer of whatever punishment might be deemed appropriate sat at the far end of the desk—a stone-faced Colombian with a gun on his lap, a hit man. If the decision didn't go our way, if the men found Paul responsible, then the punishment would be administered right there in Lizardo's hotel, whose staff Paul had no doubt, knew ways to dispose of Paul's body.

The Cali associates sitting in that conference room had just lost $59 million and wanted to vent their rage on somebody.

Paul looked around the table and recognized five of the men, our judges, all of whom had been personally involved in our lost load.

Lizardo's real name was Jose Lizardo Losada. He was a short, stocky Colombian with thick wavy black hair and a black Ricardo Mantalban mustache. He had gotten Rodriguez-Orejuela and others into our deal, so the responsibility for the loss fell squarely on his shoulders. This fact made him our biggest asset in this trial, because the last thing Lizardo wanted was for us to be found at fault. After all, he approved our airstrip, our operation, our credibility. He was responsible for Paul. If Paul was found guilty, then he would be found guilty, too.

Next to Lizardo was Helmer Pacho Herrera, thirty-five, a light-skinned, pockmark-faced guy whose picture I'd seen in a *Time* magazine article about the cartels. As overseer of all operations involving distribution of coke in several U.S. cities, Herrera coordinated the various distribution cells responsible for receiving the shipment. He had tapped Mario to receive our load, which meant that his ass was on the line, too.

Next to him was thin, curly-haired, clean-shaven Lucho Grejales, the Gilberto Rodriguez-Orejuela Organization's business manager, responsible for the financing of all loads, including ours. Grejales was involved in pulp and fruit importation/exportation, which provided the perfect way to hide the shipments of coke by mixing it with the pulp.

Next to him was Lucho Palmira, financier of coke shipments to the U.S., for whom the loss of the load meant the loss of a considerable amount of his investors' cash. He was the most sophisticated-looking man in the group. Paul told me he looked more like an investment banker than a dope dealer. He was actually both.

Finally, there was Oscar Saavedra, who as overseer of all banking and financial matters for the organization was the only man who could locate the all-powerful Rodriguez-Orejuela at any time. In his oversize five-thousand-dollar suit he was slouched in his chair like an unmade bed. He looked like he was drunk—or hungover. He was plenty pissed off, and everyone in the room knew that meant Rodriguez-Orejuela was pissed off, too.

"Good morning, gentlemen," said Lizardo, looking over at Paul.

"I've known Don Oscar for many years. He comes with great credentials and references. His partner is a well connected former U.S. senator who has great political power. We've done numerous loads with them, and we've had no problems. Our deliveries are successful, and we've made lots of money together."

Having introduced Paul to the group, Lizardo said, simply, "Don Oscar."

"Thank you, Senor Lizardo," Paul said. "We did our part. We have taken a tremendous loss ourselves. We've paid our people in Guatemala a lot of money to ensure the success of this load. But now, our business has been infiltrated by the police. We will have to change everything. We have suffered a tremendous loss and should be repaid for these losses."

Paul fanned the fake newspapers across the conference table. "Here are the New York newspapers, telling the entire story of how the arrest happened," Paul said. He let some time lapse while the men read the papers. "Where is Mario? I am here, showing my face. Mario, the guilty party, is not. Why? Because Mario knows that if he were here, he would be dead. I come and I put my face.

"I don't run and hide like Mario. With all respect, gentlemen, my partner and I have lost as much as you. We lost our warehouse in the Bronx. We still don't know how badly we have been exposed because, again, with all respect, you sent this idiot with bad plates."

Paul was lying so well. "You should have seen their faces," he told me later. Sympathy isn't an expression easily worn by Colombian dope dealers, but as the men in the room listened to Paul's spiel and read the proof in the New York newspapers, they were brought to their knees. Paul said even the hit man was nodding in agreement. They wanted blood all right, but, for the moment, it wasn't ours.

Paul couldn't leave it at that. He had to dig the spike into them even more. He picked up one of the copies of the newspaper and tossed it across the table. "This Mario could have taken down my whole operation," Paul said, spitting out the words. "But he didn't. We're in too deep for one bust to take us down. Still, we invested quite a bit of capital in this operation We did everything required of us. We did our part. Your associate did not."

Then he said the word that meant everything to the men in the room.

THE TRIAL / 101

"Responsibility," said Paul. "Someone must be responsible. Whoever is responsible for Mario will need to pay my partner Geraldo and I for our losses."

"Okay," said Helmer Herrera. "Who will be responsible for Don Oscar?"

Paul knew what that meant. Who would bet his life that Paul wasn't lying, that Paul wasn't responsible for the lost load?

Paul looked around the conference table. Two men nodded. They were midlevel Cali associates, whom he didn't know at the time, Jose Ricardo and Jorge Arturo.

"We will vouch for our friend Don Oscar," said Ricardo. "We will be responsible for him."

Of course, Ricardo and Arturo weren't vouching for Paul out of the goodness of their hearts. They'd want something in return. But at the time, Paul never dreamed of the magnitude, the sheer balls, of their demands. At the time, he was just looking at those steel bars, dying to get out of that smoke-filled room and away from these goons masquerading as businessmen.

Helmer Herrera clapped his hands and the sound echoed around the room like a gunshot. "Well," he boomed, "the determination is that Mario is guilty. Mario is responsible for the loss of the load."

Lucho Grejales, the finance manager asked, "Who does Mario represent?"

Meaning who authorized him, who vouched for Mario? Because just as someone had to vouch for us for the transportation, someone had to vouch for Mario for distribution.

"Senor Escobar out of Cali," someone said.

"We have to access the damage against him," said Lucho Grejales. "He is responsible, as well."

"I'd like to be paid for my losses," Paul repeated. "Because obviously I did my part."

"Yes, you're due your money," said Lucho. "And we'll assess the damage against Mario and Senor Escobar."

"We're sorry for Mario's ineptitude," said Helmer Herrera. "You can be sure that he will pay. We will pay you for your loss, and we look forward to doing another load with you."

"I'm sorry," Paul said. "But, as you surely must understand, we're not eager to expose our organization so soon. We wasted considerable time and money sending my people to Guatemala. We had to pay off the local police, pay for fuel, pay for the shipment."

When Paul called me and told me the news, I thought, *This is so beautiful!* We'd disrupted them from every angle, but they couldn't see the big picture because of the way their operation was set up. Because everything was compartmentalized, every aspect of their operation separate, they were playing right into our hands.

"Okay," Lizardo said in closing. "We'll release your family member. The hostage can go."

———

The moment he got out of the meeting, Paul called me. I could feel his braggadocio, an ocean away. "You should have seen them, Jerry," he said. "I had them eating out of my hand. They even apologized for having to keep Marjorie as a hostage."

Hostage? The word was like a slap in the face to me. He'd never mentioned anything about a hostage.

"Great performance," I said. "But what did you just say about a hostage?"

"Well," he said, "I had to put up someone for a guarantee."

"What are you talking about?" I asked.

He didn't seem to hear me. "I put up Marjorie," he said. "She had lots of time on her hands. And for all she knew, she was going to party for a few weeks with a few of my friends."

"Jesus, Paul," I said. "You jeopardized my career, not to mention your sister-in-law's life. How would I explain that to the brass?"

"Jerry, you do not understand," he said. "This is business. I have everything under control. Remember, point by point, Jerry," he said. "This is the way the business works. You must be able to prove responsibility and shift responsibility."

His ego was in high gear. "I told you I know what I'm doing," he said. "We're going to seize tons, Jerry. Tons! If you just listen to me, and follow my instructions, we're going to seize tons."

———

Paul had just been tried and exonerated by the Cali cartel for the biggest seizure of my career. A load of 767 kilos, sixteen hundred pounds of coke, street value of thirty-five thousand dollars a pound, meaning $59 million in coke, was in the DEA lockup. I was already a superstar among my peers, and the cartel that we had just ripped off was eager to do another load with us. At that point, I believed everything Paul Lir Alexander told me.

About a month later, when Paul said to me, "Jerry, you remember our little friend Mario? Well, he's turned up missing. I think they killed him."

But Mario wouldn't be the last drug dealer to die.

━━━

We both flew back home, Paul from Bogotá, me from Miami—and I went back to work at headquarters, while Paul went back to his home in Miami. One day not long after our return, I got an urgent call from Paul. He said he was back in Bogotá, and things weren't going well.

"Lizardo demanded that I fly down immediately," he said. "And when I got here he had the phony editions of the *New York Post* on his desk."

I felt my face flush red.

"He said the newspaper article we'd given him about the bust was a fake," Paul said. "He'd gotten all three editions of the *Post* and couldn't find anything. You gotta work fast, Jerry."

"Whaddya want me to do, Paul?" I asked.

"Lizardo said he checked all three editions of the *Post*," Paul said. "Call the newspapers and see if they had a fourth edition on that day."

I hung up the phone and called the *Post*. We were in luck. The paper had printed four editions, Lizardo only had three. I called Paul with the good news.

"Okay, run over to the *Post* and make sure they don't release the fourth edition to anybody, for any reason," he said.

So Paul's newspaper became the "fourth edition" of the *New York Post*.

Paul called me back a few hours later.

"Well, for the moment, Lizardo seems satisfied," he told me. "But he said somebody has to take the blame for the lost load."

"Like who?" I asked.

"Like anybody but us," Paul said.

━━━

One thing I learned fast about the Cali cartel: Everything—and everybody—is connected. One bust harvests hundreds of miscellaneous leads. All you have to do is pick one lead and start chasing it. After Mario went down, Paul said, "Okay, Jerry, remember, point by point. Next point, we call the second customer of the load."

Her name was Delphin Preito, and she lived in Bayside, Queens. She was a Cali native responsible for operating a New York distribution cell that handled more than 350 kilos a month in New York.

Using Delphin's pager number, which Paul had gotten through his Colombian connections, we arranged a meeting. I drove over to Queens with Paul and his major domo, Antonio Calderon, the former Nicaraguan contra general. Antonio was to meet Delphin around noon at the Bayside Diner on Northern Boulevard. Paul and I were wearing our usual Armani. We waited in the car while dark, pock-marked Antonio, in a flashy silk shirt and dress slacks, went into the diner to meet Delphin.

Thirty minutes late and looking like a hooker on a ten-minute break, Delphin Preito came clip-clopping into the diner, balanced on stiletto heels.

Antonio launched into a lament about the lost load, and how "that idiot," Mario, screwed up everything for everybody with his stolen van.

"Well, there's always next time," Delphin said. Until then, she suggested, why didn't she and Antonio get together for drinks, dinner, *anything?* She seemed genuinely lonely in New York, but he wasn't interested in playing the Dating Game.

Antonio told her we'd call her when our next load came in. Meanwhile, we had her pager number, and we traced Delphin back to her house at 207th Street and Northern Boulevard.

———

We started conducting surveillance on Delphin Preito's house, which turned out to be a very busy place. We kept seeing cars coming and going at all hours. One night, we saw Delphin rush out of the house carrying a big suitcase. No high heels tonight; she was in her traveling clothes, jeans and sneakers. She jumped into a white taxi. The cab headed for JFK Airport, and we followed it.

Halfway there, we had two of our guys, dressed in patrol cops' uniforms, pull them over as if it were a routine traffic stop. They got Delphin and the driver, Johnny, out of the cab, and while they were being questioned I sneaked into the cab's backseat and ducked down where no one, especially Delphin, could see me. Right there on the seat was a brick of cash, a page full of telephone numbers, and Delphin's cellular phone. I turned the phone on and got her cell number, then climbed back out of the cab.

We let them leave, but we continued following them to JFK, where Delphin got out with her suitcase. She checked in for a flight to San Juan, Puerto Rico, checked her suitcase, and proceeded to the gate. One of our guys, Jerry Vetrano, a.k.a. "Jerry V," stayed with the suitcase. He tried to grab it off the conveyor belt, but he was too late, so he had to tackle the bag and ride it through the luggage tunnels, until he came out on the other end. By then, we had a search warrant, thanks to Rick Gerard, who was able to get the paperwork done at warp speed. We opened the suitcase and found $150,000 in cash packed inside.

We emptied the bag, zipped it back up, and threw it back on the conveyor belt, as if nothing had happened. Then we returned to Delphin's house in Bayside, Queens, with our search warrant.

To get a better look, I climbed a tree across the street from the house. I was impressed by what I saw. This was not the typical mid-level dope dealer's hovel. It was a stacked duplex in a nice suburban neighborhood of Bayside, Queens, where kids played safely in the street and from which upper-middle-class commuters made the daily trek into Manhattan. I could see a guy who looked like an accountant sitting in the living room, counting the biggest stack of money I'd ever seen.

Group 93 stormed the house and searched the premises. I climbed down from the tree and was walking in the front door when I saw Eddie Beach coming out of a bedroom. He was wearing jeans and a work shirt and scribbling something in his little notebook, and beaming an ear-to-ear grin.

"How we doin'?" I asked Eddie.

"Pay dirt, baby!" Eddie said. "I'm tellin' you it's a fuckin' homer, Jerry! The house is full of cash!"

He wasn't kidding. That stash house looked like Fort Knox—cash was covering every available surface. Bills were piled up on tables, the floor, the beds, even in the bathroom. There were ones, fives, tens, twenties, fifties, and hundreds. There were thick ledgers and cash-sorting machines . . . so much cash that it took us all day to gather it all. When we finally were able to get it counted, it totaled $1.4 million. There was also sixty-five kilos of coke in the closest. We arrested the accountant, Pedro Sanchez, and he later got twenty-five years to life.

We never found Delphin Preito. She was nothing but a cash and coke mule, anyway. But the $1.4 million proved to me that we were on to something bigger than I ever imagined, a seemingly bottomless well of cash, coke, and connections.

10

The Costa Rica Con Job

Once Paul and I had been exonerated in the loss of the 767 kilos, everybody was eager to do a new deal with us. With Avelino and Alonso as our brokers, hungry to make their percentage on the next deal, Paul found plenty of new clients for our transportation services. He decided on a group of Colombians led by Nacho Gaitan, Pedro Paulo, and Olympo Caro.

Nacho was the leader. He was a major Cali associate who had his own international organization with distribution cells in New York City and other parts of the U.S. Like most of the cartel's dealers, he would "pool loads," participate in shipments with other associates. He was right up there with the biggest associates of the Rodriguez-Orejuela group as a major player in the cartel.

Pedro Paulo was Nacho's executive assistant, his spokesman and all-purpose aide. Pedro liked Paul, but didn't really trust him. He was the one who came up with Paul's nickname, "El Parito Loco," the Crazy Bird. Olympo Caro was nothing more than yet another broker like Avelino and Alonso, a freelance dealer hungry to make some cash. He was a short, thin, light-skinned Colombian, every ounce of his energy focused on making a deal happen, fast, so he could have a payday.

With Nacho and Company eager to do business, we needed to find a country to stage our operation. Our first choice was Guatemala, mainly because we knew the territory.

107

On June 28, 1992, Paul, Eddie Beach, and I went to Guatemala to meet with the government to try to convince them to let us do another controlled. The deal was basically the same as we'd done before. We needed permission to have a Colombian coke plane fly into Guatemala, land on a clandestine airstrip, where it would be refueled, the dope unloaded, and then flown back to Colombia, while we'd fly the unloaded coke to the United States. Shelly Katz was out of town so we had to deal with his temporary associate, Tony Lostan, and five other agents.

"No problem," said Tony. "I'll set it up, but you have to meet with Captain Yanez of the D-2, the Guatemalan CIA."

That's when the trouble began.

———

The D-2 was a group of badasses. One report called the D-2 "the Very Name of Fear," adding that the Guatemalan military intelligence group played "a central role in the conduct of military operations, in massacres, extrajudicial executions, forced disappearances, and torture."

Eddie Beach and I met with Captain Yanez of the D-2 in a room at the Camino Real Hotel, which looked like the basic all-suite hotel. There was a sitting area with a couch, a chair, and little end tables. Paul was back in the bedroom napping, letting me handle "el capitano," who with his army boots, dark green fatigues, long shaggy hair, and unshaven, expressionless face, looked worse than most of the Colombian coke dealers I'd met. Acting as interpreter, Tony Lostan, who looked a little like a South American Elvis, right between the thin and the fat stage, accompanied him.

Eddie let me do all the talking, while he just sat there with his notebook. With Lostan interpreting, I told Yanez about our operation, and then unveiled our plan.

"We'd like to arrange for a Colombian plane filled with coke to fly into your country," I began. "Then we'll have the plane land on a clandestine airstrip. We'll off-load the eight hundred kilos, refuel the plane, and let it return with the bad guys to Colombia. Then we'll take the eight hundred kilos and bring it back to the United States, deliver it to the customers . . . all while continuing wiretaps until we infiltrate the entire organization based in the United States."

Captain Yanez nodded as if I were requesting nothing more than a ham sandwich. He told us we could off-load eight hundred kilos, refuel the bad guys' plane, and allow it to leave Guatemala. "But," he added, "I would like to keep about half a million dollars, U.S., as expense money. You could get the Colombians to bring the cash with the dope—or we could seize half a million in the coke load. That's typically done in this kind of operation."

"And what would you do with the cash?" I asked.

"Give it to Senor Alexander," he said, explaining that he would ask Paul to buy the D-2 some spy-type intercept and digital-encryption equipment.

Oh, shit, I said to myself. *Eavesdropping equipment. Stuff that could be used by the D-2 against the United States.*

Eddie and I exchanged glances. We would never allow something like this to happen. At that time, Secretary of State James Baker had cut economic aid to Guatemala for humanitarian reasons. The Guatemalan government was hanging people; there were also kidnapped and missing Americans. I knew Yanez was involved because he was a part of the government perpetrating the acts. I couldn't imagine calling some NYPD chief and saying, "Hey, Chief, listen, this deal is working out great. All I have to do is trade the Guatemalans some spy equipment and we're in business!"

We weren't going to go for that, but we didn't want to tell the D-2 captain no. "Sure, no problem," I said. "We'll work it out so the Colombians will fly in a half million cash on the plane along with the eight hundred kilos. I'll personally turn the cash over to Paul and he'll buy you the spy equipment."

When we got out of the meeting, Eddie Beach was almost catatonic with rage. He had developed a nervous cough during the meeting with the D-2 captain, and he still has that nervous cough today. If you talk to him now, instead of saying, "Hey, how you doing?" It's, *Cough,* "Hey how you doing?" *Cough, cough.* He sounds like a horse clearing its throat.

After Captain Yanez left the Camino Real, I called headquarters back in the States. "I don't think things are going to work out here," I told Chief Maltz. "It just doesn't look like a good idea. I'll let you know everything when I get home."

After I hung up, embassy rep Tony Lostan came back with a transcript of my phone conversation. Yanez had tapped both of our land-lines. Yanez brought the transcript to Lostan as proof that Eddie and I were not on the level. Yanez also had a transcript of Lostan talking with his girlfriend on his embassy cell phone.

I panicked. Eddie panicked. Who knew what connections the D-2 had with the cartel? I called Maggie from a Tele-Paranda and told her, "Listen, if anything happens to me, I love you."

We decided to flee Guatemala. We packed up our Jeep, didn't tell anyone at the embassy, rousted Paul out of bed, and just said, "Adios! We're outta here." We sped out on a midnight run and got to the airport just in time to catch the last plane back to the United States—never to return to Guatemala.

We needed a new country . . . *fast.*

———

"**B**razil, Brazil, Brazil, Brazil," Paul kept telling me, in restaurants, on planes, in his house in Miami, in our office at DEA headquarters in New York.

"No, Paul, no," I'd always reply. "No Brazil. You got in trouble in Brazil, remember?"

I knew Paul had serious power in Brazil with the government, but I wasn't about to allow him to venture back into that rat's nest. I couldn't even fathom where Paul's connections in the corrupt Brazilian government might take us—so I steered him away from Brazil whenever he mentioned it, which was practically all of the time. We started shopping for another country, someplace—any place—where the powers that be would let us stage our operation without demanding either coke or cash. We shopped Panama, we shopped Belize, we shopped Mexico—all without success. Finally we tried Costa Rica.

I took the first reconnaissance trip to Costa Rica, along with members of Group 93. There were six of us: Steve Morse, Rick Gerard, Tommy Selvaggi, Jack Higgins, Jerry V, and me. In order to orchestrate the deal in Costa Rica we needed manpower. Group 93 had to do the legwork that Shelly Katz had done for us in Guatemala.

We headed to Costa Rica like the Bad News Bears, packing up our Group 93 surveillance van, which was a maroon wreck with a big Ford extended top, to the brim. Jack Higgins used the van as his portable mobile home. We packed it up with our surveillance equipment—

cameras, lenses, batteries, power converters, etc.—because our plan was to stick cameras in the bananas and film the smugglers with time-lapse videos and all kinds of other crazy stuff. We were all reved up, like a group of frat boys headed for spring break.

We unloaded the van at the airport curbside check-in, and checked everything onto the American Airlines flight to Fort Lauderdale, where we'd connect to Costa Rica. It was actually during spring break and there were three college kids on the plane in front of us, all of them drunk on airplane booze. It was a very turbulent flight, and every time we hit an air pocket they'd scream, "We're gonna crash!" The stewardesses told them to calm down, but that wasn't enough for our mountain man, Jerry V. He was like a powder keg, ready to lift them out of their seat and kick the sass out of them.

When the plane landed, Jerry V marched up the aisle, grabbed one of the three kids, and said, "Next time you better act accordingly."

One of the kids turned around and said, "Shut the fuck up, Grandpa."

I was thinking, *Oh, my God, they didn't just say that to this maniac!* The other kid chimed in, "Yeah, Gramps, mind your own business." They were pointing their fingers at him. I just knew we were headed into a major incident before we even got out of the U.S.

Jerry V dropped his bags and chased the kids off the plane, screaming, "I'll rip your heads off, you little punks." He tackled them in the airport, and pretty soon all of Group 93 was in a free-for-all.

It felt good to be back with my guys again.

———

When we barreled into San Jose, Costa Rica, I put the boys in the hotel and headed off to meet with Joe McDuff, and Jose Delgado, of the embassy staff. We met at the San Jose Palacio Hotel, another big palace hotel with white pillars, built into a mountainside. It had a grand exterior, but inside it was just another drug dealer's meeting place—a smoky lobby, a smokier bar, and a hundred rooms well worn by the footfalls of a hundred thousand hookers.

San Jose, Costa Rica, was totally different from Guatemala, for one reason. No military. Whereas in Guatemala the uniformed goons with machine guns watched your every move, in San Jose there was no military presence at all. Because they don't even have a military.

Everything seemed tranquil. The fear factor was ratcheted down significantly.

As the meeting with McDuff and Delgado progressed, I could see McDuff getting deep into the drinks. He kept knocking back white wine spritzers. Once I discovered his weakness, I pulled out the good old American cash and bought him about forty spritzers until he was ready to say yes to anything.

We were talking about finding an airstrip and doing a controlled delivery, and McDuff was slurring promises. He bragged that he'd introduce me to the head of the Costa Rican Federales, Chalo Talamantes, and we'd be able to land a 747 full of coke right in the middle of San Jose with Talamantes's blessings.

So far, so good.

———

The next day, McDuff and I were sitting at a restaurant called Las Brisas, and Chalo Talamantes came walking in, big as a Mack truck, with a head the size of a watermelon. Close to three hundred pounds, he was the biggest Central American I'd ever seen. We sat down and all the waiters came rushing up to Chalo. They put a fifth of Smirnoff vodka on the table and gave him little pint bottles of 7-Up for chasers.

As I watched Chalo slugging the straight vodka and chasing it with 7-Up, I knew we were in business again. One waiter after another would bring out a single *chicharone,* the fried pork skin, on a little plate the size of a half dollar. Chalo could eat four hundred chicharones in one fell swoop, but they brought them out one at a time. He would grunt and groan and suck down the pork skin, and a minute later they'd bring another one.

While Chalo slugged down vodka and ate the skimpy *chicharones,* I was making my pitch. I told him our requirement, an airstrip in the rain forest big enough to land, unload, and refuel a Colombian smuggling plane. I told him the whole nine yards of what we had to do.

Chalo popped another pork skin and said, "Okay, but what's in it for Costa Rica?"

"Well," I said, "you'll get the next one." Meaning he could seize the coke from the next deal, even though we knew there wasn't going to be a next one.

A big smile washed over his bowling ball face. Chalo raised his glass in a toast. "Okay, Mr. Jerry," he said. "We're in business. Let's go over to Key Largo. It's a very nice place. You'll like it."

"What's Key Largo?" I asked.

"A very fine establishment owned by a retired captain of the Los Angeles Police Department," Chalo explained. "Many Americans have settled in Costa Rica, and the captain is one of our finest citizens." Chalo extolled the glories of Costa Rica as well as any chamber of commerce rep—no military dictatorship, a tranquil country, welcomes foreign investors. "And Key Largo is our number-one place," he said.

I was thinking we were going to some fine-dining establishment. We rolled up in front of a four-story Victorian house, a gigantic place, almost a city block. There were palm trees lined up in front, a canopy that you walked under to get inside. The doors swung open and when we walked in with Chalo Talamantes, it was as if we were with the president. A gaggle of adoring women—beautiful, elegantly clad women—came running up to us. They were dressed in evening gowns as if they were going to a wedding. I was thinking, *Wow, it must be ladies' night.*

Chalo sat down at the bar, and waiters materialized with bottles of vodka and 7-Up. About that time I realized where we were, and what Key Largo was, because I was getting grabbled, prodded, and poked by the beautiful women with prom dresses.

We were in the fanciest whorehouse in Costa Rica. I stayed for one drink with Chalo. Then Steve Morse, Jack Higgins, and I left with Joe McDuff, who'd had something like twenty-five wine spritzers. He was blitzed. But he insisted on driving his government car. He steered uncertainly out of the Key Largo onto another street and almost immediately crashed into the back of a car containing a family with kids. Nobody was hurt, but all the kids were screaming.

"I'll handle this," McDuff slurred as he stumbled out of the car to assess the damage.

"Let's see how easy it is to get out of something in this country," I said to my Group 93 colleagues, Morse and Higgins.

The backseat of the car that McDuff had hit was filled with screaming kids. The parents were standing next to the dent in the back of their car. All we could see from the backseat was Joe McDuff talking to them and handing them a business card and a few bucks. The next thing you knew, McDuff was climbing back into our car. No police report, no nothing.

"Did you see that?" McDuff said, unfazed. "If the cops had come here, they'd have been busted. He stopped way too fast. He woulda been in jail. He's lucky I let him go."

The next day, we got word that Chalo liked us and was ready to approve our deal. I returned to the San Jose Palacio Hotel, where the members of Group 93 were staying. To save money, Rick Gerard and I were rooming together, as were the others.

Long past midnight, I heard a knock on my door. It was Steve Morse, our new sergeant on his first international trip, in a San Jose Palacio Hotel robe with a pair of San Jose Palacio slippers. He looked like he was having a nervous breakdown. "You've got to help me, Jerry, I can't take it!" he said. "I've gotta go home."

"Steve, we've only been here twenty-four hours," I said. "Everything is going to be fine. Chill. Don't get nervous."

"It's not the country!" he said. "It's the crazy bastard I'm rooming with! He's got three girls in the bathtub, and they're all drunk."

Morse thought I was going to go down and discipline him. "Hold on a minute," I said. I grabbed my big 35mm camera with the tripod lens and I went down to a best-left unnamed group member and Morse's room. I busted into the bathroom screaming, "Okay, you nut, group photo! Group photo! Put a little suds on her head!" I started snapping pictures and poor Steve Morse said, "That's it. I can't take it." He was on the next flight home.

Working undercover in a foreign country produced incredible stress, and everybody handled it differently. There were guys who just fell to the booze and the broads. There were guys who lost their wives because they couldn't take the extended separations. Rick Gerard's wife got so fed up with his absences she changed the locks on his front door and said, "Don't bother coming home."

When I heard about Rick's wife, I immediately called Maggie.

"Yeah, okay," she said when I laid out the whole thing about Rick's wife changing the locks on the doors. "So what, Jerry?"

"You want me to come home?"

"What, before you finish?" she asked. "You've come this far, and now you want to quit?"

"I don't know, I'm tired," I said. "I've been here for months. I just—"

She cut me off. "No, Jerry, no," she said. "You've come this far, you gotta do what you set out to do. You can do it. Don't be such a baby."

"It's just that I'd like to come home," I said.

"So now you're gonna quit?" she asked. "No way, Jerry. You do that and I will change the locks."

She hung up without another word.

———

The next day, we went to work. Our DEA contacts in Costa Rica had a pilot who worked for them; he helped us find the perfect airstrip. He had an old Piper Apache plane, and we took a ride three hours out of San Jose to Roxana, out in the middle of the rain forest. He dipped the plane to the left and there it was, the prettiest airstrip I'd ever seen, a strip of white in a sea of green. Once we landed, it looked even better—an old, abandoned airstrip on a banana plantation, about 2,500 feet of macadam, perfect for our needs.

The Colombians were talking about landing a Cessna Titan 404, a small enough plane to land on a short runway, so we knew we were in good shape. We rented the airstrip from Standard Banana. Before we flew home, Paul and I had one last order of business, opening our bogus import/export business, this one called Saburro International, in downtown San Jose.

We set up a female Costa Rican police officer as our secretary. We had stationery printed, phone and fax all set up, and then we had a ribbon-cutting ceremony. Geraldo Bartone and Don Oscar, grinning in their Italian suits and Swiss watches, made the front page of the *San Jose Times*.

———

Back in New York, the front money again arrived right on schedule from the Colombians, Nacho Gaitan and his associates. This time, we mailed checks to Avelino and Alonso in a DHL package from our bogus stateside firm. Everything was perfecto.

Olympo Caro, Nacho's gofer, called Paul to say he was headed over to Costa Rica in a few weeks to see our airstrip and check out our business operation. Paul told me that it was up to me and my Group 93 crew to get everything ready for the site inspection. We flew back to Costa Rica and set up the radio frequencies and got everything squared away.

We needed a pilot to fly us over the airfield. I enlisted Humberto, an old drug smuggler I'd met in Costa Rica, and Carlito, a local crop-duster pilot, who had once smuggled guns for Castro.

One morning Humberto and I drove down to the runway in the jungle outside of San Jose, where Carlito was waiting with an old crop-dusting plane. When we got there, Humberto checked out the plane. I could see him crawl under the wing, then touch some oil on the ground and smell it.

"What the hell is that?" I asked.

He shook his head. "Nothing, no problem. Let's go, amigo."

We took off. When we were about five hundred feet up, the engine sputtered and I could see the tachometer fluttering.

"What's the hell is goin' on?" I asked Humberto over the headset.

"Nada," he said. "Everything's okay, amigo."

"Put this mother on the ground, or I'll kill you," I said.

We banked violently, did a complete 360-degree turn, and, finally, thankfully, bounced back down on the runway. I jumped off the plane, fell to my knees, and kissed the ground.

Later that night, after we'd had a few drinks, Humberto said, "Hey, man, remember when we took off on the plane and you were sitting in the copilot's seat?"

"Yeah, I remember," I said. "You almost killed us."

"No joke, man," he said. "Carlito told me that we had a leak in the fuel bladder. If we hadn't turned around when we did, we'd both be dead."

━━━━━━

Olympo Caro flew into San Jose and stayed at Hara Dora Hotel. Paul and I met him there. He was a short, thin, light-skinned Colombian with straight black hair.

I sat in the copilot's seat and Humberto was in the pilot's seat, while Caro sat in the back with Paul. When the plane banked and he saw that white strip in the green fields, protected on all sides from police or poachers, a big, beautiful smile spread across that dope dealer's face.

"*Sí! Sí!*" he said. "Very good. Perfecto!" Olympo Caro said that his associates, Nacho Gaitan and Pedro Paulo, loved banana plantations, so this was perfect. "*Bueno, bueno,*" he said. "*Listo, listo.*" Meaning he was ready to do the deal.

We dropped Olympo back at his hotel and he left to return with the good news to Colombia. I left Jack and the rest of Group 93 at the hotel in San Jose and went back to Miami with Paul and Jerry V for a couple of weeks. The three of us needed to buy radio equipment for transmission from the jungle, fuel pumps, and other supplies. We were home for about two weeks. We didn't have to rush back, of course, since we didn't know the date when the deal would finally go down. So Jerry V and I hung around with Paul in Miami, making calls, setting up the arrangements, and waiting for the date from the smugglers about when everything would go down.

━━━

One night, a best left unnamed, married group member and I decided to go out for a drink at the Club Boca in Boca Raton. We were still in the parking lot when these two attractive women walked out of the club. "Hey, how you doing?" one of them asked, walking toward us.

I thought she was making a pass at me, because, with my group 93 colleague's mountain man beard, I figured she surely couldn't be interested in him. But she looked at me and said, "I don't want you, I want the mountain man."

They followed us back inside the club, where we had a couple of drinks. My fellow group member seemed to be getting along well with his new friend.

The next day, the group member told me, "I want you to go to dinner with me and my friend and her girlfriend tonight."

"Forget it, man," I said. "I don't want anything to do with that girl."

"Okay, no problem," he said. He asked me to drop him off to meet the woman that night in a ritzy section of Fort Lauderdale. I didn't see him for two days. When he finally walked back into the hotel, he looked like Sonny Crocket, the Don Johnson character in *Miami Vice*. He had a short buzz cut. His beard and mustache were shaved close to his face. He was wearing a Lord and Taylor silk shirt, a pair of Guess jeans, and loafers with no socks.

It was the last good laugh I'd have for a long time.

11

Blown Away in Bogotá

The date for the drop was set. I returned to Costa Rica, and along with the rest of Group 93, began the radio-frequency tests, chanting, "Omega, omega, omega, uno, dos, tres" from our airstrip in the rain forest.

A few days before the shipment's scheduled arrival, I was in the San Jose Palacio Hotel with Paul. We were on the phone with Avelino and Alonso, who for security's sake were talking from a pay phone on a street in Bogotá. Paul was on one hotel telephone extension and I was on another as we made the final arrangements for the load.

"Bueno, bueno, bueno," I could hear Avelino saying. Then I heard the sound of motorcycles, lots of them. Then, loud voices. Then, impossibly, the sound of machinegun fire. Lots of gunfire. Then I could hear the motorcycles speeding away. And then . . .

Silence.

"Hello, hello, hello," said Paul. But there was no answer. Just the sounds of the street.

Paul went to Bogotá for the funerals.

They were very simple affairs, Paul told me by phone, attended mostly by their families. Few of their coke-dealer associates or bosses showed to pay their respects for these two-bit Colombian brokers, who surely went down in some dope deal gone bad. In the collective mind of the cartel, Avelino and Alonso were filed away in the category of losers, guys who got on the wrong side of a deal gone bad.

Paul went to the funeral, not so much to mourn as to find out what the hell happened . . . and if our cover had been blown. Would we be the next to fall prey to assassination or hit and run? The reason for the execution was known by just about everybody in Bogotá. Avelino and Alonso got gunned down by the Colombian equivalent of the marine guards. Why? Because of our lost 767 load. Seven months had passed since the deal with the 767 kilos went sour, and the cartel couldn't let the lost load go unpunished. So Avelino and Alonso took the fall.

"It's a shame, yes," Paul told me on his return. "But at least it wasn't us."

━━━━

Everything changed for Paul and me. When we returned to Costa Rica, I never stopped looking over my shoulder. If the cartel had blown away Avelino and Alonso because of our screwup, what would they do if they found out what Paul and I had actually done?

Paul kept telling me that it didn't matter, that our new group, Nacho & Co., probably wouldn't communicate with the old group, Lizardo & Co. He said that justice had been done with Avelino's and Alonso's assassination, and would probably stop there. He tried to remain calm, but I sensed the first hint of doubt in Paul's voice, especially when he decided to scratch our Costa Rica operation for the time being. Paul called Nacho and said that our brokers were assassinated and we didn't know why, and that he thought it best to wait to make sure everything was in order before forging ahead.

Deaths and delays. Both are just the way of the drug trade.

━━━━

Once again, we got everything ready—fuel, the trucks, the radio frequencies. We drove toward our airstrip in Roxana, to set up our radio equipment, but the spring rains had been a deluge, swelling the Roxana River so no cars could cross it. We had to use four-by-four trucks to get across the river, and then use a winch to get the truck across. Once one truck was across and safely on the bank, we had to swim back and connect the winch to the front of the next truck to be pulled across. That river was a pain in the butt. We would end up crossing it

At age five.

In August 1989 I was promoted to detective in the NYPD.

As an NYPD undercover, I became "Crazy Jerry from Jersey," an identity that enabled me to mix with the drug dealers and users. Here I am, shirtless, ready to cop a buy.

Being "Crazy Jerry" led to my getting shot—and to receiving the Cop of the Month Award. With me are fellow officers John Lynn (left) and Ralph Rinaldi (right).

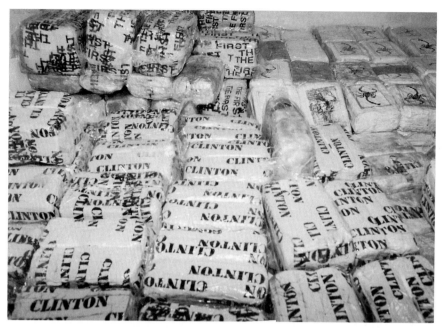

To convince the South American drug importers to trust us, we showed them a truck full of cocaine with the current brand names—Clinton, The First (for First Lady), and Scorpio.

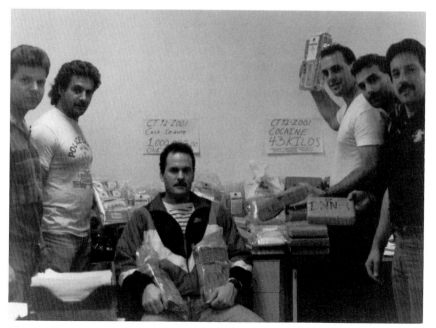

The cartel bought our story, and we were able to seize major shipments of cash and cocaine. Here Group 93 members Eddie Beach, Tommy Selvaggi, Pete Breslow, Rick Gerard, and Bobby Gomez pose with me, along with the booty we found in Delfin Prieto's stash house.

The next step in establishing our credentials: setting up a landing strip in Guatemala. Arriving in Guatemala City, we found a fearful population under martial law.

My Group 93 partner Eddie Beach, confidential informant Paul Lir Alexander, and me in front of the site of Genesis, our phony import-export business.

GENESIS
IMPORTACION
Y
EXPORTACION

Tel. 506 - 33 · 35 05 - 33 · 08 31

We worked with the local police, the Guardia Hacienda, to set up our operation in Guatemala. (Left to right) Four members of the Guardia Hacienda, Dan Brown, Frank Shroyer, Ray Mansilillo, and Major Edwin Sosa.

Here I am holding one of the 25-kilo burlap bags from the 767 kilos of cocaine we seized in Guatemala. The brand name was Gordos.

After a series of nerve-wracking flying lessons, I became good enough to copilot the Apache smuggling plane we used when we went looking for a suitable airstrip in Costa Rica.

Jerry Vetrano, known as "Jerry V," poses with Paul and me at a crop-dusting airstrip in Costa Rica.

Rick Gerard, Paul Alexander, and me (holding a flight chart) next to our Apache. Even in the jungle, Paul always wore an immaculate suit and dress shirt.

That's Paul again—and he's looking at his Bogotà bag, a required accessory in the South American drug business. Behind me is Special Agent Rick Gerard.

Rick Gerard in Costa Rica, waiting for our smuggling plane to take off.

Jerry Vetrano and me boarding the Apache.

Our pilot Carlito, Rick Gerard, and Paul Alexander checked under the wing of the plane—but they didn't detect the fuel leak that almost caused us to crash in the jungle.

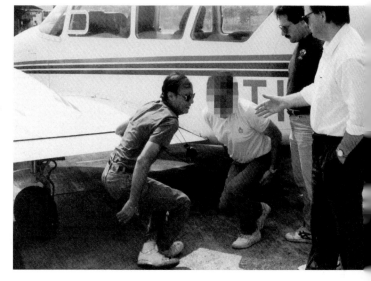

Agent Tom Selvaggi and I await the Colombians' drug-laden plane. Behind us you can see the barrels of jet fuel we would use to refuel the smugglers' Titan 404.

Tom used camouflage paint on his face to blend into the jungle.

Just as the smugglers' plane approached, a violent storm bore down on us. I used the compass skills that Bernie Kerik had taught me to guide the plane in through the break in the clouds at upper right.

Success! Tommy Selvaggi, John Gaddis, and a Costa Rican federal officer pose with our prize—a truck filled with part of the 800 kilos of cocaine we stole from the Colombians.

To get back from our airstrip in Costa Rica, we had to cross a flooded river in 4 by 4's. Above: Agent John Gaddis and I discuss the situation.

Bernie Kerik and I stand next to the 800 kilos from our Costa Rica operation.

The whole gang from Group 93 (also known as Group T-43): (left to right) Steve Morse, Bruce Stokes, Dave Henessey, Jerry Vetrano, Rick Gerard, Bernie Kerik, me, Pete Breslow, Eddie Beach, James Wood, Rosalinda Rosada, Jack Higgins, Tom Selvaggi, and Kevin Suttlehan.

Bringing our coke back to Galveston aboard the Phoenix—a job I didn't mind in the least!

The hold of the Phoenix had a hidden compartment, ideal for smuggling cocaine. When we offloaded the coke, the boat listed so badly that we had to replace some of the cargo with lead for ballast.

Yuber Tejada and Fabio Gamba were the Colombian principals in the 800-kilo deal. Tejada is serving twenty years to life in the New York State prison system.

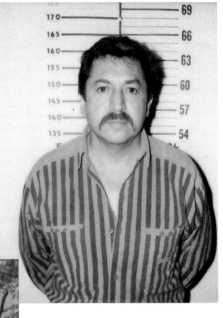

This surveillance photo shows a Bronx meeting of the late bodyguard, John Lopez, with Fabio Gamba and Yuber Tejada, while a street thug watches over them. Shortly afterward, Tommy Marmion ("Rain Man") notified us about suitcases filled with a million dollars, which we seized.

Back in New York, I set up a new smuggling operation with headquarters in the World Trade Center. To impress the South Americans, all I had to do was show them these pictures of my shrimp trawler, my uncle's black Chieftain, and our airstrip in West Milford, New Jersey.

JERRY BARTONE

Saburo International Inc

One World Trade Center, Suite 7967
New York, New York 10048
Tel: 212 524-7743
Fax: 212 524-0745
Telex: 403889

My ID as drug transporter Jerry Bartone.

Working undercover sometimes meant dining at Le Cirque; other times it meant joining the crew of a garbage truck. Jerry Vetrano is third from left with me and sanitation workers in Great Neck, New York.

This surveillance photo was taken just after we landed our Chieftain at Teterboro Airport in New Jersey with Ronnie, one of our confidential informants, and a smuggler.

The cash we seized from the trunk of John Henao's car.

Oscar Pozo, a principal of the Cali cartels, in a surveillance photo taken in Ecuador. Pozo was an ex-con who was very sharp and paranoid, thanks to his twelve-year education in the New York State prison system. After serving his sentence for running one of the biggest cocaine processing labs on the East Coast, he was deported.

Blas Uribe Cadavid, a.k.a. El Negro or 007—the leader of the Colombian assassins or *secarios*.

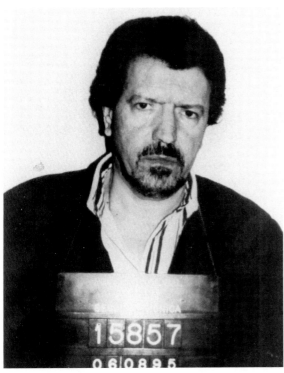

Gilberto Rodriguez Orjuella, leader of one of the "five families" of the Cali cartels, at his arrest in Colombia.

The great tomato can caper began when we saw smugglers loading pallets of tomato cans onto an eighteen-wheeler. Here it sits (at right) parked at a weigh station in Virginia, awaiting search by state troopers.

John "Big Daddy" Sager and I puffed cigars as we drove the big rig back to New York.

After nearly a week without sleep, my mind started playing tricks on me. Here I am returning from the laundry room of a Delaware motel, while the clothes I wore for five days straight were in the washer.

Members of Group 93 pulled the pallets apart in a DEA parking lot on the west side of Manhattan. That's Brian "Sneed" Sniedicker at center; my back is toward the camera. Also shown (from left): Jerry Neville, Mike Kealon, Mike Grogan, Eddie Ocasio, Kerin Timoney, and Kevin Scanlon.

Opening the boxes.

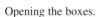

The guys ran the tomato cans through a U.S. Customs Service scanner while I stared at the screen watching for some sign of the coke or cash I was sure was in them.

Finally, we had to open each of the 5,400 cans and dump its contents into a garbage bag. By the time we found the $1.8 million in cash, I was so stressed out by sleep deprivation that I couldn't see straight.

I was proud to receive Medals of Honor from New York's Mayor Rudolph W. Giuliani (top) and New Jersey's Governor Christine Whitman (center).

Bernie Kerik and I also received awards from DEA Administrator Tom Constantine.

Bernie was at my side when I was sworn in as Chief of Police of New Hope, Pennsylvania, in 1999.

When I joined the Passaic County (New Jersey) sheriff's department, it wasn't long before I was seizing drugs and cash again. To my right is Sheriff Edwin Englehardt.

Our Passaic County undercover team included (left to right) Jose Correa, William Mullanaphy, Harry Gromb, Sheriff Englehardt, me, Scott Degraw, Herman Carter, Kevin Huha, and Carlos Carasquillo.

On my first day on the job as Sheriff of Passaic County, Bernie Kerik joined me in a tour of the jail.

Sheriff Jerry Speziale of Passaic County, New Jersey. Back home after fighting the international drug wars—an expert on cell phone and wiretap surveillance, multi-jurisdictional smuggling investigations, money laundering investigations, and organized crime—and, at heart, still a "street cop" and a "cop's cop."

dozens of times, but it was never easy. Once our radio was up and running we began our tests, every hour on the hour. "Omega, omega, omega. Uno, dos, tres."

One night after midnight, a day or two before the scheduled date of the operation, we were communicating back and forth with the Colombians. Although we didn't know it, our radio wasn't working and we missed one of the hourly transmissions. The next thing we heard from the Colombians was, "*Cancelado.*" Operation canceled. We had done all the radio checks all the way up to when the plane was to depart Colombia, but we missed one transmission and the deal was off.

I began to think Paul was playing games with me. Out there in the middle of the Costa Rican rain forest, with the deal that we'd slaved so long on canceled, I began yelling like a madman.

"If this load was called off because you are trying to double-cross me, you're a dead man," I said. "That plane better land here next week!"

Paul told me to calm down, that the missed radio transmission was only one of our problems. The bigger problem was that the pilots had gone on strike. A Colombian smuggling plane was shot down over Honduras the night before our operation. When we missed the radio transmission, our pilot panicked and backed out. That got me even crazier. Paul went down to Bogotá to meet with Nacho Gaitan and his associates to see how we could get things moving again. The news wasn't good. The pilot's strike could drag on for weeks.

I told Paul we'd send in our own pilot, Carlito.

I called Carlito and asked him if he'd be interested in flying a drug-smuggling plane from Colombia and then back to Costa Rica. I said we'd pay for his airfare and expenses, plus $20,000, and that he'd be doing the trip back with a Colombian pilot not afraid to take the five-hour trip. Carlito said sure. Paul discussed the situation with Nacho & Co. and they agreed to use our pilot. Carlito flew to Colombia for a week to be trained on a Titan 404 aircraft. He went through flight school, performing landings, touchdowns, and takeoffs.

One day, as I was in Costa Rica, waiting for the go-ahead from Paul, who was still in Miami, I got a call from Eddie Beach. "You sittin' down?" Eddie asked.

"No, but give me a minute," I said, knowing this meant trouble, and found the closest chair.

"Your boy Paul is in custody in Miami right now," he said.

"Oh, no," I said.

"It gets worse," Eddie said. "Customs caught him with half a million in cash. Caught him with the money as he was walking into his front door."

"What the hell is going on?" I asked.

"Call Bob Starkman at Miami customs," Eddie said.

Starkman told me they were tailing a drug suspect and had followed him to a Home Depot parking lot, where he was apparently preparing to do a money drop. The parties who came to pick up the cash were none other than Paul Lir Alexander and his sidekick, the former Nicaraguan Contra general Antonio Calderon.

"They were caravanning," Starkman said. "Paul was in a BMW and Calderon was in a van. They pulled into the parking lot, where Calderone met up with the guy we were tailing. Our suspect gave Calderone the box, which he put into the van, and Paul caravanned him back to the house."

I think I said, "Oh, shit."

"Then we followed Paul and Calderon back to Paul's house and hit Paul as he was walking through his front door with the box with half a million cash," Starkman said. "Paul tells us that he's a DEA informant and everything is sanctioned."

"Are you going to lock him up?" I asked.

"You bet we are," said Starkman.

I didn't know what the hell was going on with Paul, but I did know that I needed him to complete the Costa Rica deal. Without Paul, no deal. Hundreds of hours of work down the drain. I could deal with Paul later, but the deal had to go on.

"I'm asking you to wait awhile," I told Starkman.

I explained that we were in the middle of this major deal in Costa Rica, which was supposed to go down soon. Starkman said okay, that they would just seize the cash and Paul's BMW and van and release Paul on his own recognizance. Paul would have to work out everything with the Miami agents later.

"Is Paul there with you?" I asked Starkman. He said he was right beside him.

"Put him on the phone," I said.

"Hey, Jerry, I can explain," Paul said.

"You double-crossing me?" I asked. "If you are, I'll lock you up for life."

This time, Paul didn't seem like himself. The steely, all-business veneer was cracking. I thought he might even be crying. "Listen, Jerry, I didn't know what to do," he said. "Our deal was falling apart because of Avelino and Alonso, so Nacho asked me to pick up the five hundred thousand for them as a favor. I didn't want to tell you. I think they were just testing me but I had to do it in order for the deal to go through."

"You shoulda told me," I said. "You should never have done anything behind my back."

In my heart, I knew something was wrong. But in my mind, I knew that if I wanted that load to go through I had to accept Paul's story.

He promised he'd never do anything without advising me first, and we both slammed down our respective telephones.

—

I couldn't tolerate another screwup with the radio. I found a Costa Rican cop whose hobby was shortwave radios. He had a directional antenna on his roof that was as powerful as any radio station. Costa Rican police only made a couple hundred dollars a month, and his income had to support a family of six.

I bought a bunch of roasted chicken from a restaurant in San Jose and took it over to the cop's house with a wad of cash. I left Rick Gerard, my Group 93 buddy, to man the radio twenty-four-seven with the Costa Rican cop. "I'll call you by cell phone every hour to make sure that you communicate every hour on the hour so that we don't miss this deal," I told Rick before leaving him in the house with the Costa Rican cop and the take-out chicken.

We resumed test transmissions. Every hour on the hour, we'd whistle and communicate back and forth. The operation was a go.

—

At two o'clock on the morning before the plane was to leave Colombia, we left for the jungle again. Rick Gerard stayed in town with the Costa Rican cop and his family, eating chicken and sending radio transmissions back and forth. I communicated with him by cell. Carlito and the plane were waiting on a private airstrip on a farm outside of Bogotá and ready to take off early the next morning.

Around midnight, we got confirmation that Carlito had landed in Bogotá at the national terminal for flights inside of Colombia. A gate was opened for him, and the Colombian National Police and Colombian military flagged him into a hangar. Carlito thought he was a dead man. But inside the hangar the Colombian National Police, along with Colombian army officials, helped him load the coke on the plane. That's how high the power of the Cali cartels went.

After the coke was loaded, the police painted fake Costa Rican tail numbers on his plane. They turned the plane around and cleared it for takeoff. Even the air-traffic controllers were involved in the deal. They filed a flight plan as if the plane were bound for the island of San Andreas, an island off of Colombia between Costa Rica and the Central American coast. The air-traffic controllers told Carlito to drop to seven thousand feet when he got to San Andreas, where they allowed him to drop off the radar into Costa Rica.

Before I left for Costa Rica, I never thought I needed a compass. But Bernie Kerik, my best friend and Group 93 colleague, insisted on teaching me how to use one. "What do I need a compass for?" I asked him. Luckily for me, he pushed me to learn, and on the day of the plane's scheduled arrival, I had a compass in my pocket. It would turn out to be a critical tool.

As we had done in Guatemala, we had our fuel barrels ready with a couple hundred gallons of jet-A fuel. We stationed camouflaged Group 93 agents in the bushes. Tommy Selvaggi was hiding in a ditch with me, along with Jose Delgado, the assistant country attaché for the DEA assigned to the Costa Rican embassy. At around 6:30 A.M., Rick Gerard called me on my cell to say that the plane was fifteen or twenty minutes away.

Just then, the rain forest skies opened up in a monsoon, incredibly hard, driving rain. We couldn't see a foot in front of our faces. The ditch we were hiding in filled with water. Rick Gerard called me and said the pilots couldn't land because they couldn't see the runway. The pilots wanted to turn around, but they didn't have enough fuel to make it back to Colombia. They wanted to land in the closest town, Limon, which had a commercial airstrip. The pilots said that bolts of lighting could guide them in.

Great idea! I thought. I turned to Delgado in the watery ditch and said, "Let's have the plane land in Limon. We'll drive over there, unload the coke, let them refuel, and then let 'em take off." The trouble was that if the plane landed in Limon, there would be no way for us to be there in time to handle the delivery.

Delgado said he'd have the shipment seized by the Costa Rican authorities. I could see what he was trying to set up—Delgado would be hailed as a hero if things went according to that scenario. I went completely berserk.

"No way!" I said, flailing around in the rising water. "That is not happening!"

I couldn't allow this load to be busted. Paul would be dead. Our whole operation would be blown. "We might have a midair disaster here, buddy, but that plane is landing on this airstrip, right here, and everything is going according to plan," I told him. "Even if I have to mop the coke off the runway."

I called Rick Gerard on the cell phone. "You tell that pilot that they're going to land right here in the rain forest—or they're not landing at all!"

I took my compass and went out on the runway and spotted the plane through a tiny opening in the clouds to the southwest. I laid the compass down on the runway and I measured a point off the compass and started yelling to Rick Gerard over the cell phone. "Tell them to come through at 180 degrees in the southwest. They have an opening in the sky and a two-thousand-foot ceiling."

Gerard relayed the coordinates to the plane. Before I knew it, I saw that big bird drop out of the sky and—*boom!*—it bounced down the runway before coming to a stop.

A crew of undercover Costa Rican police brought out fuel barrels and began the refueling. The pilots opened the door and hurled out the burlap bags full of coke. Within ten minutes, the plane was unloaded, refueled, and was taking off again. One of our guys hidden in the bush was videotaping the whole operation.

We all ran out to the rain-soaked airstrip and stared at the mountain of coke. I ripped open a bag and pulled out a kilo. It was marked with the Metro logo, another primo brand from that time.

I called New York and told our supervisor, John Maltz, "We got it, Chief! Eight hundred kilos."

—————

The shipment would have to fly back to New York without me. I had to get out of Costa Rica. I had been there for a month and a half and it was time to go home. I had been calling Maggie every day saying, "Just wait until tomorrow, just wait until tomorrow." And she had always said, "You're in it this far, stick in there and stay with it," and she assured me that she and Franki would be okay. But now that the deal was done, I needed to go home and be with my wife and daughter.

Group 93 agent Pete Breslow flew in to watch the shipment, which was also being guarded by the Costa Rican authorities. Two days after the coke was dropped, a DEA aircraft flew into the rain forest and picked up Pete and the eight hundred kilos of cocaine and brought them both back to New York.

Next, we had to devise a plan to deliver the drugs and have the recipients both busted and clearly to blame for the bust. Paul would mastermind the delivery. Olympo Caro had given Paul a phone number and a code name, "Pastor," for the customer.

"Pastor" was Yuber Tejada, the leader of a New York–based distribution cell. Paul contacted Tejada and after they exchanged code words, Tejada instructed him to meet him at the Las Americas Restaurant in Queens.

—————

Paul and his sidekick, the Nicaraguan contra general Antonio Calderon, were waiting in a booth when the Colombians entered, all ready to receive the load.

The Los Americas was a little joint with an all-glass front on busy Northern Boulevard and 140th Street in Queens. It was always bustling, with pretty South American waitresses trying to keep pace with a steady stream of hungry, mostly South American customers. I was watching the meeting from across the street.

First, I saw Yuber Tejada, clean shaven with his thick black hair slicked straight back, in a gold, leopard-print silk shirt and black pants. Then there was John "Gordito" Lopez, who lived up to his nickname. He was a big, fat slob with long, thin black hair. Finally, Fabio

Gamba, a little short guy, who came skittering up behind the two bigger guys like Ratso Rizzo trying to keep pace with Joe Buck in *Midnight Cowboy.*

"Eight hundred kilos, arriving around the first of September," Paul said to the trio of drug dealers when they were all sitting around the table.

"Bueno," said Tejada, and the deal was sealed right there.

Since it was June, we'd have the summer to plan our strategy. We'd already set up wiretaps on Tejada and his associates at the meeting, and would follow them by both electronic and physical surveillance in hopes of catching as many of their associates as possible before the big load was to arrive.

———

About two weeks before the delivery, our wiretaps paid off. We heard Tejada and Fabio Gamba discussing meeting at a car dealership in Manhattan, where they would "pick up some cash." When they left their houses, we followed them. They didn't go straight to the car dealership, but to 524 Jackson Avenue, a rough neighborhood in the South Bronx.

When we arrived we saw Lopez coming out of the house. He walked to the corner where Tejada and Gamba were waiting. After a brief conversation, Gamba and Tejada left in separate cars.

We tailed Gamba and pulled him over. Flashing our badges, we convinced him that it was a routine traffic stop and told him that a bank had just been robbed down the street. Had he seen anything suspicious in the neighborhood? He had no idea we knew he was a drug dealer. He wanted to be as cooperative as could be. He opened his briefcase, which contained fifteen thousand dollars and a cell phone.

We released Gamba, but put a tail on him—Tommy Marmion, a.k.a. "Rainman." He was a thin guy with light brown hair, who always dressed like a preppy in plain jeans and a well-starched dress shirt. He had a great dry sense of humor and was new to Group 93, given up by the New York State Troopers. We called Tommy "Rainman" because the movie was his shtick. He did a dead-on impression of Dustin Hoffman from the film. I don't think he knew what he was getting into when he got assigned to our wild bunch, but he fit in as only a misfit can.

About five minutes after we released Gamba, I heard Marmion yell over the radio, "Whoa! Two big suitcases being dragged out of Jackson Avenue and being put into a car." They watched Lopez loading these big suitcases along with two other guys. They all jumped in their car and when they turned the corner we pulled them over. We opened the trunk and pulled out the suitcases and—lo and behold—the luggage was packed with $1 million cash.

━━━━

We brought Lopez and the two others back to DEA headquarters and processed them. But we couldn't prosecute them. All we had them for was the money, and we still had to deliver the eight hundred kilos of cocaine. So we convinced John Lopez to cooperate, to spill his guts. I was watching through a little crack in the door while Bernie Kerik interrogated Lopez in a holding area. They sat across from each other at a little table and Bernie was putting the sales pitch on him really strong.

"Listen, you're gonna get killed," I heard Bernie say.

I saw Lopez nodding his head in agreement.

"You're responsible for that money," Bernie continued. "Don't be an idiot. Cooperate. We can protect you."

Lopez was nodding his head more furiously now, and finally he blurted out, "Okay. I'll do it. I'll cooperate."

He spilled his guts right then and there. He told Bernie, who was taping the conversation, that he was working for Tejada and Gamba, who were waiting for some Brazilian guy—who was, of course, Paul—and this other guy, some "senator" named Geraldo—who was, of course, me. The Brazilian and the senator were going to deliver eight hundred kilos of coke within the next month, Lopez said.

Now we had a scapegoat who had squealed to the cops, and we could point the finger squarely at John Lopez when the load was busted. We could make a strong argument that Lopez, certainly not Don Oscar or Senator Geraldo, was the weak link.

Lopez convinced us he would continue to cooperate. He gave us some information, including a tip about a major New York distributor named "Caliche," and agreed to return the following day. Instead, he fled to Colombia, which was the worst move he could have made. Because there we couldn't protect him.

It was time for us to deliver the eight hundred kilos. We told Tejada's people to drop us a van on Seventy-ninth Street and First Avenue in Midtown Manhattan. They showed up with an old Ford Econoline. We told them that we'd return the van and the coke to the same area the next day. We took the van back to DEA, had a kill switch installed, and loaded it with the eight hundred kilos.

The next morning, I once again set up surveillance on Fabio Gamba and Yuber Tejada. We brought the loaded van to Second Avenue and parked it with all of Group 93 watching. I followed Gamba alone, while the rest of the surveillance team stayed with Tejada.

Gamba left his house and went to Tejada's. Next, Gamba stopped at a Tele-Paranda, where he met the guys who were going to pick up the eight hundred kilos from the van. To slow Gamba's roll, I grabbed a screwdriver from my trunk and punctured his right rear tire while he was meeting his men in the phone arcade. When Gamba saw his tire, he shook his head and unleashed a few choice Spanish curse words, then walked up the street and got some help to fix the flat. I was sitting there all by myself, thinking, *Maybe I should call a backup in case he gets back with his boys and, suddenly, they get wise.*

Normally, I would have called my best friend and best backup, Bernie Kerik, who would've been on the scene in a heartbeat. But Bernie was still watching the van in Manhattan, and in a few months, he would be leaving the group for good. Bernie had just been promoted. He'd become friendly with New York Mayor Rudy Guiliani through a foundation Bernie and I had chaired for Michael Buczek, an NYPD officer from Wayne who had been shot and killed in October 1988. At a recent dinner for the foundation, which attracted sixteen hundred officers from all over the state, Bernie told me he was going to be leaving the group and moving on to corrections. "The mayor's asked me to take over the department of investigations," he told me. I gave him a big bear hug and wished him the best.

So today, instead of calling Bernie, I called Eddie Beach on my cell.

"Hey, Eddie, I'm here at Gamba's," I said. "But I don't think he's going to be moving for a while."

"How do you know?" asked Eddie.

"Because I just gave him a flat tire with a screwdriver," I said. "He's gone to get help and I'm here alone. How 'bout sending a backup?"

"Okay, I've got John Saager from Group 92," he said. "He lives in Long Island, about fifteen minutes away."

Perfect, I thought. I knew John Saager. He was almost as crazy as I was. Within twenty minutes, he came rolling up in a black Z-28, which he exited like a rock star. Blue jeans, T-shirt, and about sixteen earrings on each ear. He was an NYPD detective, six-three and 220 pounds, all muscle, with a ponytail snaking down the center of his back and an equally shaggy goatee and mustache. When he let down his hair, which he did often, he looked like the popular image of Jesus Christ.

Every time we had been together in a bar, which was often, John Saager did the same thing—put a lit cigarette in his teeth, flip it back onto his tongue, and swallow it. Then, with a big swig of Captain Morgan rum and coke, he'd bellow, "Arrghh, ladddy!" We called John "Big Daddy."

We greeted each other like brothers, then receded into the shadows to wait for Gamba and his boys. They came ambling up a few minutes later. There were about five of them, swarming around the car. They fixed the flat in less than five minutes and all of them jumped into Gamba's car.

Big Daddy and I followed. Gamba drove over to midtown with his five buddies. They were headed for the van and the eight hundred kilos. But first they dropped off Gamba at a luggage store, while the other five drove on to pick up the load. I followed Gamba inside, while Big Daddy stayed on the other five.

At about the same time, I got a call from Eddie Beach saying Gamba's five associates along with Tejada were picking up the eight hundred kilos in the van. Group 93 agents, including Bernie Kerik, were watching them from a video camera in the steeple of a church, while the other agents blended in with the crowd.

The bust was contingent upon taking down Gamba as well. I had lost my backup agents because they were all involved in the van bust. I ran outside the store, grabbed two foot police officers, identified myself as a detective, and ran back into the luggage store, pistol drawn.

"Put your hands up!" I told Gamba. The guy behind the luggage counter put his hands up, thinking it was a stickup. We grabbed Gamba and arrested him. I grabbed the phone behind the counter and called Bernie Kerik.

"Bern, I got this motherfucker!" I screamed, my roll raging. "Take the load down! Take the load down!"

"We got 'em," Bernie said. "They're all in handcuffs!"

Then he said what he always said when we made a big bust. "You crazy motherfucker, you!"

———

Our snitch, John "Gordito" Lopez, should have stayed in the United States. Five or six days later, we got an anonymous call from Lopez's aunt, who said she wanted to meet us on Queens Boulevard. Bernie Kerik and I took the meeting. She told us that Lopez and his girlfriend were walking down a street in Colombia when they were both shot. Lopez died instantly, but his girlfriend survived and told authorities that the assassins were also after "a Brazilian guy," who was, of course, Paul. Apparently, once word got out that the eight hundred kilos had gone down, Lopez was blamed for the failure as well as the loss of the $1 million.

Paul went to Colombia alone to clear his name. This bust was different from the last. Months before the bust, we put wiretaps on Gamba and Tejada so that we could actually tell the press the truth. Obviously, we left some details out of our press releases. The press didn't know that we had transported the coke from Costa Rica or the mechanics of how we did the deal. But we did hold a press conference, where we released the wiretap evidence. We handed out press releases, headlined MAJOR DRUG ORGANIZATION TAKEN DOWN and FIVE-MONTH WIRETAP INVESTIGATION TAKES DOWN DRUG ORGANIZATION.

Of course, Paul and I weren't present at the press conference. Nobody knew Paul or I had been involved in the deal. Our identities, along with the specifics of the affidavits, were sealed. Nobody knew who did this operation—not the press, not the public, and, most of all, not the coke cartels.

———

Nacho Gaitan, the boss, called to explain that the van had been taken down and the whole organization taken out because of wiretaps.

"Amateurs," Paul complained, promising to hire a private investigator and lawyer to investigate. That's protocol with the cartel. Once an investigation determines who is at fault for the loss of the load, you get to present your case. After a reasonable amount of time, Paul went to Colombia and gave Nacho, Paulo, and Caro newspaper articles and police reports showing how their operatives had played right into the hands of the police, and how the cops had wiretapped everything.

Heads would soon roll. But once again they wouldn't be ours.

▬▬▬▬

We were immediately on to another bust that seemed run-of-the-mill at first, but would turn out to have bigger implications. It all began when Bobby Starkman, from U.S. customs in Miami, called me and asked me to help him with a money pickup in Queens.

He said the target was a smuggler by the name of Gustavo, and customs officers had learned that he was scheduled to drop off three hundred thousand dollars at a Wendy's in Queens. Starkman asked us to follow Gustavo and start surveillance after he dropped off the cash. Group 93 clicked into gear. We followed Gustavo, one more South American smuggler trying to keep his composure before a big payday, to an apartment complex a couple of blocks away. We staked him out for two days.

On the second morning of the stakeout, he came ambling out of the building and drove over to a house in Jamaica, Queens. We called in the address to headquarters and were told that the house belonged to a guy named Ronnie Reina. Gustavo came out a few minutes later carrying a duffel bag and a shoe box, and drove away. After he drove a couple of miles, we hit him. All he had in the shoe box was twenty thousand dollars, but it was enough to give us probable cause to secure a search warrant for Ronnie's house.

When we got back, Ronnie wasn't home, but his wife was. We searched the house and found eight kilos of coke. We took the wife into custody and waited for Ronnie to come home. He pulled up, came inside, and before he could get acclimated we busted him holding five hundred grams of heroin. It seemed like just another bust. But we hadn't seen the last of Ronnie.

12

Brazil, Brazil, Brazil

Paul taught me everything he knew about drug smuggling. Then he taught me about betrayal.

There was a price to pay for Paul's exoneration at the trial before Lizardo for the loss of the 767 kilos. When the midlevel Cali associates in the meeting, Jose Ricardo and Jorge Arturo, vouched for Paul, saying they would be "responsible" for him, I was too dumb to know what that meant.

Now I would find out the hard way.

"Responsibility," Paul always had told me. "The drug trade runs on responsibility." For being responsible for Paul, Jose and Jorge required something in exchange. They wanted Paul to help them set up an infrastructure in Brazil to help them move their cocaine.

They told him they planned to move ten thousand kilos with Paul earning fifteen hundred dollars per kilo for a $15 million payday.

Real loads. Real deals. And totally against the rules of acceptable behavior in a confidential informant.

While Paul continued doing bogus deals with me, he was doing real Brazilian deals behind my back with Jose and Jorge. Looking at it now, I have to admit Paul was brilliant. Financed by Cali kingpin Pacho Herrera, who oversaw all Cali operations in the U.S., Paul went to work point by point.

First point: establishing an alias, Jose Paulo Ferriera Rothstein, with corporate tax IDs and tax identification. He opened two import/

export companies, Illumbrias and Ameribras, and rented proper offices in Rio. Then he found an airstrip in Mato Grasso, the vast junglelike ranchland outside of Rio de Janeiro. Of course, he needed a partner, and he found one in Francisco Rebecci, a farm boy turned Cali gofer who owned a little company called Intertentcasminas in Belo Horizonte, Brazil. As manager of Paul's operations, Rebecci would be paid three hundred dollars a kilo.

With the now-deceased Avelino Devia Galvis and his beautiful sister-in-law, Marjorie de Sousa, Paul went to the Siemens Corporation's transformer manufacturing facility in Rio, where he placed an order for ten to fifteen industrial transformers, each big enough to conceal up to fifty kilos of cocaine. They were the types of industrial transformers you see hanging on telephone poles, round gray containers that look like garbage cans with wires protruding from their tops. On the same day that Avelino and Marjorie went to purchase Paul's first order of transformers, around October 1991, Paul's first shipment arrived on his airstrip in Brazil from Colombia.

The first shipment was a test—only transformers, no coke. It cleared customs without any delays or hitches.

In December 1991, Paul sent five transformers packed with 165 kilos of coke from Brazil to his Illuminare front company in Fort Lauderdale, Florida. The transformers were searched by U.S. customs officials and cleared. Paul made $250,000 for transporting the load. Two weeks later, five more transformers, packed with another 165 kilos, were successfully shipped and received in Fort Lauderdale.

Not long after, ten transformers packed with more than three hundred kilos were shipped to Florida, this time delivered to a warehouse Paul had rented under an alias in Miami. Once the coke cleared customs, Paul's well-organized team sprang into action. They could recover a load and reassemble a transformer in thirty minutes. Then the load would be delivered to Pacho Herrera's distribution team, and Paul's coke would be distributed to the New York area.

In February and March 1992, Paul sent 275 kilos of coke in even larger transformers to Miami and arranged to have the load shipped to one of several warehouses he had rented in the New York City area. In April 1992 he sent 874 kilos of coke in twenty-four transformers. In July 1992 Paul sent two shipments with twenty-four transformers each for a total of 1,886 kilos. Back in Columbia the Cali bosses began applauding his ingenuity, enterprise, and allegiance.

While I was in New York and the rain forest of Costa Rica, Paul lied to me with his very presence, plotting with me to bust loads while dealing behind my back to satisfy the cartel and his own greed.

Then he lured me to do his dirty work in the country that had blacklisted him.

———

"Brazil, Brazil, Brazil," Paul was again saying. "We've gotta go to Brazil."

We were at Paul's palatial house on Ives Dairy Road in North Miami. As always, he was in his dark Armani suit with the suspenders, the white shirt and tie and handmade shoes. Paul had invited me to visit him in Miami, and the reason was clear. He was pushing me to do a deal in Brazil.

"Listen, Jerry, we've taken a hit in Guatemala," he said. "We lost Avelino and Alonso. We took a hit with Costa Rica, and I had to take the heat. We tried to go back to Guatemala, but because of that idiot Captain Yanez it would never work. Panama is no good because they know the U.S. has interests there with the free-trade zone. Mexico is out because we can't trust the Mexican police. The Colombians are sick of Central America because they've been burned too many times."

He leaned back in his big leather armchair, stared outside at the sun glinting off the swimming pool, and sighed. Behind him, his household hummed in quiet efficiency, everyone, from maids to major domo, doing their jobs with the precision Paul demanded.

"They are asking me to go to Brazil, Jerry," he said. "It has to be Brazil, or we can't do it."

Once again, I resisted, although now a little less strenuously. With our successes in Guatemala and Costa Rica, Group 93 was on top of the world. I was feeling cocky and, okay, maybe even a little indestructible. I thought I was the Ricky Martin of drug law enforcement, and the description wasn't far off the mark. Everybody knew us—except for the associates of the Cali cartel. We'd been screwing with them so long and so well, I was ready to follow Paul anywhere, even Brazil, where he had been blacklisted in the past.

Paul knew what made me tick.

"We will be famous, Jerry," he told me in Miami that day. "We will do tons!"

Of course, I knew it was more than fame that made Paul keep pushing me to do a deal in Brazil. For him, it was about money, too, enough money for him to finally retire. I knew he was getting close to achieving that goal. Group 93 had made Paul a very wealthy man. We paid him $75,000 to $100,000 in cash per load, as well as 20 percent of any assets seized. So if we seized fifteen cars, three houses, and $250,000 cash, Paul would get 20 percent of everything. We could pay him up to $250,000 a load, according to DEA regulations, and in his years of working with me Paul had made a fortune—and I didn't even know what he was making behind my back.

"We could both go out with a bang if we brought down ten tons in Brazil," Paul told me in Miami.

He already had a plan in place. He said he knew a guy, Jose Ricardo, whom he'd met when we went down for the "trial" with Lizardo for the loss of the 767 kilos. He said Ricardo had the drugs and needed them transported.

"Okay, Paul," I said finally. "Let's do Brazil."

———

I flew back to New York and went straight to headquarters, as if Paul were at my back, pushing me forward, always forward, to where he wanted me to go. I went straight to Eddie Beach's desk. As usual, Eddie was scribbling into his little notebook, doing the paperwork he loved so much, happy for the peace and quiet, when I stormed in.

"What's up, Jerry?" he said in a flat monotone, without looking up.

"Brazil," I said. "We gotta do a deal in Brazil."

"I told you a million times, Jerry," he said. "No Brazil. You know all the reasons."

"But, Eddie," I said, "we're going to do tons in Brazil."

He shook his head. "I told you, Jerry, no Brazil, no Brazil," he said. He kept repeating the crucial point that Paul had been involved in a Brazilian corruption scandal. "So why would he want to go back to the country where he was blacklisted?" Eddie asked. He was convinced that we'd get ourselves jailed or killed—and probably both.

He put his pen down on his notebook, got up, and poured himself a cup of coffee. He slugged it down in a single gulp, then stared at me. He was my supervisor, but more than that, Eddie was my friend. He shook his head and let out a sigh, which I took as surrender. I saw a glimmer of weakness, rare for a fireplug of a guy like Eddie Beach, and I made the most of it.

With visions of busting ten tons of coke dancing in my head, I told Eddie, "C'mon, man, we gotta go to Brazil. Paul said that if we do the deal there we can bust *ten tons*." Finally, my enthusiasm was contagious and Eddie Beach gave in.

"Okay, Jerry," he said reluctantly. "But take it slowly and carefully."

I went to my little desk and called Paul's number in Miami. Eddie was back to work on his notebook, but I was already halfway to Rio, my roll raging. Paul picked up the phone on the first ring, as if he knew it would be me.

"Yes?" he said.

"Let's do Brazil," was all I said.

"Point by point, Jerry, we go point by point," Paul said.

He told me to go to Brazil to get permission from the government to do the controlled delivery. As always, we'd have to find an airstrip in the jungle, and he gave me the exact dimensions. We had to figure out how to refuel the Colombian planes. Next we would set up an office, with a secretary, letterhead, and the obligatory ribbon cutting. We would require a warehouse to store the coke until we had enough to ship to the U.S. At the time, he didn't mention shipping the coke to the U.S. He was focused on the airstrip and the refueling.

"How big of a plane you thinking about landing, Paul?" I asked.

"A DC-Seven," he said. *Oh, great, I thought, a jet! In the middle of the jungle.* With a plane that big, we could transport five thousand to ten thousand kilos of coke in one shot.

With our marching orders in place, Eddie Beach and I headed for Brazil. Paul said he would meet us there.

———

We flew into Brasília. By then, Eddie and I were international travel veterans. But I was a nervous flier. Oh, hell, not just nervous. I was petrified. My classes to become a student pilot had given me a case of the shakes that recurred every time I flew.

I tried to steel my nerves with alcohol. We could drink on international flights, because we couldn't carry guns into a foreign country, whereas drinking was prohibited on domestic flights, because we carried guns. So I drank. But it didn't help. My hands were sweating, gripping the armrest, and I was screaming at each and every bump. I was so afraid of flying that I slept *under* the seat on the floor of the plane on our first trip to Brazil. I don't know how I got under the seat, but I did.

Meanwhile, Eddie would be taking notes, watching the movie, trying to act as if he weren't with me. When we finally landed, I rushed down the jet bridge and, amid the smell of rotting fruit and stale urine, kissed the dirty ground.

"Hey, Jerry, hey, Eddie," said Peter Reef, U.S. embassy DEA attaché in the Brasília office, when he met us at the airport gate. We were in an old-fashioned train-station-like arrival area, with ancient arrival and departure boards. No computerized television screens. "Welcome to Brasília!"

Reef was a heavyset guy in his fifties with reddish gray hair, at the end of his career. Before we went to his office to discuss the controlled delivery, Reef took us to a Brazilian steak house and gave us a grand tour. Brasília (population two million) is the capital of Brazil, but it's basically in the middle of nowhere, at least five hundred miles from the nearest major metropolis. Built on a plateau in the late fifties, it has a lot of interesting modern architecture, no pollution, less crime than most Brazilian cities, and miles and miles of jungle, which surrounds the city in every direction like a moat. The politicians control the town Monday through Friday, but on weekends they all flee the city for the countryside.

"Jerry, I hate to deliver bad news, but controlled deliveries are against the law in Brazil," Reef said.

I wouldn't take no for an answer. "This is a big operation! Ten tons! Ten thousand kilos!" I told him about Group 93's proven track record with our Guatemala and Costa Rica deals. "We've disrupted the cartel and tied a fishnet around their dealers all across America."

Although he said we probably wouldn't get anywhere, Reef gave us a contact with the Brazilian feds, Jetulio Brazero. He was the head of the Brazilian Federales, or the DPF, the Brazilian equivalent to the head of the FBI.

We met Brazero in the state building in the heart of Brasília. We walked into a ten-story office building and were led to Brazero, who was waiting in a big conference room with a conference table. Not impressive, but not that bad. Along with Brazero were Peter Reef and seven Brazilian feds.

We didn't tell them that our CI was Paul Lir Alexander; they knew him from his past screwups. I just said that a stateside CI wanted to do this operation with us. I went over our needs, point by point: the landing strip in the Amazon, the shipping containers, the bogus business operations.

The Brazilians were more difficult than the Guatemalans. They were more sophisticated. They insisted on following their constitution, which forbade controlled deliveries. Where the Guatemalans and the Costa Ricans looked the other way, the Brazilians would take more convincing. We were used to promising the next deal to the government, hanging them on their own greed, getting our way, and then slipping away. The Brazilians wouldn't bite at that bait.

After about an hour of meeting, I had them interested. They said that if everything checked out with the higher-ups, including the president, they'd probably go along with our plan. As per Brazilian custom, one of Brazero's underlings poured each of us a cup of Brazilian espresso with water chasers.

Eddie stuck his spoon in his coffee, which was as thick as mud. He was shaking, the little spoon quivering in his massive hands. Watching this big bulldog, Eddie Beach, more than two hundred pounds, freaking out over the dangers lurking in a cup of coffee, looked kind of funny to me. But I knew what he was thinking. Eddie was flashing back to when we were in Guatemala and I popped a raw pork skin and came down with a knee-knocking case of amoebic dysentery.

Eddie looked at the muddy espresso, then looked at the general. "No, no, no!" he said, words pouring out. "Really, not the water. I'm afraid of the water here. I don't want nothing to do with the water or the coffee, I'm afraid to get one of those bugs in my stomach."

He might as well have told the general, "Your country's a filthy hellhole. I'm not touching your food, your water, or your coffee."

I couldn't believe what I was hearing. To show them that I took pride in Brazil, I grabbed my coffee and water chaser, slammed them both down, then grabbed Eddie's coffee and water and slammed them too. That seemed to appease our hosts.

"Please do not to do anything in our country until you hear back from us," the chief federale said when departing. "We will give you our decision in two weeks."

I didn't know that Paul already had the entire operation set up behind my back.

———

It was a Friday, carnival season, November 1992. We rushed to the airport and flew out of Brasília to Sao Paulo. A few hours after our meeting with the general, Eddie and I were getting out of a taxi at the Sheraton Mafahez in São Paulo when a white stretch limo pulled up. The doormen rushed to open the doors, and Paul Lir Alexander stepped out.

Paul looked and acted like a drug lord. He was wearing his usual immaculate dark Armani suit and suspenders. Trailing behind him was an entourage: the de Sousa sisters, Antonio Calderon, Paul's gofer Nielsen, and a slew of bodyguards, with the addition of a pack of dirty undercover Rio de Janeiro cops. I thought I saw the telltale powder of cocaine underneath one of the women's noses.

"Welcome to my country," Paul said to me, giving me an *abrazo* while the rest of his entourage, all of whom knew me and Eddie and our DEA mission with Paul well by now, greeted us warmly.

I was a big believer in Paul Lir Alexander in America. But now that he was on his home turf of Brazil, he acted as if he owned every inch of the country. "Come with me," he said.

Eddie and I trailed after him, two more members of his entourage. After a few drinks in the hotel lobby, Paul took us all to a concert by the Brazilian pop sensations Leandro and Leonardo. When we exited the limo at the soccer stadium, I could hear the roar of sixty thousand people, all so crazy for music that there were chain-link fences in front of the stage so none of Leandro and Leonardo's fans could climb over. I could feel Paul's power as we waded through the crowd at the soccer stadium full of Brazilians. Now there were bodyguards with machine guns around him.

He pointed to a sign that read ALEXANDER PRODUCTIONS. "That's my company, Jerry," Paul said, proudly.

"What, you're in the concert business?" I said.

"Yes, my friend, and business is booming, no?" he said, gesturing to the throng. "If anybody asks, just tell them you and Eddie are producers from Hollywood."

Before I knew it, we had backstage passes and we were actually onstage, looking out at the sea of music-loving Brazilians. Eddie Beach and I were, per Paul's instructions, two Hollywood producers. I fell into the part a little more naturally than Eddie did. "Yeah, we gotta couple productions goin'," I kept telling everyone in my broken Spanish, and they had no reason to doubt me. I was with Paul, and that was proof enough.

After the concert we went to a small private club, Limelight, which, Paul told us, was a favorite hangout of the president of Brazil. We sat down with Paul and his entourage. Marjorie de Sousa, who had been held hostage during our Guatemalan operation, kept staring at me. She was wearing a skimpy red dress with matching stiletto heels—and slugging down Cristal champagne. Paul kept sending over prostitutes to me all night long, because, of course, if he could compromise me with a hooker he'd have a lot of leverage against me. Finally, he put Marjorie on me. She came over to where I was standing and tried to climb me like a flagpole.

"Come on, Geraldo Bartone, let's have some fun," she said.

"Whoa, now, slow down," I said, wrestling myself free.

Later that night, after Eddie and I had got away from Paul and his entourage, a knock sounded at the door of the hotel room we shared. I opened it and there was Marjorie in her red high heels and holding a bottle of Cristal champagne. She looked at me as if I were the love of her life and was headed toward me, full steam ahead, when Eddie bolted out of the bathroom, big as a house and pissed off at this woman who dared delay his sleep, shouting, "None of this stuff! Get out! Get outta here!" I swung Marjorie around and sent her on her way.

Marjorie wasn't my only visitor that night. Paul stopped by not long after she left. He wanted to talk to us, but he wasn't making any sense. He just kept saying over and over that he wanted to retire.

Everything had become so difficult for him. I didn't know it then, but he must have had tremendous guilt building up. He was about to ship six tons of cocaine behind my back, and he must have been getting scared.

"I want to give you information about this guy, a big-time distributor in New York," Paul said. "His name is Caliche, and he's a big distributor for this organization we're going to be transporting for."

Paul didn't exactly *give* me the information. Instead, he sent me on a wild-goose chase. Maybe he was trying to sidetrack me. Paul gave me a phone number that he said belonged to Caliche.

"When this gets going, Jerry, you should look into this group," Paul said.

But when I tried to track the number, I discovered that it was Caliche's old cell phone number, one that Paul had used three months ago to discuss one of his covert transformer shipments. I left Brazil and returned to New York, not suspecting anything was the least bit odd about Paul.

Later, Eddie and I would remember Paul's visit that night in the hotel. We'd both agree that Paul was trying to come clean. But he just couldn't do it.

Instead, he went ahead with his double cross.

——————

After Eddie and I left Brazil, Paul gave the order for Rebecci to ship two more containers loaded with two tons of cocaine to Miami and New Jersey. But in typical dope dealer style, Rebecci couldn't be satisfied with his three hundred dollars per kilo commission. No, he had to steal seventeen kilos off of one transformer load and another ten off a later load.

In late 1992, Paul got an urgent call from Rebecci, not from his shipping facility, but from a Rio jail cell. Rebecci had been busted trying to sell the dope to an undercover Brazilian Civil Police officer, and the cops now wanted six hundred thousand dollars in bribe money for Rebecci's release.

Paul called his original benefactor, Jorge Arturo, who had vouched for Paul in our lost 767 kilo load with Lizardo. But this time Arturo was not about to accept responsibility for Paul. He said it would take at least one or two weeks before he could come up with the cash. By then the Brazilian Federal Police would probably become involved . . . and, if Rebecci talked, the whole operation would be busted.

Rebecci was Paul's responsibility. Paul was holding a load when the load went down, and Paul knew what that meant.

Rebecci gave up Paul's entire operation to the Brazilian Federal Police. He told them that he had shipped two containers for a smuggler by the name of Paolo Ferriera Rothstein. The load had already left Brazil destined for Miami and New Jersey. With his Colombian contacts hanging him out to dry and his operations manager in jail, Paul was faced with losing his operation and possibly his life.

───

It was just before Thanksgiving, 1992. Eddie and I had just returned from Brazil, and we were in the office when the phone rang.

"Jerry, a friend of mine has some information about a shipment that's coming to the States," Paul said.

"From where, Paul?" I asked. "And whose shipment is it?"

"Oh, the usual—some Colombians and a Brazilian friend of mine," he said.

I got hot. Here he was, beating around the bush, and I didn't have time for it. I'd gotten a new phone number from the disconnected Caliche number that Paul had given me, and I was trying to push forward the deal that seemed to be going nowhere in Brazil. "Well, Paul, where's the load coming? New York? Jersey?"

"No, I think it's coming to Miami," he said.

I didn't have the time or the interest to do a deal in Miami, which had its own DEA group. "Well, look, Paul, if it's coming to Miami, call Bobby Starkman in customs down there. You know him, remember?"

"Yes, sure, I know him," said Paul.

Right, of course you know Starkman, I thought. *He wanted to bust your ass, but I protected you.*

But I didn't say that. I just told Paul to call Bobby Starkman and give him the information. I thought it would be a good way to repay Starkman for not popping Paul when he caught him with the half million in the Home Depot parking lot. Paul's cooperation would show Starkman that Paul was on the level, just as I said. "Tell Bobby to consider it an early Christmas gift from me," I said.

Paul called Starkman. He gave the identification information about the container. Starkman said he'd check into it.

Within the hour, Starkman called me. "Whoa, Jerry, big problems," he said. "That container is flagged by the Miami DEA-Joint Customs Group." He told me all about the arrest of Rebecci and the situation with the Brazilian Civil Police. "We're working on this guy Paolo Ferriera Rothstein, who supposedly shipped the stuff from Brazil."

I was dumb as a box of rocks.

I didn't know Paolo Rothstein was an alias of Paul Lir Alexander.

So I told Starkman to call Paul for help.

I still thought Paul was on the level and that he could help the Miami DEA's case. Paul met with the Customs Group and played a complete charade. He said he knew a guy in Brazil who knew Rothstein, and he would call him and see what he could find out.

Later that day, Paul set up a call from his elaborate telephone-switching station in his house in Miami, placing a controlled call to one of his stooges in Brazil and letting the Miami customs and DEA guys listen in. I can only imagine how well he pulled it off. "Hi, brother, it's me, Paul Alexander. I'm trying to find out about this guy Rothstein," he'd probably say. I can also imagine how well the decoy on the other end spoon-fed Paul what he wanted the DEA to know about the load and where it was supposed to go in Miami.

I can see his strategy. Paul thought the agents would bust the warehouse, give him his reward for helping them, and move on. But Paul forgot a critical point, that *he* had rented the warehouses, had even visited them. The agents assembled a "photo array"—Paul in a dozen settings and poses—and went to landlords who leased the warehouse to Rothstein.

The landlords did what I couldn't do. They ID'd Paul as Paolo Ferriera Rothstein.

So now the Miami agents knew that Paul Alexander was a liar. Instead of sailing off in a coke-white limo, Paul found himself in a fluorescent-lit conference room, with Bobby Starkman and his colleagues, Joe Vigna and Frank Gomez, firing off questions.

The agents in Miami didn't tell me about this. Had they shared their evidence, I would have locked Paul up myself. But instead they kept me, and the rest of Group 93, out of the loop.

"**P**aulo Ferriera Rothstein?" Joe Vigna from the Miami Joint Customs Group kept asking me by phone. "Who is Paulo Ferriera Rothstein?"

I must have said, "I don't know" a hundred times.

I was in my office in Group 93 headquarters, in my jeans and sweatshirt. It was December 1992, a couple of days before Christmas.

A name like that I would have remembered. There aren't that many Rothsteins involved in the Colombian coke trade. I didn't think too much about it . . . until my supervisor, John Maltz, called me into his office and told me Miami DEA wanted me and the members of the group who dealt with Paul Alexander to go down to Miami and give the U.S. Attorney a sworn deposition.

"No way, they don't know what they're talking about, the guy's clean," I said. "He made more cases for the government than they know about."

"Did you give him permission in Brazil to ship anything in transformers?"

"Listen, chief, you know we were there to build an airstrip, that's it," I said. "We didn't actually ship anything yet."

"I know," said Maltz, "But they need you to come down and give them a sworn deposition to that fact."

"Who wants it?" I asked.

"Miami Joint Customs Group," he said. "Joe Vigna."

"For what?" I asked.

"For this," Maltz said, sliding a photograph across the table. I looked at the picture. "So what? This is Paul."

"No, it's Paolo Ferriera Rothstein," Maltz said. "He just transported seventeen hundred kilos of coke from Brazil, and Miami says that your group is involved."

Comprehension hit me like a bombshell.

Then things got dicey. Alex Segarra, the U.S. Attorney in charge of the investigation, hated Paul from the get-go. The DEA agent in charge of the Miami Joint Customs Group, Joe Vigna, didn't particularly like me. I think he thought I was too big for my britches and he wanted to take me down. He put two and two together and figured that I was as dirty as Paul—and, considering I was in Brazil running with Paul, that wasn't a bad guess.

Geraldo Bartone was in big trouble.

Back on West Fifty-seventh Street, Paul called Group 93 headquarters, saying he was headed back to New York. Eddie Beach picked up the phone and, after a minute of conversation, held it out for me.

"Just talk to him," said Eddie

"I'm not trusting that scumbag," I said. "That's it. I'm done."

I never saw or spoke to Paul Lir Alexander again.

Eddie held out the phone to Bernie Kerik.

"Okay, Bernie, you talk to him," Eddie ordered. "Tell him he better not be lyin' to us."

So Bernie went to see him. As usual, Paul was staying at the New York Hilton in Midtown Manhattan. Bernie got there early, when the hotel was still asleep. He banged on Paul's door. When Paul opened it, still dressed in his pajamas, Bernie yanked him into the hallway. He frisked him for wires and, when he didn't find anything, interrogated him. Paul didn't give an inch. It was all a misunderstanding, he said, and would be cleared up immediately.

"Listen, I think the guy's clean," Bernie said when he returned. "He swears he's not doing anything."

"I don't care," I said. "I'm not going near him. I don't trust that motherfucker."

Paul flew to Colombia and explained the situation to his bosses in the cartel.

"Welcome to the club," Cali kingpin Pacho Herrera told Paul, meaning, "Paul, your trading days are over." He was ordered to remain in Colombia, never to return to the U.S., and promised that, for his allegiance, Paul and his family would be taken care of forever. He was ordered never to discuss the case.

But Paul didn't stay in Colombia.

His life wouldn't be worth a dime if word got out, as it surely would, that he was working with us.

On April 18, 1993, Paul and Erica arrived back in Miami. At the airport, they were surrounded by agents of the Miami DEA. Paul was arrested and charged with smuggling seventeen hundred kilos of cocaine into Miami.

Once Paul was in jail, the U.S. Attorney's office in Miami wanted to bring me down for questioning. I didn't know what kind of defense Paul was mounting or how he was characterizing my involvement. I went to the deputy chief of the task force, Kenny O'Brien, and said, "I'm not goin' down there if they think I'm dirty. Am I a target of this investigation?"

Kenny advised me to refuse to fly to Miami without a grand jury subpoena. He told me that a grand jury subpoena would protect me if they compelled me to testify.

I followed Kenny's advice. A day or two later, the grand jury subpoena arrived. I told Maggie to be prepared to hire an attorney or put the house up for bail money—I had no idea what they were planning for me.

I flew down to Miami alone. Vigna met me at the airport. He couldn't have been more polite. He had no idea that I knew what he was saying behind my back: "Don't trust the New York guys. They're going to warn their CI that some shit is about to go down, and their CI is dirty."

I was the first to be interrogated because I was the closest to Paul. They put me in a little room across the table from Vigna and Segarra. Both of them were completely straight-faced. They took a full deposition.

"Did you authorize Paul to ship the transformers and set up the airstrip in Belo Horizonte?" asked Vigna.

I said I had proposed a plan to the Brazilian government to set up an airstrip in Mato Grasso and was waiting on authorization.

They told me that they had instructed the Brazilian chief of police to investigate my stay in Brazil, and he had come up with some interesting information.

"Do you want to tell us about sleeping with Marjorie de Sousa in the São Paulo Sheraton?" Joe Vigna asked me.

I almost jumped across the table. "Never happened," I said. "Ask Eddie Beach. He was right in the room with me. If you think you're going to drag my wife and family though the mud, you've got another thing coming. You'll have to kill me first."

"Okay, Jerry, calm down," said Vigna.

"You got me mixed up with Santo," I said, referring to Santo Giambelli, a Miami DEA agent who was sleeping with Marjorie. But behind the bluster, I was blowing a gasket. I knew if I walked into a courtroom and Marjorie walked in, and the jurors were sitting there, nobody would believe I didn't go to bed with her. I could see my marriage and my career both coming to an end.

The agents obviously believed that I would get on the stand and change my story to protect Paul. After they persuaded me to calm down, they asked me to write my statement. They read me the perjury statute before I signed it. That threw me for a loop. It was uncommon in the law enforcement community to read the perjury statute to an agent. Normally an agent's word is golden and the story an agent gives the U.S. Attorney is the story they stick with.

I told the truth, that I'd never known Paul used Rothstein as an alias, that I never knew about an operation involving smuggling coke in electrical transformers, that I never knew that Paul was doing anything except leading me to some of the biggest dope busts in U.S. law enforcement history.

After the depositions were complete, I went straight to the airport and flew back to New York. All I had been trying to do was seize coke, cash, and the cartel players, but now the tables had turned.

———

When Paul went on trial, I gotta admit, I was sweating big time. He could easily have taken me down with him. Days before Paul's shipment of the seventeen hundred kilos in the transformers, I was in Brazil, proposing to do a deal that was similar to what he actually did. He could have said I knew all along. He could have finagled a lighter sentence or made it look as if he were sanctioned. He could have said that the government, meaning me, gave him permission to do the load and if he was breaking the law, then I was, too. He could have pointed the finger at me, and the judge and the jurors would have believed him.

I was cursing myself, because I should have figured all of this out before the DEA in Miami did. At the time of Paul's arrest, Brazil was the world's number-one cocaine connection, with an estimated 60 percent of the U.S. consumption coming from what's known as the Cocaine Triangle of the Amazon, where Brazil, Peru, and Colombia meet. Four major Rio gangs controlled the Brazilian cocaine trade, one of them led by Paul. Of the four gangs, it was later estimated that Paul's was the richest, worth some $20 million in cash, real estate, and various businesses.

The Miami DEA found his yachts in Italy and Spain, millions of dollars in various domestic and international bank accounts, his various businesses, property, and holdings in Brazil. He was using not only Rothstein as an alias, but also Pedro Chamoro and several others. In his Miami mansion, agents studied his telephone-switching room, the elaborate setup where Paul could have calls relayed via forty different cell and landlines to wherever he might be doing his double-dealing, from Bogotá to Jersey to Miami, leaving the callers—including me—thinking that he was being a good boy at home.

———

I was in New York when the case went to court.

"Your boy took it on the chin," Bob McConnell from the Secret Service told me over the phone. On the stand, McConnell told me, Paul told everything straight. He said the transformer deal was all his own doing. He pled guilty and said nobody in Group 93 had anything to do shipping coke in transformers. In a plea bargain, he got twenty-three years to life.

He'd let me off the hook. But by then, he had already screwed me. When it hit me, I had to sit down to keep from falling.

"Brazil, Brazil, Brazil."

BS, BS, BS.

13

Caliche

Gloom hung over Group 93. We all sat around our evidence locker of a headquarters, thinking our operation was over. We'd lost our star CI. Everyone was freaked by the accusations and innuendos from the Miami Joint Customs Group. After suffering for a couple of months, I said, "Fuck it" and went to Eddie's office. I found him, as usual, scribbling in his notebook.

"Wait a minute," I said, "who needs Paul Lir Alexander? We can do it without him. Let's give it a shot."

Eddie stayed at his desk, still signing papers, while I bounced around him like a jack-in-the-box. Finally, he looked up and said, "Yeah, yeah, whatever you wanna do, Jerry. Just get outta here and leave me alone."

As I walked out the door, I heard Eddie yell after me, "Remember, we don't need no heat. I'm going to keep a tight leash on the operation—and on you."

I didn't need Paul's help anymore to pass as a drug smuggler. With the tools at my disposal, I could pass the toughest test. I knew that appearances are everything. Being in the right restaurant with the right people in Bogotá, and carrying the required Bogotá bag, could be the beginning of serious cred.

I knew the places where the coke smugglers stayed, dined, and drank. I knew their superstitions. Primarily Roman Catholics, they would shut their operations down on the first week of December until after the Feast of the Three Kings. If you called them on Christmas Eve, or any other religious holiday, they'd bust you right away. I knew that they wouldn't walk behind a black cat or under a ladder.

I knew their lingo, their allegiances, their points of reference, that their aspirations were to send their kids to the best schools, that Isla de Providencia is a tiny Colombian island off the coast between the Yucatan Peninsula and South America, and how rough the ocean can get there. I knew the things that only a smuggler would know.

I'd learned it all, point by point. I'd listened to all of the stories from the real smugglers we'd locked up—cages full of dealers: distributors, pilots and mules, who had sailed through the gut-roiling storms and crashed small planes on windswept jungle runways. I knew how to use those stories in my own dialogue with the dealers. "Hey, I remember the time Carlito was praying in the lightning storm and he crashed the plane and got the dope off and buried it with a backhoe on the runway."

Their stories became my stories. Their lives became my life. I got so good at lying to drug dealers, I thought I should get an Academy Award.

———

By the late winter, we were in our new offices at the new DEA headquarters on Tenth Avenue. Eddie Beach had a real office and every member of Group 93 had a little cubicle on the sixth floor. Best of all, we had a state-of-the art wire room on the seventh floor.

After Paul gave me the expired phone number of the New York–based distributor known as Caliche, I went to work. I figured Paul knew Caliche from the transformer loads he had shipped to the United States. He had used Caliche to distribute the coke and probably told Caliche to destroy his phone. I figured Paul thought it was safe to give me Caliche's old number, because what good could it do me? I did what's called a telephone pattern analysis, and I found all the frequently called numbers on Caliche's disconnected cell phone, numbers for people like his mother, sister, and girlfriend. Then I asked the cellular carrier to locate phones that had also called these common numbers using a dial digit search. I soon had Caliche's new cell phone. I had probable cause and was able to secure a wiretap.

We started by wiretapping only two of Caliche's phones, and it sounded like Grand Central at rush hour. This guy Caliche was talking to everybody: a guy named Jota about a coke drop; a guy he called El Matador, who told him to pick up "the bicycle from La Tia," which I knew to be a major load from Los Angeles. The calls were red hot, and this was just from two phones!

I would stand in the wire room, listening to those crazy loud tones and conversations, and it was as if somebody hit me with a shot of adrenaline. I would go racing down from the wire room straight toward Eddie Beach's new office, spinning in a cloud of energy like the Tasmanian Devil.

"We don't need Paul," I told Eddie. "I found the phone pattern analysis."

"I thought those phones were dead," Eddie said, referring to Caliche's old phone numbers.

"No, I did the check for the common number routine, and you won't believe what I found," I said. "He's talking to thirty-five phones and beepers to dozens of people." I rattled off a few of the names. "I wanna get on Jota's phone. I want to get on El Matador's phone. All of them! We gotta go up on all thirty-five phones and devices."

"Thirty-five?" he said. "You're out of your mind."

"Eddie, you don't understand, this is big, bigger than anything we've done yet," I said.

"No, Jerry, you don't understand," Eddie said. "Thirty-five phones. Two monitors per phone. Twenty-five thousand dollars per phone. A month! Do the math, Jerry. You're asking for a quarter-million dollars every month."

I think I said, "So?"

"So who do you think is gonna authorize that?"

"Are we in this for real, or are we just playing games?" I said. "This is a major organization. We can really take down something big. Are you with me or not?"

"Yeah, Jerry, I'm with you," he said. "But the bureaucrats aren't gonna go for this."

"We'll never know if you don't help me," I said. "Our guys are standing around, waiting for something to do. Just help me get the authorization. Go see Maltz and whoever else we need to do to get up on the phones."

Eddie did just that. Pretty soon we were wiretapping Caliche on thirty-five phones and paging devices.

======

"**A**ll right, guys, listen up," I said, calling all of the group out of their cubicles. "We're going up on thirty-five phones!"

I started pointing and barking orders like a madman. First Bernie Kerik, our subpoena expert.

"Hey, Bees, start pulling the subpoenas for ATT wireless," I said. "Big Daddy, start doing some dumps on Caliche's phones to see who all of the incoming calls are. Kevin, you start looking at the records of the cell phone calls."

Then I returned to the wiretap room, where now almost seventy monitors, two for each of Caliche's target phones, were working in cubicles. Each cubicle had a big cassette recorder with three separate compartments for tapes. When a tapped phone was activated with an incoming or outgoing call, the recorders would be cued up to start, and we could hear the dial tones rolling through overhead speakers. Then the wiretap attendants would start monitoring conversations and passing on information to the agents in the field.

We hired Spanish-speaking translators to monitor the wiretaps; we had them sworn in as special deputies to the special narcotics prosecutor's office. Group 93 members Bruce Stokes and Jack Higgins managed the wiretap room. I ran the field operations. I would call in and say, "Whaddaya got?" and they would pass along the tips.

Point by point, I thought, *just take it point by point.*

======

Caliche's real name was Carlos Torres. He was a dealer who was the Cali Cartel's point man on Long Island. He rented houses in the suburbs, and pretty soon we were intercepting instructions we heard from his Colombian bosses, most prominently Don Francisco, an FBI fugitive also known as Hernan Prada. They also called Don Francisco "El Senor," and Don Francisco called Caliche "King."

"Listen, my King, I need you to rent houses with attached garages in the suburbs of Long Island," we heard Don Francisco tell Caliche.

"It's very important that you show that you are like the Americans. Bring a woman and kids with you and keep them in the house."

"Okay, El Senor," said Caliche. "I will begin immediately."

"King, every day you get in your car at eight in the morning. Every day, have your woman kiss you good-bye on the porch and then leave with your briefcase. Even if you have to go and ride around the city all day long while the others are doing the deals and receiving the loads, you must stay away from your home until five in the afternoon. After that time, you will go back and have your wife come out and greet you so you look like the all-American family. That's how the Americans are."

"Okay, El Senor," said Caliche.

"And, King, I want you to subscribe to the American bible."

"What is that, El Senor?" Caliche asked.

"*TV Guide*. Every American home in the suburbs gets the *TV Guide*. Even though you don't speak English, you must subscribe to *TV Guide* and many other American magazines."

Caliche followed Don Francisco's instructions and became, for all outward appearances, the all-American husband and father.

On January 7, 1993, we intercepted Caliche on a call to someone whom he called "sir" at least seventeen times in the conversation. That, we felt, meant he was talking to El Senor or another one of his superiors. In our transcripts, "sir" was listed as UM-1, meaning unidentified male number one.

CALICHE: Do not worry, you know that I already have everything set up over here, sir!

UM-1: Well, King.

CALICHE: Sir!

UM-1: Tell me.

CALICHE: You are, you are pleased with the office, right?

UM-1: Of course, I am pleased with you.

CALICHE: God bless you, sir.

UM-1: No, everything's fine, everything's fine. I am very pleased with you, Palo.

CALICHE: I already got the other house, sir, for the other coban [bank, or stash house].

UM-1: Well, King.

CALICHE: I already have the people that you authorized and everything is normal, sir.

Tracking Caliche provided new insights in how the cartels do business. He was an expert in evasion. When he drove a car, he would change lanes constantly and pull U-turns on major thoroughfares, to evade tails. He gave explicit instructions to his workers on how they should conduct themselves while doing business, and he and his associates spoke in a sophisticated code, which was soon crackling across our airwaves.

There were hundreds of code words, such as "coban" for bank or stash house, "tickets" for kilos of coke, "pesos" for dollars, caleta for the hidden compartments in cars or trucks where the coke was hidden, and "sick" describing an associate who was arrested. As for the police, he called them "animals," as in, "There were animals crawling all over the street, brother, and they left with about a hundred tickets and a couple guys got sick."

Here's one of hundreds of hours of conversations we intercepted, this one between Caliche and an unidentified male:

UM-1: There was a holdup last night, brother.

CALICHE: A what?

UM-1: A holdup! But nothing was taken, brother. [*sighs*]

CALICHE: Really?

UM-1: Brother, when some of my employees entered the house—

CALICHE: Hm . . .

UM-1: They were held up at gunpoint, brother Belten said . . . When he knocks, he has to knock three times.

CALICHE: Hm . . .

UM-1: A guy enters with a shotgun, brother. Boom, boom, boom, and we started shooting through the window, brother.

CALICHE: Hm . . .

UM-1: I think we killed someone, brother. [*sighs*] I don't know, the cops grabbed two around the corner.

CALICHE: Two what?

UM-1: They got two of them, brother. They didn't take anything, man.

We called headquarters and, sure enough, there had been a homicide the previous night involving one Hector Barona. He was shot twelve times as he was getting out of his car at his house—retribution for a Caliche coke deal gone sour.

———

One day, we picked up a wiretap between Caliche and one of his underlings. Caliche was talking about somebody he called "Code Twenty-five," who had driven a van loaded with 150 kilos of coke from California. Code 25 had dropped it somewhere on Northern Boulevard in Queens late that evening. But Code 25 had forgotten where he'd parked the van. Before it could be retrieved, the van was either stolen or towed. Either way, it was never found.

Caliche held Code 25 responsible. He called his boss, Don Francisco, and told him that Code 25 lost both the van and the 150 kilos. Don Francisco was livid. He instructed Caliche to kidnap Code 25 and have him tortured and killed if he didn't come up with the load. Our wiretaps followed Caliche as he called the beeper number of Blas Jimenez Uribe Cadavid, who was known as 007. We soon learned that 007 was an assassin. The assassin instructed Caliche to meet him at a pay phone in front of the Casa Del Pacho Restaurant.

One of Caliche's workers was also using a cell phone that we had tapped. We heard 007 get on the line and call the bosses in Colombia. "Send him to heaven," we heard the bosses say. "Let the honeymoon begin."

I was in the New York District Attorney's office when I got word that all of this was going down. I knew enough about the mechanics of the drug trade to put two and two together. Clearly, the cartel was going to kill Code 25. Even though he was a drug dealer, I couldn't allow that to happen.

I ran out of the prosecutor's office and jumped into my car with lights and sirens blazing. Twenty minutes later, I was at the pay phone booth where 007 was talking to Caliche. I got a good look at the hit man. He was a short Colombian guy, and every inch of him exuded ruthlessness.

Next thing we heard over the wiretap was Caliche telling Code 25 to meet 007 at the restaurant to discuss the loss of the van. He told Code 25 that 007 was an "investigator" from the cartel. We set up surveillance and watched Code 25 arrive. He was short with long brown hair. We saw him meet with 007 and two of his assistant assassins. Then we saw 007, Code 25, and his two assistants leave the restaurant and get in a car.

We tailed them as they drove around all day. As the sun was going down and the long afternoon was headed into what was beginning to feel like a bloody night, they took him to La Samuna Espanol Bar, where they proceeded to get Code 25 drunk.

Eddie Beach and I gathered a bunch of uniformed cops and hit the bar like troopers on an enemy beach. We grabbed everybody, including 007, who was packing a pistol. He also had a roll of duct tape in his pocket. Code 25 was so drunk that he didn't realize what was going on.

"Buddy, this ain't no party! You're about to be killed!" I told him.

"What are you talking about?" he said. "These guys are my friends."

This presented a problem. We could only federally arrest 007 on the gun charge. If we arrested him based on the wiretap information, we would have to end our investigation of the entire Caliche organization—a big price to pay, when we had only seized 150 kilos of Caliche's vast resources. We had them on kidnapping, but we wanted to go further into Caliche's organization and see what else we could get on them.

We charged 007 with the federal gun offense. We ended up getting Code 25 deported because he had no immigration papers. The feds put a $250,000 bail on 007, which he made. Once he was out of jail, he skipped bail and fled to who knows where.

As the Caliche investigation dragged on, first into months, then into a year, fatigue took its toll on Group 93. We had been following Caliche for so long, we were getting dizzy from the multitude of deals and personnel. Automobiles became a liability for me. I was having car accidents, one after another. At the height of the investigation, I was wrecking a car a month.

Caliche and his group were so widespread and tough to follow that I suggested to Eddie Beach that we could best do it with a helicopter. We were following two of Caliche's dealers in separate cars up the Harlem River Drive. I was in one car, Eddie Beach was in another car, close behind. The other members of Group 93—Big Daddy, Jimmy

Grace, Terry Hartman—were also in hot pursuit, each in his own car. Eddie gave me the go-ahead to radio for helicopter assistance.

"Bring the chopper in," I said, calling for the Flint Unit, which is the universal call sign for a helicopter unit in the DEA.

"Flint, spot me first," I said. "I'm in a BMW 750, champagne colored. Sunroof open. I'm in the left-hand lane on Harlem River Drive at about 140th Street."

Next thing I heard was *thump, thump, thump.* The chopper radioed back that they saw me down below. Along with a pilot on a surveillance chopper, there is what's known as a spotter, who looks out the window to follow the suspect with high-powered glasses.

"The silver car in front is the target car," I said over the radio. "Keep an eye on 'em so we can lay back a little."

Thump, thump, thump, I heard the chopper overhead, and the pilot or spotter said, "Okay, ten-four, we got one of the cars." With the copter overhead and Group 93 behind me, I followed the target car into the neighborhood of Washington Heights, and the chopper personnel told me where to turn to follow the target vehicles. I swerved through traffic, trying to keep pace with the speeding silver car. Another turn and—the next thing I heard was a loud, earth-shattering *crash.* A black guy in a white butcher's coat and a motorcycle helmet landed on the front hood of my car.

"The spotter fell out of the chopper!" I screamed over the radio. "Oh, my God, the spotter fell out of the chopper!"

In the same split second, a guy in a motorcycle helmet crashed through the side window of my BMW. Now I was hysterical. "May day! May day! The pilot's out of the chopper! The chopper's coming down!"

I fully expected the helicopter to come raining down upon me. But then, the next thing I heard was *thump, thump, thump,* and I knew the chopper was still in the air. "Flint to 2304," the pilot radioed me. "We're still in the air. You've run over a motorcycle. It's still under your car."

I had been making a right turn when a guy on a stolen motorcycle slammed into the back of my car and went flying up in the air and landed on the hood. Caliche's guys in the target car were getting away.

I was stranded, with a motorcycle under my car and a guy on my hood, who suddenly slid down and took off on foot. By now, my

Group 93 colleagues, Terry Hartman and Kent Fullenweider, were on the scene, surveying the damage. Kent Fullenweider, a great African-American cop with a beard and mustache, could blend into the scenery on any type of surveillance. He was also the fastest runner in our group. Terry Hartman was a fourth-degree black belt and also very fast. I stayed with the wreckage while Kent and Terry took off after the guy who'd fallen from the sky.

I called Eddie Beach on the radio. "You better get over here," I said. "I've got a motorcycle under my car."

Eddie drove over to where I was parked. He got out of his car and said, "What the hell is wrong with you?"

"I didn't see it," I told him.

"How could you not see it?" he said. "It's a motorcycle! It's as big as a sofa!"

By then, I had called headquarters to trace the motorcycle's license plate. "Guess what, Eddie?" I told Eddie Beach. "The bike came back a hit. It's a sixteen." Meaning it was stolen.

Kent and Terry brought the guy back to the scene. But he didn't work for Caliche.

For now, his guys had gotten away.

———

Now every member of Group 93 was focused on busting the elusive Caliche. We'd all head from our office on the sixth floor of DEA headquarters up to the wire room on the seventh floor watching the wiretap monitors work.

Each wiretap operator, or monitor, was set up in a gray office cubicle on the seventh floor. Each monitor handled one wire. They had what's called a DNR (Dialed Number Recorder), a small gray box with a little LCD screen. When a wiretap became active, you would hear a beep and a set of tones that sounded something like *be bo bop be bo,* and then you heard another series of tones, and you would see the tape start pouring out with the number being called. We had another three Panasonic tape recorders hooked up to this machine, recording everything. There were usually two Spanish-speaking supervisor monitors wearing headsets and holding yellow steno pads, writing down everything that was being said over the wire.

We continued wiretapping Caliche's cell phones, all of Group 93 gathering on the seventh floor wire room, awaiting a break. On February 22, 1993, we heard Caliche say he was going to deliver a half million dollars to a guy named Fiero. One of Caliche's mules, John Henao, was to deliver the cash to Fiero's house in Long Island City. We set up surveillance on Henao's house.

He lived in a beautiful neighborhood in Valley Stream, Long Island. On a gray winter morning, Henao came out of his pretty single-family home to find twelve inches of snow in his driveway. We didn't think he'd do the move because of the snow, but he shoveled the entire driveway. We watched as he followed "King's" instructions to the letter.

He kissed his "wife," who was actually a woman paid to sit in the stash house by the cartel. He put a bag, which we knew was full of cash, in the trunk of his Mazda 626 and pulled out of the driveway. I was leading the surveillance in a silver Cutlass. Nearby were two members of Group 42, who were also working on busting the Caliche case. First was Gene Torriente, a dark-skinned Cuban agent, in a black Porsche. Then, in a red Pathfinder, there was Matty Martucci, an Italian kid who looked like a neighborhood tough, also from Group 42, and our group's Jack Higgins.

We all tailed Henao down Astoria Boulevard. We watched him turn off onto Steinway Street. At that point, Henao apparently noticed Torriente tailing him.

"I've got this black guy in a black Porsche following me," I heard Henao say over his tapped cell phone, thanks to the wire room monitors who relayed the conversation to me. "I think I'm being tailed."

Instead of dropping back, I gave the order to stay on him, hoping Henao would panic and do something stupid, and he did—in spades. We had originally only planned to take the cash from him and release him. But what actually happened was much better.

I parked my car. From a safe distance, I watched Henao slow to a stop, and from where I was parked I could see Henao jump out of the car and walk away. He abandoned the car on the side of the road and left the cash in the trunk! I watched him go into a store, where he bought a baseball cap and a new shirt, and he changed in the store's dressing room. In his "disguise," he walked to a pay phone and called Caliche. Once again, the wire room relayed the conversation.

"I was being tailed," Henao told Caliche. "This black guy was following me. So I dumped the car. There are five hundred shirts [meaning more than five hundred thousand dollars] in it. I'll come back later and pick it up."

I radioed Martucci and Higgins to pick me up in the red Pathfinder. We parked near the abandoned car and I called Assistant District Attorney Mary Maloney. "We heard over the wire that this guy made our surveillance," I said. "Requesting permission to break into the trunk and take the bag out."

She told me we had enough probable cause and to proceed as planned.

Martucci and Higgins had a hammer and screwdriver in their trunk. I got out and went over to the abandoned Mazda, and punched the lock out of Henao's trunk. Sitting inside, like a birthday gift, was an old leather satchel stuffed with cash. I grabbed the bag and put the lock back on the car and left it there as if nothing had been touched. We took the money, which turned out to be $770,000, back to the DEA and continued the wiretaps.

We heard Caliche call one of his other workers, a guy named Mongoya. "Hurry and take a look at the car that idiot Henao abandoned!" he said in code. "Make sure that everything's okay."

When Mongoya got to the scene, we heard him call Caliche and say the car was there and everything looked fine. But later, when they actually went to retrieve the car, the money was missing. We listened in as Caliche and Mongoya placed a painful call to Don Francisco in Colombia.

"Find Henao," Don Francisco ordered in code. "Torture him and find out where he put the cash."

Next thing we heard was Caliche reporting that he had found Henao, and was going to question him, along with Mongoya and other members of their group, later that evening. We heard Caliche call 007, the assassin. *Here we go again,* I thought. I knew that they were going to torture and kill Henao. I didn't know where the killing would occur.

We set up surveillance on the places that Mongoya and his cronies frequented. More often than not, they could be found at a place called Colombian Realty in Queens, which, like many bogus real estate offices in those days, rented stash houses to the Caliche organization.

Colombian Realty was run by Johnny Suarez, a small, thin, well-dressed Colombian with dark straight hair. He was well trusted by the

Cali cartels. Suarez would go into the multiple-listing book, find a house with an attached garage in Valley Stream or one of the other Long Island suburbs, and then prepare all the fake documents the potential tenants would need.

"I have a lovely Hispanic family interested in the property," he would lie to the local Realtor. "He's a machinist who works in the city." It was Johnny's job to make coke traffickers appear to be upstanding citizens.

The next morning, Mongoya drove up in front of Colombian Realty in a silver car. I was alone on surveillance, watching from an Exxon station, which had a bank of pay phones and three repair bays across from the offices. I could see 007 sitting beside Mongoya. After Mongoya went inside the real estate office, he and 007 drove off. I followed them over to an apartment on Yellowstone Boulevard. Through the window, I could see Henao being aggressively questioned.

While I continued to watch through the windows, I received information from "the plant," the wiretap room. They said they'd heard a Colombian voice, certainly Don Francsico's, command, "Send him to heaven and let the honeymoon begin."

"We have the wedding rings," said somebody in the house.

I knew what that meant.

The wedding rings were handcuffs.

The honeymoon meant murder.

I called Bernie Kerik. He was in court. "Listen, Bern, I'm at Yellowstone Boulevard in Woodside and they've got John Henao in the car," I said. "I think he's being kidnapped. I'm on the move with them, but I'm by myself. You gotta get out here. I don't know where I'm going. But get the troops out there, fast!"

"I'm on my way," he said.

Bernie alerted Group 93 and was flying lights and sirens out toward Queens. Meanwhile, I continued tailing the assassins and their intended victim out toward Long Island. They drove out toward Littleneck, Queens, the Long Island border, where they took the kidnap victim, Henao, into a vacant house that sat on a little hill overlooking the Long Island Expressway.

I parked at the bottom of the hill so I could look up at the house and watch its occupants through binoculars. They couldn't see me. I did a drive-by and got the address. Then, while awaiting the arrival of Group 93, I called 911 on my cell. "I'm with the DEA task force and I need backup assistance," I said.

Pretty soon, the anticrime unit cars from the one eleven precinct started arriving, parking beside where I'd set up down the hill. I heard the roar of an engine and saw Bernie Kerik's battered old Cutlass careening over the hill on two wheels with brake smoke burning, like the wheels were on fire.

"Bees," I said, using the nickname I always used for Bernie, "we gotta go in. I spoke to the plant on the way out here and they said they were going to send this guy to heaven."

Bernie and I met with the anticrime cops. They had a sledgehammer in the back of a squad car. I borrowed it and Bernie and I prepared to break down the door for a rescue. By then, the rest of Group 93— Big Daddy, Terry Hartman, Kent Fullenweider, Jimmy Grace—all started arriving.

We huddled and I quarterbacked. "Kent, you take the back door," I said. "John, you go with him. Jimmy, you and Terry come in after Bernie and I get through the front door."

I grabbed the sledgehammer and we all walked to the front door. I slammed the sledgehammer and the door collapsed like a piece of cardboard. We all burst into the house, me first, then Bernie with his gun drawn, and finally Terry Hartman, Jimmy Grace, and Kent Fullenweider. We walked through the vacant living room, then to the kitchen, where we saw the stairwell leading to the basement.

Three nasty-looking, ruddy-faced guys were already at the top of the stairs, headed for the back door. Terry and Jimmy gang tackled two of the guys and cuffed them, but the third guy got out the door in a flash. Kent Fullenweider, the fastest guy on the scene, took off after him like a greyhound after a jackrabbit.

I tried to follow, but being neither particularly fast nor coordinated in a chase, I fell down one of the five-foot drops that separated one yard from another in that neighborhood. When I looked up, I could see Kent leaping short fences like a track runner leaping barricades.

I was lying there, thinking about what to do next, when I heard a car squealing around a corner on the road near me. There was Bernie in his Cutlass, leaning over and holding the passenger door open for me while the car was still rolling. I got up and jumped in. We followed

Kent, still in hot pursuit of the assassin. They ran onto the Long Island Expressway, where Kent chased the guy against traffic.

Bernie reached behind his seat and grabbed a bubble light and slammed it on the roof of the Cutlass. We were following Kent, chasing the would-be assassin down the wrong way of the Long Island Expressway, with the bubble light blazing on the top of the car like Kojak.

Kent was going over the center median, across eight lanes of traffic. By the time Bernie and I drove across the eight lanes, Kent had the scumbag tackled and cuffed.

We returned to the house, where we had all three would-be assassins handcuffed. We found Henao still handcuffed to a chair, his shirt wet with blood and sweat. He said they had interrogated him for more than an hour with guns pointed at his head. They had used stilettos and a hunting knife to cut the buttons off of his shirt and were getting ready to start slicing him up, piece by piece, and depositing the pieces in a freezer box that they had ready beside the chair. They were recording the whole ordeal on audiocassette so they could send it down to Don Francisco as proof that they had carried out his orders. When we played back the tape, we could hear them saying, "We're gonna kill you! Where's the money? Tell us, or die!"

We arrested all the members of the assassination crew.

———

Henao became the best informant I've ever had.

We took pictures of him in a DEA T-shirt, which we got to Caliche's associates, making them think they'd been infiltrated by a DEA informant. Once again we were pinning the blame back on their guys, instead of ourselves.

Later, we intercepted a call between Caliche and 007.

"There was a problem, a big problem," 007 told Caliche.

We heard Caliche call Don Francisco and say, "There were about fifty animals [code word, cops] at the house."

"How did they find out?" asked Don Francisco. "Did they know about the house through the phone?"

"No, because we did not speak about the house over the phone," said Caliche.

We kept the heat on Caliche, and our wiretaps formed a web across his entire organization. The chart we'd created about the Caliche organization looked like the organizational chart of a major corporation, until we began drawing lines through the cells and associates that we'd taken out. Pretty soon, we'd taken down another million dollars and raided four more of Caliche's stash houses.

―――

On May 7, 1993, we launched seven separate raids, seizing $600,000 and arresting five dealers, including Caliche. I'd been watching his home at the Boulevard Apartments in Bayside, Queens. It was a high-rise apartment complex with basement parking. The building's superintendent had helped me install a surveillance camera in the basement so we would know when he was coming and going. The morning of the sweep, we put additional surveillance on Caliche.

After we took everyone except Caliche down, we noticed Caliche was loading his television and personal belongings into his Nissan Maxima. He drove out with a woman companion. We stopped him about a mile and a half from his apartment building and handcuffed both Caliche and his associate. He didn't say a word. We offered him a plea bargain and deals to get him to flip, but he insisted on going to trial.

Busting the Caliche operation resulted in the seizure of more than four tons of coke, $10 million in currency, and the arrests of twenty-five Cali cartel operatives nationwide.

Caliche was convicted and sentenced to thirty-three years to life in prison. Shortly after his incarceration, he tried to commit suicide, cutting all the main arteries in his legs and wrists. He was unsuccessful, but the attempt left him semiparalyzed. He remains in the New York State Prison Facility, where he'll probably stay for the rest of his life.

14

The *Phoenix*

After the debacle with Paul, when he was in jail and I had been cleared of any wrongdoing, I couldn't shake the sting of being double-crossed. I vowed to prove to the brass, and, even more importantly, to Paul, that I was nobody's chump, that I was a first-rate under-cover. The only way to do that was by dismantling the cartel, one bust at a time.

I lived at the office, haunting the wiretap room at all hours of the day and night. I'd get there at ten in the morning and wouldn't leave until way past midnight. An eighty-hour workweek was a holiday; there was no end to my obsession or my work. I was sleeping too little, drinking too much. Maggie and Francesca rarely saw me, except when I left the house before dawn and returned home after midnight. Some nights, I never came home at all.

I'd roar into our new state-of-the-art wire room, which, thanks to Eddie and me, was now packed with seventy young women monitor-ing thirty-five phones and beepers. It was always crazy in that wire room. There weren't enough cubicles for the monitors, so they were practically sitting on top of each other. Bruce Stokes, the plant manager, was trying to keep order in this chaos, but the place was always crazy. It sounded like a Las Vegas casino, a cacophony of sound and sweat.

I heard those beeping tones that the wiretaps made in my sleep.

Most of the monitors were a little edgy around me. I'd walk into

166

the room and somebody would say, "I think Mongoya's gonna meet Caliche." Or some other smuggler. And I'd wheel around and stare the monitor down. "Whaddya mean, you think?"

"Well, they had a conversation, and I think Caliche [or some other smuggler] is going to meet him. "

And they couldn't give me the particulars. "What are you talking about? Either he's gonna meet him or he's not. You don't think he's going to meet him, unless you're a fortune-teller."

Then I'd storm out and head down to Eddie, demanding that so-and-so get fired, complaining that one monitor was lazy, another apathetic, and we'd both head upstairs and fire somebody. By the time we'd done that a couple of times, you could hear a pin drop. Everybody thought we were crazy, which, of course, we were.

Caliche and his group had been like an ant farm. One arrest led to a dozen leads, one bust led to a hundred possibilities.

One day, we were doing a wiretap on some of Caliche's associates' digital pagers. We had duplicates so when they got a page, we got the same page. While monitoring one of the associates pagers, I saw a phone number pop up. Then there was a dash and the numbers 1105, which I knew was a hotel and a room number.

I was standing there amid the church-mouse-quiet monitors when the number came up. I roared out of the wire room, Eddie behind me. By then, we had traced the number to the New York Hilton on Sixth Avenue at Fifty-fourth Street in Manhattan, room number 1105.

I called the Hilton to see who was in the room. I thought it was a transporter who had brought in a load of cocaine from California, because that was their normal MO—from Colombia to Mexico to California to New York for distribution. I figured they'd gotten the load to the hotel and were ready to turn it over to Caliche's boys.

I raced over to the Hilton, picked up a house phone, and called the room where the digital page had originated. A man with a Boston accent answered.

"How you doing, Joey?" I said.

"Who?" he said. "There's no Joey here. Who's this?"

"I'm looking for Joey. Is this Joey?"

"No, you've got the wrong number."

And he hung up. Now I knew the guy was in the room.

I called Bernie Kerik on his cell. He was already at home. "Bernie,

I just got a page from the New York Hilton, room 1105," I said. "An American guy answered the phone in the room. I got it covered in the hallway on the eleventh floor. Get the rest of the group and get the hell out here."

He was there within the hour. I stayed in the hallway. Bernie went down and talked to the people at the front desk. The room was registered to a guy named Jim Lewis. Bernie got security to get us a room across from 1105. By then, everybody was on the scene. Bernie and I were in the hotel room, while some of the guys staked out the hallway and lobby, and the rest waited outside in their cars for the guy to make a move.

We hooked a camera lens into the peephole on the door across the hall, so we could watch what was going on inside the room on our television set. We watched that room for twenty-four hours. Our suspect was a white guy, about sixty, bald, a beard and mustache. He looked like Pa Kettle. Not your typical drug smuggler. I was baffled. I figured Caliche's associate was using this guy as a mule.

The next morning, Lewis came out of the room and placed a page to another beeper we were intercepting. All of Group 93 followed him down to the street. He walked against traffic for a couple of blocks. I watched him go to the corner of Fifty-second Street and Sixth Avenue, where he got picked up by a gray car driven by an old associate of Caliche. They drove around the corner, and we watched Jim Lewis get out of the car with a duffel bag in his hand.

I continued tailing the car. By the time Jim Lewis returned to the Hilton's lobby with the duffel bag, Bernie and the rest of the group surrounded him. The bag was filled with one hundred thousand dollars cash. Possession of one hundred thousand cash is not a crime, but Bernie and the group seized the money, handcuffed Lewis, and hauled him back up to his room for questioning.

"I'm not talking at all," said Jim Lewis.

I followed the drop car through the midtown tunnel to a house out in Queens. After I saw the car park and the guys go inside the house, I called Bernie to see how it was going.

"You better get back here," said Bernie. "The guy is clamming up."

I told him to put Jim Lewis on the phone.

"Listen, buddy, just relax," I said. "I'm the boss. I think we can work this whole thing out. Tell us everything you know and we'll set you free."

I really didn't have much to pin on him. But he thought I did, and that was enough to get him talking. I went back to the room, I found Jim Lewis handcuffed and scared.

"Take the handcuffs off him," I said, and sent everybody else out of the room. I cracked open the minibar and smiled at him, "How about a drink?"

He said bourbon, rocks, and I poured him a stiff one, along with a vodka for myself. We sat down and each had a drink.

"Look," I said, "cooperate with me and this whole thing will work out."

"Well," he said, "I do know about some 'merchandise' in Australia," and he started talking. Jim Lewis turned out to be a former Navy Seal. He spilled his guts about four hundred kilos of coke in Australia that he moved for Don Francisco and his group. He said he could work it out so we could seize it.

"Great," I said, pouring him another bourbon. "That's real good. Look, we're going to let you go home. We've got to seize your hundred thousand dollars, but give me a call tomorrow and we'll work this thing out a little further."

I think he was shocked that I let him go, and I think he thought I knew more than I really did. Like Paul, I'd learned how to bluff, and this bluff would pay off big time.

———

The next day, I got a call from Jim Lewis. He'd gone back to his home in the Northeast.

"Look, there's a lot more about this I want to tell you," he said. "I transport merchandise for two big Cali players out of Columbia, Don Francisco and a guy named Jose Urdinola."

I knew all about Don Francisco and his associate, Jose Urdinola. He was a Colombian cartel boss, responsible for Caliche in the U.S. and other distributors around the world. He was the biggest player I'd come into contact with yet.

Jim Lewis told me that Urdinola had spent about a million bucks building a sixty-five-foot, twin-mast, steel sailboat, the *Phoenix,* which was designed to smuggle drugs. "The entire keel is a hidden compartment that can be filled with cocaine, fifteen hundred kilos, almost a couple of tons," Lewis told me.

He said he was going to be one of the main distributors for the load when the *Phoenix* arrives in the U.S. But at the time of our conversation, it was broken down in Ecuador with some mechanical problems, and a couple of tons of coke in the keel. He said an American guy was staying on the boat, guarding it until the needed parts arrived.

He also told me that he had a partner named Rocky, who was a boat captain. They both wanted to get out of the soup with the cartels. Jim Lewis's skin was as red as a beet because his blood pressure was sky-high from nervousness. And he always blushed deep red whenever he was around me.

Pretty soon, Jim Lewis introduced me to his partner Rocky, who weighed more than three hundred pounds. A big Italian guy, he'd eat pork rinds and drink pure fat. He had the nicest personality of anyone you'd ever want to meet. The three of us got along really well, as I always did with smugglers. I just felt comfortable around them. From everything I'd been through with Paul, I understood their lifestyle. Normally, drug smugglers do not trust DEA agents. But because I could talk the talk and walk the walk, the smugglers I "flipped," or brought to our side, had confidence that I would follow through on my promises.

I thanked Jim Lewis for the information and went to work. First, I called our DEA office in Ecuador over what we called a "stew phone." A stew phone is an encrypted phone, which the military uses during a war because it cannot be intercepted. Group 93 was doing such high-level cases that we would communicate internationally with a stew phone. You pick it up like a regular phone, but it has a key on the side along with a number of buttons. I would first call the regular number and say, "This is Speziale from the DEA in New York, and I need to talk to you on your stew phone. What's that number?"

I'd get the number, which looked like a regular international number, and I'd call back. Then I would say, "Let's go to secure mode six." I would turn my key on the side of the phone and push the number 6. Then we'd talk almost like airplane pilots, going back and forth, ending in "over."

When I called the U.S. embassy in Ecuador, a guy named Freddie Villareal answered the stew phone.

"Freddie, listen, we've got a boat that's in Ecuadorian waters with fifteen hundred kilos of coke on it," I said. "We want to take it out of there without the Ecuadorians hitting this thing."

Freddie said okay, he'd go to the Ecuadorian government to get permission. We'd send our guys to take over the boat and sail it back to the U.S., where we'd remove the coke and take the *Phoenix* out of commission. A few days later, Freddie gave us the green light. We sent Terry Hartman and Steve Morse, from Group 93, to get the guard and crew off the boat and replace them with our personnel.

Morse and Hartman enlisted the Ecuadorian cops to help them con the guard off the boat. The guard went to the dentist, and when he was returning to the boat, the Ecuadorian cops stopped him, asked him what he was doing in the country, and told him that they were going to keep an eye on him. The guy got so scared that he split the country without a word to anyone.

Once he was out of the way, we installed a GPS-tracking device up on the mast of the boat so we'd know the coordinates once it started moving. Then we hired an independent delivery crew, telling them only that Eddie Beach and I had bought this sailboat and we wanted it sailed back to the U.S. In a twenty-one-day cruise, the boat sailed back to the U.S. and, when it arrived on the Gulf Coast of Texas in May 1993, Group 93 was there to unload it.

———

I went down to Texas with Eddie Beach, Rocky and John Chase, an agent I'd met when I did my first smuggling deal in Guatemala. He was an old New Orleans vet who knew his way around ships, and looked like a salty dog—a Cajun in his early fifties, rail thin with gray hair and an appetite for adventure. He was perfect for helping us get the *Phoenix* to a coast guard station where we could off-load the cocaine.

The rent-a-crew were completely in the dark about John Chase, Rocky, Eddie, and me. All they knew was that we were rich New Yorkers who bought a sixty-five-foot sailboat. So when they delivered it to us about ten miles south of Galveston, we took command of the boat and paid them for the delivery.

"Hey, thanks for bringing our baby home," I said, and Eddie Beach, Rocky, and John Chase, and I got onboard.

We acted our roles perfectly. It was early summer and the crew had no reason to think we were anything but four businessmen off for a summer of ports of pleasure. I was at the wheel of that beautiful ship. I had my shirt off, a bandana tied around my head, and was wearing nothing but a pair of cut-offs and sneakers. I had a beer in one hand and the wheel in the other and two tons of coke somewhere below.

I steered the *Phoenix* about ten nautical miles to the coast guard station in Galveston. Once we docked, it hit me: I'd never *seen* the cocaine that was supposed to be in the boat's keel. I had taken Jim Lewis's word that the boat was loaded with coke. We never checked.

We searched for the coke for seventeen hours and practically dismantled the entire ship. Finally, we found the water tank, an intricate compartment in the keel, which had been hidden beneath a layer of poured concrete. Once we cracked open the concrete, there it was, fifteen hundred kilos, each package stamped with the Nike "swoosh" logo. It was prime.

Jim Lewis called Urdinola and said that the boat had landed safely in Galveston but he needed $250,000 in expense money to off-load the boat. Urdinola gave him the number of a trafficker, Ovideo, who would give him the $250,000 in New York City. Urdinola told Lewis to tell Ovideo, "I'm Jim on behalf of Jose Urdinola. I understand you have 250 shirts for me."

Ovideo took the $250,000 and met Jim Lewis at a McDonald's on Thirtieth Street and Second Avenue. They met inside the restaurant, then walked around the corner to a parking lot, where Ovideo opened his trunk and gave Jim Lewis a duffel bag with the money. Ovideo drove away.

We seized the $250,000. From the probable cause we gathered from Jim Lewis's phone calls to Ovideo, we placed a wiretap on Ovideo's phones. His calls turned out to be a gold mine of information for future coke and cash seizures.

Back in Galveston, it took all day to unload the coke in the *Phoenix*'s keel. In the late afternoon, all fifteen hundred kilos sat on the side dock, and we could hear the boat creaking as it leaned to the side from the uneven load. We put lead weights on the opposite side to keep it from tipping over. The load would have made the cartel $100 million on the street. Instead, it was taken to the DEA's Houston Field

Division, then flown back to New York in a borrowed military transport plane.

We would use the coke to bait its benefactor, the Cali boss, Jose Ricardo.

——

Back in New York, I had Jim Lewis call Urdinola in Colombia. I had shopped for a country that would allow extradition, and Italy had complied.

"Tell him that the shirts have made it to the U.S., and we're ready for delivery," I said. "But, tell Urdinola to meet you in Rome, so you can negotiate how you're going to hide all the millions that will come from the sale of the coke."

He did as instructed. On June 22, 1993, Group 93 agent Terry Hartman and I went to Rome with our new ally, Jim Lewis, armed with a provisional arrest warrant for Jose Urdinola. It was beautiful. We awaited Urdinola's arrival at the Rome Hilton Hotel with the Italian authorities. Jim whispered, "There he is!"

I could see Urdinola strolling into the lobby. Before he could get his bearings, we formed a daisy chain of cops around him. I saw his face turn purple. I watched him turn on his heels and . . . and the guy was trying to escape!

I was revved up. First, from the anticipation of wondering if the guy was going to show. Then, from the idea that I'd traveled so far to watch the biggest smuggler I'd ever cornered just run away. He was walking through a double-glass revolving door. I was walking out as he was walking in. So I stopped the door midspin, then pushed it fast and he came flying out on the other end, landing on his ass. He was still rolling when Terry Hartman tackled and cuffed him.

One more bigwig bagged, tagged, and extradited to the United States.

Urdinola, with help from Don Francisco, had been running an estimated $12 million a week in coke over a ten-year stretch of dealing. He was the biggest Cali cartel figure ever extradited to America on state charges.

——

A few weeks later, Eddie Beach called Bernie Kerik and me at Group 93 headquarters and told us to meet him downstairs, where he was waiting for us in his car. Once we got downstairs, he swore us to secrecy, then let it rip: Jeff Beck and Joe Termini, two NYPD detectives from another DEA task force, along with a state trooper named Bobby Robles, had sold heroin to an undercover agent for internal affairs.

We were shocked, of course. Not merely because dirty cops are the scourge of law enforcement, but also because Beck and Termini were losers, low-on-the-totem-pole guys. None of us thought they had the street smarts to even think of anything dishonest, let alone try to pull something off. When I was a ninety-day wonder in Bronx narcotics, Jeff Beck was in the same unit, already working as an undercover. But he was lucky if he could find a stoplight.

Bernie and I looked at each other. "Sellin' heroin?" Bernie said. "Those two zeroes couldn't buy aspirin in CVS. They couldn't find drugs in a drugstore!" I nodded in agreement.

The next day, Bernie, Eddie Beach, and I went down to Miami on another investigation. We had a rare day off before things got rolling, so we were sitting by the pool at the Hollywood Beach Hilton. Bernie, who avoided the sun, was laid out like a big Buddha, wearing a white towel on his head to prevent sunburn. Eddie was calmly reading a book, as usual. And I was coated in oil, trying to get as tanned as I could.

"Heroin!" I was saying. "Where did those two idiots get heroin?"

That's when it hit me. "Ronnie!" I said. "It's gotta be Ronnie."

It was so obvious. When we busted Ronnie Reina coming home with the five hundred grams of heroin, Termini was there. I called Bruce Stokes, who had filled out the drug voucher for the five hundred grams of heroin we'd busted Ronnie with. "Bruce, after you submitted the voucher, did you ever see what came back from the qualitative lab report?"

He said that he hadn't.

"Well, go look at the file," I said.

Bernie called Ronnie—who was, by now out of jail—and asked about how much heroin he had when we hit him in his driveway. Ronnie said it was five hundred grams to the T. He remembered because he had just weighed it a half hour before we pinched him. When Bruce Stokes called back, he said that something was strange. The lab reports had shown that there was 420 grams, eighty grams difference, precisely the amount Beck and Termini had stolen.

"Did you ever leave Termini alone with the heroin?" I asked Bruce Stokes.

"Yeah, I had Termini put the H in the evidence bag and take it to the vault," he said.

We took the first flight back to New York. Eddie, Bernie, and I went directly to Chief John Maltz's office.

"Listen, Chief, we know about an internal affairs investigation into some dirty cops in the task force," I said.

He played deaf, dumb, and blind. "Get outta my office," he said. "I don't know what you're talking about."

We got up to leave, but before we walked out, Eddie Beach said, "We heard Beck, Termini, and Robles were dirty."

I added, "Chief, we know where the eighty grams of heroin came from."

He exploded. "Who the hell told you about this?" he said. "Get back in here!" He shut the door, made some calls, and then shuffled each of us into three different offices. Within a half hour, Maltz's office was buzzing with brass, including the chief of NYPD Internal Affairs. When our stories panned out, and they were finally convinced that we knew something, everybody wanted to talk to us.

———

The next day, I was in federal court in Brooklyn, preparing to testify on a different case, when the U.S. Attorney's office paged me. I called the office and was told to report to an address in lower Manhattan. I was suspicious. My first thought was that maybe Bernie had been locked up over those dirty cops, and they were calling me to see if our stories matched. It was the usual tactic. They'd lock up one of us and see if the other's story jibed.

I ran to a pay phone, which we primarily used in those days. Cell phones were still relatively new and expensive, and the DEA was cheap. We had maybe six cell phones for our entire unit. So we primarily used pay phones, where our DEA calling cards allowed us to call long distance. I called Bernie.

"You get a strange beep?" I asked.

"Yeah, you get one?"

"Sure did," I said. "You going downtown?"

"Yeah."

"Okay, see you there."

The address we'd been given was for the U.S. Attorney's secret investigation office in Lower Manhattan. When we got there, the brass was sitting around a long conference table. Chief William Beatty, head of NYPD Internal Affairs, along with New York State Police Major Mickey Cahill and U.S. Attorney David Fein, who went on to become President Clinton's counsel in Washington, D.C. Around them were assorted uniformed and dark-suited personnel, everybody wearing serious expressions.

"We've got three dirty cops, and we need your help," Fein said.

"Well, what do your wiretaps show?" I asked.

The internal affairs brass all looked at each other. They had no clue how to even start.

"Okay, here's what you need to do," I said. And we laid it out, point by point. Number one, get all of the call detail records for Beck's, Termini's, and Robles's phones and see how, when, and where they were communicating with each other and others.

"Then you gotta do their beepers, do a reverse dump so you'll know everybody calling into their beepers," I said.

"Reverse dump?" somebody asked. "What the hell is that?"

None of these men even had a clue about phone surveillance technology. These were the highest members of law enforcement, both federal and state, in New York, but when it came to what Bernie and I had been doing with wires they were just a line of blank faces.

Bernie and I gave them a lesson in eavesdropping. "A reverse dump is like a dial-digit search—" I started to explain.

Bernie interrupted me and cut to the chase. "If you listen to us, we'll catch your crooked cops," he told the brass. "If you think you're going to do it on your own, like the typical internal affairs thing, where you hold stuff back from us, then we can't help."

I jumped in. "If you tell us everything you've got, and everything you know about the case, we'll take them down," I said to Bernie.

"They're not cops," I added. "They're criminals wearing badges. So we're not going to protect them."

So we did it ourselves, reviewed the phone and beeper numbers, did a pattern analysis, traced cell phones, until finally we had their

MO. Beck, Termini, and Robles didn't just pinch the 80 grams of heroin, they were monitoring our radio transmissions, then tipping off their mobsters, who would hit the houses and strip them of dope and cash before we could take them down.

By the end of the week, Bernie, Eddie, and I were back in the downtown conference room, filling out subpoenas and pushing them across the desk for signatures from the internal affairs chieftains. We'd come up with a hell of a trap. We wrote up a bogus report that there was $2 million in a stash house out on Long Island. Then we put suitcases stuffed with money and coke and the whole nine yards in the house as bait.

We bragged about the case over the radio, which we knew Beck, Termini, and Robles were monitoring, so they'd know exactly which house we were zeroing in on. "Home run!" I'd yell. "We got the place, Eleven Cottonwood Drive. We'll hit it in a week! It's loaded with cash!"

Sure enough, Beck, Termini, and Robles showed up to fleece the place, and when they did they were surrounded. After his arrest, Beck went on television, on *20/20,* and fed them a load of crap. He claimed he was so corrupted by being an undercover cop that he got used to the lifestyle—the expensive, lavish cars, the drugs and the cash and the women—and thought he deserved some of that, too.

After internal affairs took the dirty cops down, Ronnie became another great informant on our side. He would eventually introduce me to Javier, a major distributor who handled the New York area distribution for another Cali bigwig, Oscar Pozo. And we were off on another major case.

15

Wiretaps

I was buried under a mountain of coke and Colombians, deluged with leads, and deprived of sleep. We had been so successful for so long, both before and after Paul's arrest, it was inevitable that the other side would find a way to slow our roll. I should have seen it coming, but I didn't. And I certainly didn't expect it to arrive in the form of a seemingly meek, mild, milquetoast wiretap monitor named Monica Brozowski.

She was a civilian monitor hired to listen to the wiretaps, a young, attractive Latina single parent in her twenties from the Bronx. Monitoring the wires, she'd helped us seize millions.

Other groups would hire apathetic monitors who felt no personal involvement in the cases. We had a different philosophy. We wanted our monitors to feel like they were important to the investigation, because, of course, they were. When we came in from a million-dollar seizure, we would invite the monitors from their seventh-floor wire room down to our sixth-floor office and ask them to pose with us while we took our trophy picture. It was a great moral booster. With Monica, the opposite occurred.

She first came to our attention when she called Bernie Kerik from the wire room, saying that she'd just heard about ten grand being left by a couple of dealers in the trunk of a parked car on Fourteenth Street in Manhattan. Bernie and John Comparetto drove to the scene, found the car, and popped open the trunk.

Nothing.

They went around the corner and spotted two Colombians carrying suitcases and running toward the car. Bingo! Bernie and Comparetto called for backups. When the Colombians were gone, Bernie rushed back to the car, opened the trunk, and removed the bags.

Instead of ten thousand dollars in the bags, there was six hundred thousand.

When Monica saw how much money we were hauling in from the drug trade, she apparently wanted a cut. With Caliche in prison, and his operation burned to the ground, the cartel needed a replacement to lead in the rebuilding. They found one in a midlevel broker by the name of Juan David. Monica also knew that we were looking for Juan David and his brother, Johnny. Juan and Johnny had been part of the Caliche organization, and continued working for Don Francisco after Caliche went down.

The wire room alerted the group that the Juan David wire was communicating with a phone in Houston. I flew to Houston to show probable cause to tap the Houston phone.

I met with Pete McCormick, group supervisor of the Houston Field Division. He was a tall, redheaded guy, about forty, with a full red beard and mustache. McCormick and one of his agents, Alfredo Cristolieb, a young Hispanic guy who was ready to bust the world, told me to meet them in an old warehouse in Houston's Westhiemer entertainment district. We sat on broken chairs and boxes.

"Exactly what do you have?" McCormick asked.

"Look, we got this guy Juan David, he's talking to a guy named Muneco, (which means "Baby Doll,") from Houston," I said. "Here's Muneco's number. I want to give you the probable cause to go up on the phones."

Both McCormick and Cristolieb were exactly what we needed for the team. They were ready to kick ass. Historically, agencies have always been touchy about their territories. The Houston agents couldn't understand why a New York agent would fly down and hand them a huge case, instead of taking it for himself. They thought our task force wanted something in return.

"We don't want anything except to expand the team," I told them. "If this wire spins to somewhere outside of Houston, we'd ask you to do the same thing we've done and share your information. We can all work together as a team to take the entire Cali organization down."

They cooperated, and ultimately our joint venture was responsible for seizing three tons off of the Juan David wires in Houston, the biggest bust in Houston history.

━━━━

The Houston DEA investigation spun to Miami, where we presented the same probable cause we'd given in Houston. We asked the Miami DEA to set up on a dealer named Tribolene and see where the wiretap led. Now Miami, Houston, and New York were up on wires.

We received a call from Houston, informing us that it sounded like the cartel had loaded a stash house with over three thousand kilos of cocaine. They had only been on the wiretap three days and were unsure of how to proceed.

"Pal, we would be calling you from the guy's living room if I knew there was three thousand kilos," Eddie and I told the Houston agent. "We appreciate the heads-up, but if you've got three thousand kilos, this is tremendous. So get it."

They did, and another three thousand kilos went into the DEA's coffers.

Now, everyone was a believer in the interstate power of DEA.

Except Monica. She picked up a phone number over our wire that turned out to be Juan David's number in Miami. Deciding she could make some cash, she called Juan David's brother, Johnny on a Miami cell phone, and told him she had some important information about two DEA agents, "Kerik and Speziale," who had been busting their business. She said she wanted to meet him to discuss a potential deal. But our associates in Miami heard all of this over their wire and gave us a heads-up. We traced the call to a pay phone in Monica Brozowski's neighborhood in the Bronx.

We had to find Juan David's brother, Johnny, before he met her. We knew Johnny lived in Queens and traveled frequently to Miami.

I checked the parking violations bureau to see if Johnny had any outstanding parking summonses. He had plenty, specifically early-morning parking violations in the One-Ten Precinct. That told me the guy lived nearby and was oversleeping the parking meters. Bernie Kerik and I drove out to the One-Ten precinct and I addressed the officers at roll call.

"Listen, I'm from the DEA task force. Would everybody here like an all-expense-paid vacation to Miami?"

Everybody yelled, "Hell, yeah!"

"Well, we're looking for a car that parks early in this area. If you locate this car, call me on my cell or my home number."

I told them they'd have to testify at Johnny's brother's trial, but they'd get the three days on us. I left the roomful of cops salivating.

At four that morning, my telephone rang; they'd found the car. We set up surveillance, and sure enough, early next morning, Johnny came out to get it. We grabbed him and I said, "Look, we know about the call from Monica and we want you to help us out."

He told us that she was ready to sell us out for ten grand. We found an undercover Spanish detective that Monica didn't know from a up-state New York State Police unit. The agent posed as Johnny and set up a meeting.

I suggested he try to get a bargain. "Offer her a thousand, and let's see what she does," I said.

She agreed to sell out Bernie and me for a measly grand! In exchange for the thousand dollars, she told the agent, she'd give him our home phone numbers and addresses.

On the day of their meeting, I was hiding in the courtyard of a high-rise building in the Bronx, just off Sedgwick Avenue. Monica was a little late, and while I was waiting it started raining, really pouring. By the time she showed up, I was lying in the mud in the rain.

I waited until the undercover gave her the cash, then jumped out of the bushes, looking like the Loch Ness Monster.

"You're finished!" I said, as I snapped the cuffs on her. "You're going to jail."

Monica got seven years in prison.

———

Not long after Monica was taken down, our old informant Ronnie's wife, Maddie, called me in the middle of the night, crying hysterically. Finally, I got out of her that someone had called Ronnie and instructed him to meet them near his house. When he arrived, a van pulled up, several men jumped out, threw Ronnie into the van, and drove away. Shortly afterwards Maddie got a call that her husband had been kidnapped and they were holding him for ransom.

"You gotta help me, Jerry," she said.

"Okay, I'll do my best," I said.

Late that Sunday night, I called Group 93 together and asked them to meet me with the Trigger Fish at a Dunkin' Donuts near Ronnie's neighborhood. Then I went over to Ronnie's house to wait for Maddie to get another call. Sure enough, the kidnappers called back, this time demanding $120,000 or six kilos of cocaine.

She held her hand over the telephone receiver and said, "What do I do?"

"Agree to the six kilos," I told Maddie.

I flew out the front door and ran down to the closest grocery store and bought forty-eight bars of Ivory soap and a roll of duct tape. Eight bars of Ivory soap taped together make a very convincing kilo. The kidnappers wanted it delivered to a phone arcade on 187th and Roosevelt. The group and I helped Maddie into the passenger's seat of the van. With the group hiding in the back, I drove the van over to 187th Street with the "coke" in tow.

Waiting on the corner were a couple of swarthy-looking guys in a junk heap of a car. I stopped the van. Maddie jumped out and handed the package to the driver.

As soon as Maddie handed the guy the bogus load, the group jumped out of the back of the van in SWAT gear and pointed machine guns. My stress level must have been off of the chart. I jumped out ahead of the group and grabbed the head guy and threw him on the ground with a machine gun pointed at his head.

"If Ronnie dies, I'm going to blow your brains out," I said.

Yes, Ronnie was a drug informant. But he was our informant. And no scumbag was going to hold him for ransom. Another kidnapper must have been watching everything go down because within the hour Ronnie was dropped off at the 115th Precinct. We later found out that he wasn't an angel. Ronnie had been double-dealing behind our backs. We revoked his probation. He's currently serving eight years to life in prison.

First Paul, now Ronnie and a dozen others. Whatever faith I continued to have for the characters in the drug world was slowly fading. In my metamorphosis from Jerry Speziale into Geraldo Bartone and, eventually, into Paul Lir Alexander, I had become just like Paul. I didn't trust anybody anymore.

━━━

Since Paul's arrest, I had seized more coke and busted more cartel associates than I'd even done under his tutelage. Group 93 had wiretap operations in thirteen cities across America, and our wires had formed a virtual net around the cartel's operations. We were reeling them in, one by one.

My experience in these cases had made me the country's authority on wiretaps. Chief Bill Mockler, who had worked with us in the task force, was promoted to start a unit called the Special Operations Division in Washington.

One day, Mockler called and said he wanted Bernie and me to fly to Fort Lauderdale and help him and his associates write a wiretap manual. So there we were, Bernie Kerik and me, in a conference room, looking like a couple of characters out of *Miami Vice*. Sunglasses, hair slicked back, short-sleeved shirts, jeans, and sandals. The resulting manual about wiretaps and large-scale dope ops was entitled "Use of Cellular Intercepts in Organizational Targeting" for the U.S. Department of Justice. It's still used today.

———

After we took Urdinola down, Ovideo got scared and threw out his phones. I did a pattern analysis, just as I had done with Caliche. I found three new phones that were calling the same numbers that Ovideo was calling. I tapped them. Two were Ovideo's new lines. The third was one that Ovideo had purchased from an arcade where the lines were all registered under real estate office names.

Drug dealers would purchase phones from these arcades and when they were done with the phone they would simply return them. A real estate agency in Jackson Heights didn't return their phone after Ovideo was finished with it. They just gave it to another dope dealer, a Colombian named Ricky.

———

Group 93 was getting so busy that we turned the Ovideo investigation over to our sister unit, Group 91, but for some reason I decided to stay on Ricky. He was a transportation specialist who would deliver all the shipments that arrived into New York to the customers of Caliche's boss, Don Francisco, and various other cartel leaders. It turned out that Ricky was running one hell of an operation.

One day, I got a call from the wiretap room that the monitors were picking up conversations between Ricky and a 904 area code. I ran upstairs to listen to the call and discovered that Ricky was speaking with a guy who I'll call Dan Rich in Vancouver, Canada. In the background, you could hear jazz and classical music, and Ricky walking across creaky wooden floors as he spoke to Dan.

We continued the wiretaps, both on Ricky and on Dan Rich. "We have two-twenty ready for Poncho," Ricky told Dan Rich. We heard Rich send a sixty-year-old white guy (code name "Poncho") in a motor home with Canadian plates to a hotel in LA to pick up the load. We stayed on Poncho. We heard him tell Rich that, once he picked up the load, he'd drive from LA to New Jersey. Pretty soon, thanks to our LA wiretaps, we had the group's MO.

Based out of Canada, this group of middle-aged white guys would transport loads of four hundred to five hundred pounds of Cali coke across America in motor homes and tractor-trailer trucks. The coke would be hidden in boxes of onions, so if the truck was stopped, it would seem to be transporting only produce.

The group had developed elaborate codes of communication, including names for each other, and had perfected a way to vacuum-pack coke in plastic as a precaution against drug dogs. By the time I rolled up on them via wiretaps in 1994, Dan Rich (code name "El Feo") owned a fishing lodge outside of Vancouver, Canada, as well as an impressive chalet-style home, seventeen acres of investment property, and much more.

With Ricky as their New York point man, the Canadians would send one of their ten couriers in his Winnebago down to LA, where he would receive the coke from a guy known as "the S," short for Salazar, who apparently ran the organization. Ricky was just a controller; he would have the Canadians respond directly to Los Angeles.

We eventually had wiretaps on all their pagers and cell phones. Dan Rich and his mules had voice-mail systems on their Skytalk pagers. One of Rich's transporters would drive a Winnebago to LA, and Dan Rich would leave him a voice mail with instructions like, "You're going to meet the S at the Holiday Inn in Monrovia, California. You're to park in the back parking lot and go get dinner. The S will load you up. Once you are loaded, head across the desert and call in for further instructions."

Then Ricky would tell Dan Rich where to deliver the goods. They had established a code. "The street you are going to deliver at is eleven, twenty-one, thirty-five, fifty-six. . ." Ricky would say, as if they were calling plays in a football huddle. The numbers were codes on the typewriter. If you look at a keypad on a typewriter, number 1 would be the letter Q, number 11 would be the letter under Q on the keypad, which is A; number 111 would be the letter underneath that, which is Z . . . so on until the drop location was spelled out.

Big Daddy John Saager and I sat in a Red Roof Inn for days, smoking cartons of cigarettes, trying to break that crazy code. It took us forever. But early in our surveillance, Ricky had called somebody and said, "I need you to drop something off at my post office box. It's in a little hardware store on the corner of . . ." and then he gave the address in code. I already knew where he had a post office box. Bingo. We had a start to crack the code.

When I heard on the wiretap that Poncho was headed to Los Angeles, I jumped on the first plane to explain to my LA associates in the DEA that "the S" was delivering merchandise to these Canadians in area hotels. I called back to New York and told the rest of Group 93 to keep playing me the wiretap intercepts so I could keep abreast of what was going on. I heard Dan Rich talking to Poncho, who said that he had picked up the 220 kilos and just stopped off at his home in Pennsylvania on his way to New York.

"A Winnebago with Canada plates!" I said out loud.

I went to the DEA office in LA and, sitting in a borrowed cubicle, called our Canadian DEA guys and asked them if they ever had any calls to Pennsylvania and, if so, to please check the phone numbers. They called back an hour later.

"Well, yes, we do have some communication between Canada and Pennsylvania," the agent on the phone told me. Poncho had a phone number in the Carlisle, Pennsylvania, area. It was the middle of the night in California, but I called the Carlisle Police Department and asked them to check it out. They called me back and told me the number was for a residence at 200 Drexel Road in Carlisle.

"Do me a favor," I said. "Send an undercover car past that address and tell me what they see in the driveway."

They called me back ten minutes later. "Listen, there's a Winnebago in the driveway with Canadian tags on it."

"Do me another favor and stay on the Winnebago while I get in touch with our people in New York," I said.

I called Eddie Beach at home and woke him up. "Eddie, listen, get all the guys and start heading for Carlisle, Pennsylvania, 200 Drexel Road," I said. "It's a home run. There's a big shipment sitting in a Winnebago in the driveway."

I could hear Eddie groan. "Look, Jerry, it's Saturday night. You want me to wake all the guys up and send them to Pennsylvania on your hunch? Forget about it. Call me in the morning after you've had a good night's sleep."

I blew a gasket. "This ain't no hunch, Eddie," I said. "This is a home run! Haven't I been right about these guys for the last hundred times? Get the group to Carlisle, and I'm flying from here to Philadelphia with Big Daddy. We'll rent a car and drive up to meet you."

"Jerry, you're runnin' on empty," Eddie said. "I want you to go hell home and get some rest."

"Fuck you, I'm not tired," I said. "I'll see you in Carlisle."

"You're gonna kill yourself, we'll handle it, go get some rest," he said. And he hung up the phone.

Oh, boy, was I steamed! Here I'd worked for days to crack this thing and all I get is a "Go home and be a good boy and we'll handle it" from Eddie Beach, who's supposed to be my longtime ally. I was ready to roar out of California on the first plane east. But a minute later, the phone rang.

It was our division chief, Steve Krajci, a tall, stocky guy in his fifties, who was one step lower in the chain of command than John Maltz. Unbeknownst to me, Bernie Kerik had called him, saying, "Listen, Jerry's been running for ten days, sitting in a hotel room, trying to crack a code. You know Jerry, he's gotta get some rest."

Krajci ordered me to take it easy. "Bernie's concerned," he said.

I slammed the phone down and looked over at John "Big Daddy" Saager, big as a house, his long hair back in a ponytail, and flashing me a rare expression of concern.

"Fuckin' Eddie and Bernie!" I said. "They want us to go home."

"You gotta be kiddin' me!" said Big Daddy. "We worked this hard on this code and now we're not gonna see it end."

"Fuck it!" I said. "Come on."

We raced downstairs into the street, jumped into the car, and raced at eighty miles an hour down the 405 Freeway to the Newport Beach exit. I drove straight to Maggie's brother's house, my wealthy brother-in-law, John Reinhardt, who owned a hotel on the beach and was a divorced guy, a player. He looked at us as if we were two wharf rats just off a third-class steamer.

"Go upstairs and take a shower," John told us.

We did as told. John lent Big Daddy some clothes, as his usual biker jeans and T-shirt wouldn't work in Newport Beach's haughtier social locales, and the three of us headed off to Margaritaville, a local bar. We started banging down drinks, drowning in our sorrow, cursing everybody from Eddie to the lieutenant to John Maltz, to everybody we'd ever been involved with in the task force.

At around 2:00 A.M., closing time California time, 5:00 A.M. in the Northeast, the three of us, Big Daddy, my brother-in-law, Johnny, and I were standing at a pay phone. I called Bernie Kerik and started slurring curses. "You mother! I'm your best friend! We break the code and I'm left outside of the bust?"

Bernie gave it right back. "It's for your own good, you idiot! Go the hell home! We don't want you flying to Philadelphia and then driving a hundred miles an hour and arriving on the crime scene all jet-lagged! You're gonna kill yourself, Jerry! I'll handle it!"

Big Daddy was jumping up and down and screaming in the background like a cheerleader. "You tell 'em, Jerry!" he said. Then, to Bernie: "You fuckin' turncoats!"

I was rolling now. "You and Eddie and the whole bunch of you can go fuck yourselves!"

We were too drunk to realized how dumb we looked, screaming into a pay phone in the middle of the night. Finally, Big Daddy picked me up and slung me over his shoulder like a sack of potatoes. He carried me to the car, loaded me inside, and we went back to the hotel and crashed.

———

We were up bright and early the next morning, hungover as hell but determined to get back to New York. I don't think Big Daddy and I said two words to each other from takeoff to touchdown. But we were both thinking the same thing. *Screw them. Let them do the operation on their own. See if we care.*

I was so pissed that Eddie, Bernie, and the group didn't seem to want me and Big Daddy on the scene, after we had broken this whole deal wide open, that I didn't take Eddie's phone calls. He was calling from Carlisle while they were sitting out in front of the house at 200 Drexel Drive, watching the Winnebago.

"It's Eddie again," Maggie kept saying. "Maybe you should at least talk to him."

"I told you, I don't care if I ever talk to him again," I said. "Tell him to get lost."

Eddie was relentless. He called so many times. By the thirty-fifth call, I grabbed the phone and snipped, like a petulant little baby, "Listen, dude, I ain't coming. Remember you didn't want me?"

"We need you, Jerry," he said at last. "This is our group. We need you on this case. You were right about this thing."

As soon as I heard the words "We need you," I dropped the phone, got dressed, jumped in the BMW, and hauled ass down the highway, a hundred miles an hour, toward Carlisle. As soon as I crossed into Pennsylvania, Eddie got me on the radio.

"The guy is coming out of the house, and we're on the move. The Winnebago is just about dragging on the ground." Eddie told me that early that Sunday morning, sixty-year-old Poncho ambled out of the house, climbed into the Winnebago, and drove to the Mill Creek Shopping Mall in Secaucus, New Jersey. Once Poncho arrived at the mall, the wiretap plant called his pager to pick up his messages. There was also a message from Dan Rich, which said, "There's a white Taurus in the lot with plates 123 XYZ. The keys are in the ashtray. Load it up and park it in front of the Haagen Dazs against the bushes."

By that time, Eddie and the group had also been relayed a conversation on Ricky's wire saying that a woman in her mid-twenties named Blanca was watching to make sure everything went smoothly. While Poncho was driving around the rear mall parking lot, we dressed Group 93 member Bruce Stokes, who resembled Poncho, in a baseball cap and glasses. Then, after Poncho got out of the Winnebago, in the back of the mall and out of view, we jumped him.

We had the disguised Bruce load up the Taurus with the kilos, then park the car exactly according to the instructions, except that he parked in a handicapped parking spot. We had the local cops rush over and tow the vehicle away.

Blanca saw this all happen and we heard her say to Ricky over her wiretapped phone, "That Poncho is an idiot!" Once again, we had shifted the blame from us onto them, just as Paul had taught me.

We still had to find Ricky.

16

Snowing Coke in Canada

Eddie, Bernie, the rest of the group, and I used a "Trigger Fish," a cellular tracking unit that sits in the back of a van and indicates the direction of cell phone signals, as a target suspect speaks on the phone. Ricky didn't talk a lot on his phone, which made tracking him tough. I listened to the tapes of his conversations over and over. I could hear classical music and hardwood floors but didn't have any other clue as to his location.

I called the cell phone company for more information. They gave me the mile-and-a-half radius for Ricky's cell tower, which originated on the corner of Houston Street and Broadway in Manhattan. On one of the tapes, I could hear a siren in the background. At first, it was faint. Then it was very loud. Then it faded away. The call was made at 10:13 on a Sunday morning.

I called the New York City Fire Command Center to find out what fires had occurred at that time on that Sunday in the southern Manhattan area. There was only one, and it had been handled by Ladder 15 on Lafayette Street.

I went over to the station and found out who had answered the call. Then I found out the route they took. I asked a fireman to help me drive at the same speed they would have traveled, and I wrapped a pair of headphones to my head with an Ace bandage so I could listen to the tape while I was driving. Then I turned the tape on. When the siren on the tape became loud I stopped the car. The siren was loudest on the corner of Broadway and Prince.

I set up on that corner, got the Trigger Fish, and waited for Ricky to make a call. Sure enough, he did. As soon as he got on the phone, the Trigger Fish went crazy. We followed the arrow, which pointed at the downtown branch of the Guggenheim Museum. I thought he must work there. I spent hours in the Guggenheim looking for someone on a cell phone whenever the Trigger Fish would go on. Nothing.

I had the crazy idea to walk down the street, stick my head into a business, and just scream. If the guys in the van monitoring the Trigger Fish heard me, we would know we were in the right place. The people in the art galleries, restaurants, and shops looked at me as if I were crazy. No one knew I was a cop, of course; they thought I was a deranged street person, who kept haunting their doorways. I walked the streets, and the group worked the van, for an entire day with no success. The Trigger Fish still pointed at the Guggenheim.

I had to leave for Canada, because we were getting ready to take down Dan Rich. A few days later, I got a call from Group 93 agent Bruce Stokes. He said the Trigger Fish had been fooled by something called RF deflection. Ricky's cell phone signal was bouncing off the glass of a skyscraper. He wasn't in the Guggenheim; he was in an office called "Manhattan Investments," which he owned, across the street.

Bruce Stokes and the rest of Group 93 were in SoHo, set up on Rickys's office, while the DEA group in LA was set up on one of Dan Rich's associates there, and I was in Vancouver, Canada with Big Daddy and the Canadian DEA office, getting ready to arrest Dan Rich at his house. Simultaneously, we all hit our targets.

Big Daddy and I flew to Vancouver. We were met at the airport by the local DEA agents, a brace of bearded agents in flannel shirts, who drove us out to Dan Rich's neighborhood. It was in the middle of nowhere. We saw a caribou eating the top of a tree, big as a house. We were sitting in the back of the squad car, in our Guess jeans and New York wise guy appearances, half frozen and petrified that the caribou would eat us next.

We went straight from there to the DEA office, where the resident agent in charge tossed us the keys to his brand-new 4-Runner for Big Daddy and me to use while we were there. It had like three miles on it. Big Daddy and I climbed in and several of the Vancouver DEA guys led us back out to Dan Rich's house. It was an enormous log cabin set deep in the snowy mountains.

We staked out the house, and I could hear Big Daddy's teeth chattering from the cold, even though I had the heat blasting. I climbed up on a big wooden deck. I could see Rich in his living room like any other middle-aged guy, sitting in a La-Z-Boy recliner, watching television with his wife.

We stormed the place as if it were any other stash house, and probably almost gave Rich a heart attack. I identified myself, and he denied everything.

"I don't know what you're talking about!" he said. He thought he was so sophisticated, but to me he was just another drug mule

"We know about Ricky!" I said. "We know about the S! We know about Mr. T! We know you're El Feo!"

Rich's face dropped. He put his hands up. We cuffed him and the Vancouver DEA guys drove him back to headquarters. Big Daddy and I high-fived each other, then jumped into the 4-Runner. Once we were on the road, I called New York and got word that they, too, had gotten their suspects. Everybody was in custody.

Big Daddy and I were so revved up that when he pulled out into an icy intersection we got broadsided. It was a small truck with only the driver inside, but it was a direct hit. The brand-new 4-Runner flipped over. We were lying on our side in the middle of the street. Big Daddy and I climbed out of the passenger side of the truck. Within minutes, the Vancouver DEA agents arrived back on the scene, more worried about the boss's brand-new, and now totaled, 4-Runner than about Big Daddy and me.

"What's the big deal?" I asked. "It's only a car accident!"

"We've never had one with a DEA vehicle," said one of the agents.

"Listen, it's no big deal," I said, rattling off the forms and procedures they needed to follow.

"Man, how long you been a DEA agent?" one agent asked.

"I'm not a DEA agent," I said. "I'm an NYPD cop on loan to the DEA. But we've wrecked about thirty cars each."

Dan Rich went to trial, pleading not guilty. He was sentenced to thirty years to life.

━━━━

Back in New York, as Ricky was walking out of his investment firm, Bruce Stokes grabbed him around his neck, dragged him to the ground, and cuffed him. Bruce took Ricky back to Group 93 headquarters.

After we had Dan Rich, I called Bruce. "We're secure in Vancouver," I said. "Do you have Ricky?"

"Yeah, I've got him in the interrogation room," Stokes told me. "Jerry, you'll never believe what this guy looks like. Curly hair, pale, doesn't look at all like a doper."

"Put him on the phone," I said.

"Hold on," said Bruce. "He's still cuffed, but I'm going to put the phone to his ear and you talk."

I lit into him. "Listen, buddy, we got you, we got you!" I was beyond excited. I was ready to jump out of my skin. "You're going to jail for life. I'm telling you right now, we know about the S and everybody. I'm in Vancouver with your buddies Dan Rich and Jimmy and the rest of the crew. You're all going to jail."

When I finished my tirade, Ricky looked at Bruce and said, "Who the hell is that guy?"

———

When I got back to New York, I discovered that Ricky was no ordinary dope dealer. He was from a wealthy Colombian family, which owned the equivalent of the McDonalds hamburger empire in Colombia. Ricky came to the U.S. and wanted to prove to his family that he could be successful in his own right. When his investment business failed, he turned to dealing cocaine to keep it afloat. But he didn't even know what a kilo of coke looked like. He was a middleman, a logistical coordinator. Cartel operatives would have the dope delivered to him and he would call the shots for distribution by telephone.

Ricky was now facing twenty-five years to life in prison.

———

We always reached out to small fish, hoping that they would lead us to bigger game. A few months after Ricky was arrested, I contacted him to see if he would cooperate. By then, he had a new lawyer. They agreed to a proffer conference. I sent my new number two, Eddie O'Casio, a Hispanic undercover newly transferred to Group 93, and several other agents over to Riker's Island. They picked up Ricky and brought him over to the Special Narcotics Prosecutor's Office, where I was waiting in the conference room.

At first, I didn't recognize him.

Eight months in prison will change anybody, but this was beyond belief. Ricky didn't look at all like the dapper New York businessman, with the curly dark hair and immaculate clothing. This was a scraggly guy with a sunken face and a long beard.

I must have said out loud, "What the hell happened to you?"

He sort of broke down after that, and a deluge of words poured out.

"I've embarrassed my whole family," he said. "My father made his millions the hard way. I wanted to prove to my dad that I could do it on my own. I didn't want to be like my brothers and sisters, who live off of his money and work in the family business. I love business, dealing with clients. But when my business was failing, I couldn't let my family down. I wanted to show them that I was doing well and living the American dream. Now I'm only embarrassed and ashamed."

He could have talked forever. But he didn't have to convince us; his physical appearance was proof enough that Ricky was sincere. Being a former wild kid, I could understand . . . I almost put myself in his shoes. The tough cop melted away, and I became compassionate.

"Okay, Ricky, here's the deal, pal," I said. "You know you screwed up royally, and you got yourself probably in the toughest jam anybody could ever be in. You're facing most of your life in prison. It's time to get yourself out of this."

He nodded. He was ready for any way out.

"Now, I don't know if anything will ever come of this, and there's no promises here, but you gotta take a shot," I said. "You're a very big risk and your family will have to come up with substantial bail, if we are even able to cut a deal."

"The bail is no problem," he said.

"Okay," I said. "First of all, how can you get me something that's bigger than life in the cartel? Can you get me somebody who's on the outside, somebody who can give me the structure of the Salazar organization, and the Cali cartel organization that's behind it? I mean the principals, the CEOs, the directors of finance, the smugglers, the routes, and the transporters . . ."

I went through everything I knew about the cartel, and when I was finished, Ricky was giving me a look of amazement.

He told me that he knew the command and control phone number down in Colombia, where everybody in the Salazar organization called the daily tallies in. He said he'd give it up in exchange for his release.

"That, in itself, is just not enough," I said. "In order to get more probable cause, I need to talk to someone who can substantiate it."

"Okay, then, I'll give you Tocayo," he said.

"Who's he?"

"He's the guy you picked up on the wiretaps, giving me instructions from Colombia," he said. "Tocayo's my best friend. We grew up together. We went to college together. He'll do anything for me."

I held up my hand. "You gotta realize something," I said. "Tocayo's entrenched in the cartel. I doubt he's going to risk his life and his family's life in Colombia for you. You're in jail, you're captured. He's going to write you off."

"No, I know Tocayo. I'm telling you, Tocayo will come forward for me."

"Okay, will Tocayo come to the States?"

"No, he will be afraid he'd be grabbed in the States. You would have to go to Colombia."

"Okay, if you can get Tocayo to commit to meeting me, I'll get my people to commit to send me to Colombia," I said.

The trap was baited. Now all I had to do is wait for Tocayo to bite.

———

I heard from Ricky a few days later. He said his brother in Colombia convinced Tocayo to meet with me. "He told him, 'You got my brother into this, you gotta help him out,'" Ricky told me. They promised Tocayo I wouldn't burn him; if he would give me the information I wanted, nobody would ever find out that it came from him.

I agreed to those stipulations, and got Ricky released on $10 million bail. At that time, it was the highest bail posted in New York State history.

Eddie Beach and I went to our division chief, Lieutenant Mike Gervasi. He was a veteran NYPD lieutenant who had recently been reassigned to our task force. Gervasi didn't want to make waves. He had a take-home car, a cell phone, an expense account, and I knew he wasn't going to put any of that on the line for us. Still, I pleaded with him to let me go to Bogotá

"Listen, we got a deal set," I told him. "Ricky has got his friend ready to cooperate. He's a major connection. We picked him up on a wire. He's going to help us, and help Ricky with his problem, but I need to go to Bogotá to meet with the guy."

"Forget that, you're not going to Bogotá," Gervasi said. "What am I going to tell the chief of this department if you get killed down there, and I signed off on you traveling?"

Eddie and I looked at each other.

"What about what you'd have to tell my family?" I said.

"My ass'll be outta here if you get killed in Bogotá," he repeated.

I did an end run around the lieutenant. I went to the Special Narcotics Prosecutor, Robert Silbring, and Judge Leslie Crocker Snyder of the New York State Supreme Court. They called the New York City Police Commissioner and told him they wanted me to do this operation. Next day, Lieutenant Gervasi got a call from the commissioner's office telling him Jerry Speziale was going to Colombia.

I landed in Bogotá a few days later with Group 93's Big Daddy as my backup and bodyguard.

By now, Big Daddy and I were traveling everywhere together. I always marveled at the sheer size of the man. He was a mountain. With a ponytail down to the center of his back, big muttonchop sideburns, and a goatee hanging down his chin, he could pass for the biggest, meanest dope smuggler both domestically and abroad.

Whenever we would hit a city, Big Daddy and I would jump in a cab or rent a car and head for the first bar, where we'd drink, hang out, meet the locals, and plot our strategy. We considered it part of our job. Of course, we could have left the bars before closing time. But we rarely did. Like me, Big Daddy was happily married, but, like me, he enjoyed talking to the women without ever going any further than a quick good-bye kiss.

Whenever we'd go to Washington to meet with the DEA brass, which was often, Big Daddy had to pin his hair up and stuff his mountainous hulk inside a suit and speak like a professional. But after the meeting, we'd head back to the hotel. After working out in the hotel gym, we would put on our jeans and head back to the bars. We were like brothers. We even stayed in the same hotel room, like two fraternity boys, talking all night after having a night out on the job, going back and forth about our wives and kids and where our lives seemed to be heading.

One night, we got so loud and rowdy in our conversation that a pilot staying across the hall pounded on our door. I had just fallen asleep, when I was awakened by a loud voice. I looked up to find Big Daddy standing in the doorway frame, wearing only his underwear, hair as long as Jesus Christ's. The pilot was standing before him in full uniform, hat and all. Big Daddy grabbed him by the suit and practically lifted him off the ground and shouted into his face. "If you ever come to my fucking door again I'll throw you through your door without opening it." Then, he shoved him—hard.

I thought I was dreaming and went back to sleep. Then, a few hours later, the phone rang. I heard Big Daddy just burst out laughing.

"Who the hell was that?" I asked.

"The pilot," he said. "He said he'd never seen such a big guy in his underwear with such a small package."

"So what are you laughing about?" I asked.

"Because I told him, 'That's not what your wife said.'"

On the morning of our arrival in Bogotá, as Big Daddy and I flew over the old aluminum-roofed shacks, the one-family pueblo houses with chicken and goats bidding us welcome, we were both psyched, headed into enemy territory.

The local DEA agents met us at the *aduana,* Colombian customs, with a gang of bodyguards. They yanked us out of the line, got our passports stamped, and within a half hour we were in a bulletproof Suburban with inch-thick windows. We drove into a subterranean parking garage that would later be used in the movie *Clear and Present Danger,* a dark, cavernous, foreboding place. We rode an elevator up to the embassy.

In the conference room, I presented my plan. When I was finished, everybody seemed impressed. "Okay, I'll call Tocayo and arrange to meet him in town," I said.

The agents stopped me right there. "No way, pal," a beefy red-faced guy said. "We can't let you go out of here. You've got to meet him here at the embassy."

"No, no, no, it's just a restaurant here in town," I said.

"You don't get it, kid," they said. "You're in Bogotá. You're not meeting him anywhere but the embassy."

I called Tocayo. No way would he come near the embassy. "You're not snatching me up there," he said. "That's American soil."

I told him I'd get back to him soon. The embassy agents weren't budging, so Big Daddy and I decided to get back to them in the morning. Before we left the embassy, the reps gave us all the usual warnings and showed us a video about current events in Colombia. There were endless warnings and instructions: what to do if anyone tried to recruit us as spies, how we should stay far away from the *zona rosa,* the red-light district, where all the guerilla fringe operators were kidnapping people on a regular basis.

The embassy issued us a bodyguard, a quiet little guy who didn't look like he could guard us against much. He took us to our hotel to unpack and change clothes. Once we got downstairs from our room, the bodyguard asked where we wanted to go. I pulled Big Daddy aside.

"You thinking what I'm thinking?" I asked.

"Hell, yes," he said. *"Zona rosa!"*

"How are we going to get rid of this guy?"

"Shouldn't be too hard," Big Daddy said. "He probably makes about three bucks a month."

I went over to the "bodyguard" and slipped him twenty dollars. "Go get yourself something cool to drink," I said. "We're going to bed and we'll see you tomorrow morning."

He flashed me a big grin, took the money, and was gone.

Big Daddy and I jumped into the first cab. *"Zona rosa,"* we told the driver. It was a brightly lit quarter of endless bars, loud music, loose women, and dangerous-looking men. We chose a little bar in an old hotel, and after a few drinks we had the bartender crank up the music, and Big Daddy and I led the whores and the patrons in an impromptu salsa dance exhibition.

We went back and forth about where to meet Tocayo for days. Finally, I threw a fit, insisting that I had to meet Tocayo in a restaurant or my trip would be wasted. The agents agreed to let me meet him in a little café across the street, where they would guard me from all sides. Before I left for the meeting, they gave me a long-nosed 9mm Beretta that I stuffed in the back of my pants. The gun was so big it stuck out of the middle of my back.

I walked outside, playing Gerry Bartone to the max—suit, tie, Bogotá bag. I stood on the corner outside of the café, agents covering me on all sides. A silver SUV pulled up, driven by Tocayo. He was only in his early thirties, but his hair had prematurely turned gray. He was a thin, clean-shaven, light-skinned guy who looked and acted like a New York City kid, although he was full-blooded Colombian. He was wearing dress pants and a nice shirt. Only the big bodyguard in the passenger seat gave any indication that he was anything other than a middle-aged businessman.

Tocayo cracked his window.

"You Jerry?" he said.

"Yeah, you Tocayo?" I said.

"Yeah," he said.

"Why don't you step out and we'll go inside the café and have some coffee?" I said.

"No, why don't you step in the car, and we'll sit down and have some coffee in here," he said.

"Hey, pal, you're not taking off with me here," I said.

"Hey, pal, you're not taking off with me in there," he said.

"Well," I said, "why don't you lower your window, and we'll do it right here?"

The window went down. For four hours I stood on that curb, like a carhop at a drive-in, taking an order. Finally, he agreed to meet me the next day at the Tecandamo Hotel.

We sat down in a room, me with the 9mm Beretta at my back and John "Big Daddy" Saager sitting in the bodyguard chair in the hallway with a machine gun. Every ten minutes, Big Daddy called me from the house phone to make sure I was okay.

Over a six-hour conversation, Tocayo laid out the whole structure of the Salazar organization. "Salazar" was the code name for a Colombian named Rudy Pito. Tocayo told me that he looked like New

York shock-jock Howard Stern. He had been dispatched to Los Angeles by the cartel bosses to handle a vast distribution network that stretched across America. His loads were transported from Colombia into Mexico, where Salazar received them from the Mejias, a cartel group known as the "Mexican Federation."

Working under Amado Carillo Fuentes, the leader of the Mexican Federation, the Mejias were responsible for transporting coke across the U.S.-Mexico border. They would take the loads into Arizona, where Salazar would take over. He kept the coke in stash houses in Los Angeles, where it was distributed by transporters who came to LA from all over the country.

"Salazar's main guy in Colombia is Juan Carlos Ramirez, and his partner, Victor Patino," Tocayo said

"Tell me about them," I said.

"Well, Patino thought his wife was cheating on him and had her killed, only to later discover that he was wrong," Tocayo said.

"Okay," I said.

"The office in Cali is run by a guy named Carlos," Tocayo continued. "He owned a car dealership in New York but left year before last to return to Colombia because he was getting too hot in New York. Carlos has an assistant in the office named El Polito who handles all the coordination between Salazar and the Mejias.

"The Mejias beep Salazar with code 00, so he knows it's them," Tocayo continued. "He then sends his people down to the San Diego border crossing and picks up the trucks and brings them to the stash houses in LA, and it's distributed by truck from there.

"And if anything goes wrong—or if anybody screws up?" he added. "Salazar has Valentine. He's the organization's enforcer, in charge of a group of *secarios*—assassins—in the States."

———

Tocayo turned out to be a gold mine. He broke Salazar's entire operation down for me. The principals, which consisted of an executive board of twenty-five people. The phone numbers for pagers, landlines, and cell phones, both domestically and internationally. The routes. Everything.

The ring had been in business for five years and was responsible for $40 million worth of coke sales annually.

I flew to LA with all of the information and gave it all to Dave Marzullo and Mike Ferguson from the Los Angeles DEA task force. Dave and Mike were able to secure wiretaps of two LA-based cell phones, one of which belonged to Rudy Pito, a.k.a. Salazar.

I worked the case on my end with Jimmy Grace, a fairly new Group 93 agent, a T-shirt and jeans guy from Queens with a lot of balls who became one of my best friends. Jimmy had come into the group at about the same time as Big Daddy. About six years younger than me, he was a quiet guy who usually wore jeans and a sweatshirt and chewed tobacco. Another misfit, who somehow fit.

Starting as my junior agent, Jimmy went on to become one of the best in the DEA, an expert in wiretaps. Pretty soon, Jimmy and I were monitoring nationwide wiretaps in the case. We were able to tap Salazar's phones in California. From there, we discovered, Salazar branched out to Seattle, Philadelphia, the Rocky Mountain states, North Carolina, Miami, Houston, Chicago, and New York, fourteen cities in all. Eventually, the agents from the different cities met at the Houstonian Hotel in Houston to devise a plan for a national takedown of the Salazar organization.

———

On the morning of the bust, I was communicating closely with the LA office. "Do you have a line on Salazar?" I asked.

"Believe it or not, he's at Disneyland," special agent Marzulo told me.

"You gotta be kidding!" I said.

"No, I'm not," said Marzulo. "This guy loves Disneyland. He goes there all the time. He's in the park right now with some friends. We've got agents on him, following him from ride to ride."

The DEA agents grabbed Salazar as he was getting off of Disneyland's 20,000 Leagues Under the Sea ride. Because we didn't want to divulge the wiretap investigation, the LA agents posed as INS agents and arrested him on immigration charges. Meanwhile, DEA agents across the country did a simultaneous bust of the entire Salazar organization, resulting in 166 arrests in fourteen cities, the seizure of six tons of coke, $13 million in cash, and various bank accounts. It was the largest and most comprehensive and coordinated law enforcement investigation against the Cali cartel to date.

We knew the Colombians would send a replacement, and they did, a smuggler they called El Loco. Through our existing wiretaps on the Mejias' phones, we were able to get up on El Loco and continue to take down the organization. Salazaar resulted in something like five major takedowns, crippling the Mexican distribution ring.

With that bust, Group 93 became the home run hitters of the drug war. Accolades arrived from every corner of the law enforcement community. A New York State judge sent letters to the New York City Police Commissioner recommending that I be promoted, and every member of Group 93 got the DEA Administrators Award. Attorney General Janet Reno sent us a letter of congratulations, applauding our "unprecedented" operation.

In Washington, there was a major press conference about the case. DEA Administrator Thomas Constantine did the press briefing, along with President Clinton and Janet Reno. Constantine called Eddie Beach and me personally. He told us that it was amazing to see such a skilled case of law enforcement; in all of his years he never thought he would see anyone achieve what we had accomplished against the cartel.

There were articles in newspapers from New York to Seattle. Big Daddy and I were given Attorney General Citations Letters for our initiation of the investigation. Group 93 was given the Administrators Award, the highest award given by the DEA, and we would go on to win the award again in 1995 and for my work in Passaic county in 1999. Our bunch of misfits had become heroes.

Everyone in the group was so high on our accomplishments that we didn't really care about the accolades. The press conferences started to become meaningless. We were so satisfied by our success that it didn't matter what the outside world thought.

———

After we took down the Salazar organization, agents from all over the country met in Miami to discuss the bust. We went out for drinks at a place called Christopher's on a Wednesday night, which was ladies' night. We all got pretty gassed up. Eddie Beach, my roommate, got nervous when he saw that things were getting crazy. He took a cab back to the hotel.

Before we knew it, a woman at the bar convinced us without much prodding to do "body shots," an acrobatic feat that involved putting a shot glass between her breasts, flipping her over, and drinking the booze out of the shot glass. The bartenders and waitresses got in on the action. They locked the door and the party continued.

I got back to the room in the dark at 5:00 A.M. Suddenly the light clicked on, and Eddie Beach, in his pajamas, was standing over me. I felt as if I were in an interrogation. He started waving his notebook at me, showing me where he had documented the name of the taxi driver who brought him home.

"I have proof I left at nine-thirty," he said. "So if you were up to any of your shenanigans, I have evidence that I wasn't there."

"You're nuts," I said. "Turn out the light and go to bed."

The next day we flew back to New York as heroes.

I should have been satisfied.

But I wanted more.

17

Becoming Paul

Point by point, Jerry, point by point.

Paul was in jail, but his voice was always with me, whispering in my ear, saying that I wasn't good enough, smart enough, slick enough, to do things as well as he could. I could hear him pushing me to do things bigger and better than he did.

Following Paul's lead, I did my homework and laid new groundwork to catch even bigger Cali players. Still playing the role of Geraldo Bartone, I rented an office suite on the seventy-sixth floor of the World Trade Center and created a dummy import/export company called Saburo International. I set up a phone system, hired two professional-looking women as secretaries, and wired the whole place for sight and sound, with surveillance cameras in the ceilings in our big conference room and audio bugs in every corner of the office.

Just like Paul, I'd dress up in my Italian suits and bark orders to my "assistant," Eddie O'Casio. Like the rest of us, he was another live wire who didn't fit with his former unit, Group 91. Eddie was from the south side of Brooklyn, a short, stocky Puerto Rican American who was going bald before his time. I took him shopping, and pretty soon he was wearing Armani, a fake Rolex, and learning the menu at Le Cirque. Just like Paul had Nielsen, I had Eddie O. "Get us some coffee," I'd say, just like Paul, and Eddie was all "Yessir, yessir, yessir . . ." just like Nielsen.

Eddie and I would work the front of the office, with civilian secretaries we'd hired, while the rest of the group—Big Daddy, Eddie Beach, and the others—hid in surveillance rooms monitoring cameras and recorders.

We would have the visiting smugglers on our wires from the moment they entered One World Trade, where you had to pass a security desk. This was just after the first bombing of the Trade Center, and security was tight. Visitors were required to show photo IDs before being allowed to go into an elevator. When smugglers came to meet with me to discuss an operation, we would know their true identities (or at least who they were purporting to be) because they would show some form of ID at the security desk.

We had everything ready. All we needed was a new case. Our old informant Ronnie handed it to us on a silver platter when he introduced me to Javier, who suggested we meet to discuss our flying loads from Colombia for him.

———

We met in S.P.Q.R., one of Paul's favorite restaurants in Little Italy. Of course, we never let the restaurants know we were cops. We would play the restaurant like we did the smugglers. For all they knew we were mobsters, and in the early nineties restaurants in New York were well accustomed to dealing with that kind of clientele. Eddie O would call the restaurant and say that Mr. Bartone would be coming in and wanted a quiet table in the back so the conversation would be private.

When I arrived for my meeting with Javier, in my immaculate Armani suit and with my overcoat hanging off my shoulders, the maître d' rushed up like a hungry puppy. "Mr. Bartone! How are you? So nice to see you again, sir."

Eddie O, walking behind me in his twin Armani, hit him with a crisp fifty.

"We've got your table ready for you, sir, private, just like you requested," the maître d' continued, leading me to the table, where Javier, a dark-skinned Colombian in his thirties in an open sports shirt and an undersized jacket, was drinking scotch as if it were water, with several mongrel-faced bodyguards watching from surrounding tables. Once I had my cocktail, and Javier drank three to my every one, I started looking for weaknesses, and I found an obvious one: Javier was a major drunk.

I told Javier that we could help him with a "route," meaning a transportation network. We discussed references, past operations, strategies, and my string of successes.

Javier might have been a drunk, but he was no dummy. He asked me to give up a family member as a collateral, a request that got more common as the deals got bigger. They never call it a hostage, but that's what it was. It was one condition I could never accept.

Pin it back, pin it back on them, I could hear Paul saying.

"Okay, my friend, I'll send a relative down to Colombia if you'll send me one up here," I said. "But, please remember, if you don't pay like you're supposed to or something gets lost on your end, then, well . . . it's just another expense of doing business."

"I'm sorry, my friend, that's not an option," he said. "Two family members cancel each other out. There has to be only one—and it must come from you. I need a guarantee."

"Yes, I understand," I said. "And I'm ready to give you one."

I slid my index finger across my neck, and said what Paul Lir Alexander had instructed me to say in this type of situation.

"My guarantee is my life," I said.

The next day, I got a page from Javier. He wanted to see more, and I was ready to flash him our offices.

For our next meeting, Ronnie brought Javier to my offices in One World Trade Center. As always, we had choreographed his arrival as carefully as a Broadway play. Eddie O'Casio would, of course, serve as my assistant, while our Group 93 informant Donny Blakely, an old country boy smuggler from Florida in his sixties, would act as my wealthy uncle. I'd pay him $2,500 per meeting, which was good pay for a retired smuggler. He had a million stories, like the one when they buried an entire smuggling plane with a backhoe after a crash landing and unloading a hatch full of coke.

"Okay, ladies, make sure you know Ronnie, really know Ronnie," I told my secretaries.

As soon as Ronnie arrived, trailed by Javier and a couple of body-guards, the secretaries went into action. "Oh, Ronnie, how ya doin', Ronnie!" they said. "C'mon in and make yourself comfortable. The boss is in the back with his uncle, but we'll let him know you're here."

As if they'd known him forever. Just then, Eddie O came out, in full-dress Armani, speaking perfect Spanish and shaking everybody's hand. He led Ronnie and Javier and his goons into our beautiful, spacious conference room, with its big conference table and everything wired for sight and sound.

"I'll get the boss," Eddie said.

He walked into the back room, where my "uncle Donny" and I were waiting. "It's show time," he said.

Donny and I walked in, both of us in our suits and ties. Eddie O started bringing in the cappuccinos with espresso chasers. Once again, I told Javier about our global transportation operation and looked over at Donny Blakely.

"My uncle's got this beautiful plane that you've gotta see to believe," I told Javier.

"Can you do anything through Polonia?" Javier asked.

Meaning Poland.

"No, we don't have any routes through Poland," I said. "But any through South or Central America is no problem."

He wanted to know where we landed the loads in the U.S.

"Right here in the New York area," I said.

"Where?" he asked.

"Why don't we show you?" I said.

———

Early the next morning, we picked up Javier at his home in Washington Heights. On the way out the door, he motioned to two of his bodyguards, two nasty scar-faced mules, to follow us. He got into our car and we drove him out to Teeterborough, the private airport in New Jersey used by all the high-rolling businessmen of Manhattan.

Donny Blakely, Eddie O'Casio, and I drove Javier up to the Executive Air private jet terminal, and I stepped out of that BMW as if I owned the place. I was wearing a short-waisted, baby's-bottom-soft black leather Italian leather jacket that I'd picked up in Milano, black Rayban aviator sunglasses, designer jeans, and a mock turtle-necked cashmere sweater. Eddie was dressed just like me, and Donny Blakely had on his country boy apparel—jeans, cowboy boots, work shirt.

We walked out on the tarmac, and let Javier take in Donny Blakely's beautiful black Piper Chieftain. It was a twin-engine, jet-black beauty with red pinstriping and steel wing-tipped fuel tanks.

"It's one of several in our fleet," I said. "You oughta see her land, hombre. We fly in five hundred feet under the radar, and when we get close to the landing strip, we shut down the running lights. Because it's black, you can't see it coming in. It's practically invisible."

He almost began drooling right then.

We got into the cockpit, me at one control, Donny Blakely at the other. Being an experienced pilot, Donny took us up; then I took over with his instructions once we were airborne. Javier settled into the plush leather seat, everybody ready for the show. We flew up over Manhattan, where the skyline seemed to beckon good morning; over to West Milford, New Jersey, where there was private airport, with a pristine landing strip.

"Bank a forty-five-degree turn to the left," Donny Blakely told me. I did as he instructed, while shouting back to Javier, "Look down! Look down!"

He could see that airstrip shimmering in the morning sun. "Perfecto," I heard him say under his breath.

By the time I set the plane back on the ground at Teeterborough, Javier was ready to do business with us.

———

"The old man's tired, he's getting old," I said to Javier, as Donny bade us good-bye. Then Eddie O, Javier and his two bodyguards, and I went to celebrate at a Jersey City nightclub called Foxes. Tailing us were most of the members of Group 93, along with a new sergeant, Dominic Gentilli. He was a straitlaced, dictator-strict Italian American in his mid-thirties, transferred from NYPD. He was driving a gray Oldsmobile that I used occasionally when I would crash my car, which I was doing more and more frequently. Every time the BMW was in the shop, I would use Gentilli's Olds Cutlass.

After an hour or so in Foxes, both Javier and I were pretty drunk. I always tried to keep a lid on the drinking, but I had to do something to take the edge off of everything. I'd never get drunk to the point where I'd get stupid, because that's a sure road to ruin. But I'd drink enough to take the edge off of my nerves.

We hit the dance floor, both Javier and I dancing with whatever spare women we could find, while Javier's bodyguards watched their boss as if he were dancing with nuclear bombs. After we got done dancing, Javier and I returned to our table to continue our business conversation.

We had just ordered another round when one of Javier's bodyguards came over and pushed a napkin across the table toward Javier. I read the note, which was in Spanish, upside down. It said that a suspicious car had followed us to Foxes and was still outside in the parking lot. The license plate number was written on the napkin. I knew right away that it was Dominic Gentilli's Oldsmobile. I took a deep sip of my drink; I was afraid they would kill me right there.

Pin it back, pin it back on them, I could hear Paul saying.

"Do you know anything about this car, Geraldo?" Javier asked.

I took another slug of vodka. "What kind of car?" I asked.

"A gray Oldsmobile," he said. "My bodyguard saw it in the Lincoln Tunnel, saw it by the restaurant, and now he sees it here."

I went ballistic. "I told you, I'll kill you if you screw this up," I told Javier. "I'll have your people taken out! If you contaminated my office, if you have the heat on you, you're dead!"

That made Javier forget about the cops, but he couldn't forget about the hostage. He was like a broken drum. Hostage, hostage, hostage. He must have said it a million times. "I need one of you to be with our people down in the pueblo," he'd say. "I need one of you, as a guarantee."

"What happens if the plane crashes?" I asked. "We've both been in this business a long time. We both know there are liabilities, risks, it's part of the business. I'm sorry, but I'm not able to provide you with a hostage."

But he didn't hear me. "Don't worry, they will be treated like a king or a queen," he said. He slammed his fist on the table and the entire barroom seemed to shake. "It's a condition of the deal," he said.

Once again, I could hear Paul whispering in my brain, *Pin it back, pin it back on them.* I knew I couldn't stall Javier forever. So I excused myself and went to the nightclub's pay phone and called Javier's boss, Oscar Pozo, in Colombia. I was able to get him on the phone right away.

"Listen, sir, with all due respect, I've got a problem with Javier," I said. "Frankly, the guy's a liability. He's a drunk. I can't take the chance. He's too loose."

I told him about the incident that had just happened at Foxes, where Javier said he'd seen a cop car. Of course, I knew that Pozo would soon hear the story from Javier, which would make me even look better.

"Javier already brought the heat down on us, and we haven't even started our deal," I continued. "I'm sorry, sir, it's either him or me. I've been in this business far too long to work with amateurs."

To appease me, Pozo eventually cut Javier out of the deal, and I was, once again, home free.

With Javier out of the way, I was ready to fly down to Ecuador to meet Oscar Pozo, the half-Colombian, half-Ecuadorian who needed a transportation broker for his load. I did a little homework before my flight and discovered that he'd come to America in the early 1980s to open one of the first cocaine-processing labs in upstate New York. He had planned to ship the coca, the base, into the States and process it like they did in the labs in Colombia. But the feds hit him and locked him up for eleven years in the New York State Penitentiary.

At the time I was to meet him, Pozo was a gung-ho ex-con, thoroughly pissed off at New York. I discovered that he was an independent broker for a number of cartel bosses, a very hands-on guy who knew the business inside and out.

Before I flew to Ecuador to meet with Oscar, I picked up the *New York Times* and read about Colombia's new shoot-down policy. The government was going to fire on any plane that didn't have an approved flight plan. I knew the U.S. government wouldn't let me fly an operation. So, thinking wistfully of that beautiful black Chieftain I had shown to Javier, I had to change the entire operation to a boat deal.

I called my old friend Rocky, the three-hundred-pound skipper who helped us steer the coke-laden *Phoenix,* and he agreed to serve as my captain for the Pozo deal. On the five-hour flight to Ecuador, Rocky gave Eddie O'Casio and me a crash course on boat smuggling—routes, fuel, speed, capacity. By the time we arrived, we were ready to roll.

As Paul had taught me, I arrived in Quito, Ecuador, like a big American smuggler ready to throw his weight around in a foreign country.

At my side was Eddie O'Casio, my all-purpose assistant and body-guard, dressed in full-tilt Armani, exactly like me.

We took a cab from the airport to the Hotel Oro Verde, the best in Quito—a marble-floored, plush palace with a casino and the best restaurant in town. Eddie and I exited the cab in front of the hotel like two drug kingpins, dressed in our suits and tipping excessively, just in case anybody was watching. We checked into a suite, and I called our contact to alert Oscar Pozo of our arrival.

"I'm in place for the Oro Verde and I'm looking forward to seeing Don Oscar for dinner this evening at seven, as planned," I said.

"El Senor left for a day trip to Turcan on the border early this morning," said the voice on the other line. "But he's returning by car late this afternoon to meet you."

"Okay, I'll be waiting," I said.

—————

That night, Eddie and I were sitting on a couch in the lounge area of the bar when Oscar Pozo walked in with three of his goons. Tall and dark, with jet-black hair slicked down and parted on the side and a thick mustache that hung down his chin, Pozo looked menacing—and the harelip that he was trying to hide with the mustache didn't help.

I walked over and said, "*Buenos noches,* El Senor. *Mucho gusto.*"

Pozo scanned me up and down with black and steely eyes.

"*Mucho gusto, mucho gusto,*" I said, pumping the hands of each of his goons. Everybody shook hands, and I introduced Eddie as "Generette," my manager.

With the introductions out of the way, we all sat down for drinks in the lounge. I told Pozo that although we had discussed transporting the load by plane, I had other ideas.

"The plane thing was something I did with my uncle, but my real business is shrimping," I said. "We can load off the corner of Isla de Providencia and sail the goods back to Miami."

"*Comprendo, bueno, bueno,*" Pozo said. His harelip made him speak with a lisp. He knew Isla de Providencia well. We reviewed my maps and devised a plan. We'd get the load into Providencia by plane; then we'd have two shrimp boats standing by. An empty shrimper would have the load in its hole, while a second boat would bring shrimp to dump on top of the covering where the load would be stored.

The boat with the dope would return to Miami, while the other boat would continue shrimping.

"Perfecto," said Pozo. He clapped his hands. "*Listo.* I'm ready. Let's celebrate."

We all walked into the hotel's three-star restaurant. We were waiting for the maître d' to seat us when I spotted a silver tray bearing the nightly catch. On the tray were a lobster, a steak, and a giant shrimp with the head still attached. Up to that point, I had only seen cocktail shrimp. I looked at this giant crustacean and said to Eddie O'Casio, "What the hell is that?" Not a smart line from a supposed shrimper.

Eddie turned white as a ghost. Just then, thank God, the maître d' came over to see us. We didn't know if Pozo overheard. Eddie and I sat through dinner thinking we were going to be killed. He must not have heard my comment, because after dinner we went up to our room and mapped our route on the navigational map.

Pozo suggested a transportation route from a point off of Cozumel, Mexico, back to the U.S.

I did just as Paul taught me. "For my expenses I'll require seventy-five thousand dollars," I said. "Once that's received, I'll start the operation."

He asked me for a hostage as collateral, but I refused. "I've been in this business a long time, with many successes," I said. "No hostage and seventy-five thousand up front in expenses."

He extended his hand, and we were in business.

━━━━

I returned to the U.S., leaving instructions with Pozo to have somebody in his organization contact me on my Skytel pager when he was ready to deliver the $75,000. Back in the city, I soon had a page with a phone number from one of Pozo's reps.

He wanted me to meet him on Second Avenue at Thirty-fourth Street, right outside the Midtown Tunnel in front of the Citibank. Eddie O'Casio and I waited on the corner by the pay phones in our Armanis. A black Buick LaSabre with tinted windows pulled up. A tall, dark-skinned Colombian with straight black hair got out and walked over to us.

"Are you Jerry on behalf of Oscar?" he asked.

"Yeah," I said.

"Good to see you, man," he said. "Come on over to the car, I have some papers for you."

Eddie and I walked over to the car, where the guy popped the trunk and handed us a small duffel bag. Inside, there was $75,000 cash. Eddie and I got back in our car and drove around for a while to make sure there was no countersurveillance on us, and then we headed back to the DEA offices.

There was only one problem. Pozo's conversation with his New York operative who was to deliver us the cash was picked up on a foreign wiretap in Medellín, Colombia. So Pozo's instruction to give $75,000 to "Geraldo," and to alert him via a Skytel pager when he was ready for me to pick it up, was passed on by the Colombian government to the DEA in Bogotá, which then passed the information on to the Jackson, Mississippi, DEA office, where my Skytel pager was based. The Jackson DEA did a search, which showed that the pager number belonged to a New York–based DEA agent named Jerry Speziale.

Wouldn't you think they would figure that, maybe, this was an undercover operation? *No.* They assumed that it was a dirty operation run by a dirty cop. Once again, they came at me with double barrels loaded.

———

The Jackson, Mississippi, DEA office passed the information on to DEA's internal affairs division, the Office of Professional Responsibility (OPR). They saw that the case involved a New York City detective on loan to DEA Group 93, so they called in NYPD Internal Affairs. The New York State Police was also called, because Group 93 was a tri-task force, with State Police personnel involved in any internal affairs incidents.

Representatives of all of these agencies were already headed to New York, all loaded for bear, when my lieutenant, Mike Gervasi, called me. "Uh, Jerry, you've got problems," he said. "You may want to get yourself an attorney."

"What are you talking about?"

"Well, representatives of internal affairs, OPR, and the State Police Internal Affairs are upstairs and they want to talk to you."

What have I done? What could they be looking at me for?

I was starting to panic. Deep down, beneath the bluster, beneath the loud and shiny packaging that Paul Lir Alexander had created, I was still Jerry Speziale, just another street cop on a mission. But then, I thought, *What the hell? I haven't done anything wrong!* And I was Geraldo Bartone again. I walked upstairs, taking my reports with me. I was soon staring at a line of somber faces sitting at a conference table as if somebody had died—or were about to be buried.

"Do you want to tell us about seventy-five thousand dollars you picked up?" one of the officers asked.

"Yeah, sure, I want to tell you about it," I said. "Don't you people read reports?"

I slid a report across the table that spelled everything out. "This was a sanctioned action, approved by the attorney general for trafficker-directed funds," I said. "The seventy-five thousand is in an operational account in Miami. There are teletypes proving what I'm telling you. This action was sanctioned."

They all seemed to exhale in unison, and then the backpedaling began. "Well, you've got to understand, Jerry," one of the officers said, attempting warmth and friendliness. "When you were picked up on a foreign wiretap, there was some concern for your safety."

"Oh, yeah?" I said. "So this is a safety squad here? I've got the State Police Internal Affairs, NYPD Internal Affairs, and DEA OPR, and you're telling me you're all here because of my safety? No, you are here because you thought you were going to lock up a cop. Your business is to lock up cops, pal!"

I wouldn't let it end at that. I had to drive the spike deeper. In a weird way I had become Paul, and, like him, my ego was running out of control. "I want to explain something to you. I'm the number-one expert in wiretaps in America."

I took my beeper off my belt. "If I ever did decide to go bad, you would never catch me on a pager, nor would you catch me on a phone. The only way that you would catch Jerry Speziale is if you were in a swimming pool naked, right beside me, and I decided tell you the whole story. Now if you'll excuse me, I've got work to do."

And I walked out of the room.

———

Oscar Pozo was starting to get antsy.

Too many things were going bad with too many loads for any coke dealer to feel secure. Foremost on his mind was Javier. After Javier was cut out of my deal, he got on to another load that he was to deliver for Pozo. That load turned out to be a controlled delivery from another DEA task force group, and Javier was left holding the bag. Coupled with what I had told Pozo about Javier being an amateur and a magnet for cops, Javier's loss of the load was the last straw.

"Remember Javier?" a Cali mule asked me one day. "Won't be seeing much of him anymore."

"What happened to him?" I asked.

"Poor guy got kidnapped," the mule said. "Not only did they kill him, they put him through a meat grinder. Never found even a bone."

━━━

I was on the road in Houston, teaching the FBI and the local DEA about wiretaps, when I got Pozo's call. It was good to have Pozo call me in a different city, a different area code. That was the MO of a coke smuggler, always traveling from port city to port city, perpetually on the run.

"Listen, I need you to pick up eleven hundred kilos off the coast of Mexico in two days," Pozo said.

Two days? I thought. *How the hell can I do that?*

But, of course, I yessed Oscar Pozo, telling him there would be no problem.

When we were getting ready to negotiate to do the deal, we ran Pozo through the computer and discovered that the Miami DEA group was already negotiating with him for a Mexico boat deal. They had secured an informant as the boat captain.

I called Pozo and told him that I had a guy lined up to help him do the boat load. I then worked the deal with Miami and we sent the informant boat they were originally sending. Pozo thanked me, and Miami dispatched the boat.

The Miami DEA arranged for their operatives to pick up the 1,100-kilo load off the coast of Cozumel. When the shipment got to Miami, all of Pozo's clients who received the load were arrested. When Pozo's people were taken down, I called him.

"The load arrived safe and sound, but some things went wrong on your end," I said. "Let's meet in Bogotá to discuss the problems and how we can avoid them in the future." He agreed to the meeting

I thought I'd pull the same con that I'd done with Jose Urdinola in Rome—get him on foreign soil and extradite him to the U.S. Because Oscar Pozo had dual citizenship, both in Colombia and Ecuador, we could treat him as a citizen of Ecuador, whose statutes allowed the U.S. Department of Justice authorization for a Provisional Arrest Warrant, the formal term for an international arrest warrant.

We went through the State Department Office of International Affairs, which put an international arrest warrant out on him, and then we flew to Colombia. When I flew down to Bogotá, it was the first time an undercover had gone into Bogotá to set up somebody for the Colombian National Police to arrest in conjunction with the DEA.

———

I went to Bogotá with Jimmy Grace. Ready to discuss what had gone wrong with the delivery in Miami, Oscar Pozo came walking into Bogotá's Tecandamo Hotel, where we were waiting in the lobby.

"Welcome, amigo," Pozo said. I greeted him with an *abrazo,* and we sat down to talk, surrounded by Colombian undercover agents and DEA agents from Bogotá. As soon as I shook his hand, the agents knew that it was Pozo.

After I identified him to the agents, I said, "We're going to be here for a while, Oscar. I'm going to hit the head." But instead of going to the bathroom, I walked straight out the door of the hotel—never to return. The surrounding Colombian feds and DEA guys stood up, stormed in, and took Oscar straight to jail.

Another home run, I thought.

Wrong.

Oscar Pozo was powerful in Bogotá. He was able to persuade the Colombian government to release him. There were many accusations and innuendos. But this time, the cartel's power and money proved to be stronger than ours. A judge in Colombia refused to sanction the extradition of an Ecuadorian citizen to America. So Pozo was sent back to Ecuador, where he still remains at large.

Rocky and Jim Lewis retired after helping us bring down Oscar Pozo. They made good money working with us. They decided to go straight and became involved in a medical software business, which didn't turn out quite as successful as their work with us had been. Their engineer turned out to be a drunk and they lost their shirts. Desperate for cash, they kidnapped an old Colombian smuggler with whom they were once in business. Apparently, the guy owed them some money from years back. They held him for ransom. When nobody wanted to pay up, they ended up stun-gunning their hostage in a bathtub in Florida. They're now serving life sentences for kidnapping.

I flew back to New York and started scouring snitches, streets, and wires for my next big deal.

18

Big Man in Bogotá

I was stressed out and fearful of retribution over Oscar Pozo. I'd put my life on the line to get this big target all set up and busted, only to have a corrupt Colombian judge set him free.

I should have just taken it in stride and flown home to Maggie and Francesca for some long-needed R&R. But, of course, I couldn't. I was running on adrenaline. I had become Paul, and I needed a big bust to show that I had become better than him. I was sitting around Bogotá, fuming, when a name bubbled up into my brain. Marcos Vargas, a major smuggler in Bogotá.

I had been introduced long distance to Vargas by Ronnie, the stateside Dominican CI I'd flipped after busting him for the five hundred grams of heroin. Undercover work in Colombia was not sanctioned by the DEA, and so I'd stayed away from Marcos Vargas. But with the freeing of Oscar Pozo, I realized the Colombian government didn't play by the rules. So why should I? If I could bust Vargas, I could beat the corrupt judge at his own game and gain some sort of twisted revenge on him for setting Oscar Pozo free.

I called Kenny McGee, an agent with the U.S. embassy who ran the fugitive squad for the DEA in Bogotá.

"Kenny, listen, I've got this old contact, Marcos Vargas, who runs a *casa de cambio*, a money exchange, in Bogotá, and I want to pop by real quick undercover just to show my face and possibly start my next smuggling routine," I said.

"You know it's against policy," Kenny said. "But I know you're going to do it anyway. Be careful, and remember, I didn't give you permission. Call me later and let me know everything's okay."

My strategy was simple. *Put your face,* Paul had always said. Meaning show your availability for work. Jimmy Grace, my hard-working and ever eager preppy-looking backup agent, and I were sitting around our hotel room when I called Marcos Vargas.

"Hey, Marcos, Geraldo Bartone, how you doin', brother?" I asked. "Remember, we met through Ronnie, our *compadre* in New York? Well, I'm here in Bogotá on another deal and I'd like to stop by and say hello."

"Sure, I remember you," he said. "Come over to my *casa de cambio* at around five."

Jimmy and I were there within the hour. The *casa de cambio* was a dingy storefront with steel gates on the door and bars on every door, window, and crack. Across the street was a cantina with tables outside. I told Jimmy to hang out around the corner and keep an eye on me. I went to the bar, sat down on a stool, and ordered a beer while I kept watch across the street.

Pretty soon, a white Range Rover pulled up and a dark little guy, presumably Marcos, got out, followed by a bodyguard, the biggest Colombian I'd ever seen. They both walked into the *casa de cambio,* which was basically a cage, locked up tight with double steel bars.

I clanged on the bars, saying, "Hey, Marcos, Geraldo Bartone!" The big bodyguard came to the gate, unlocked it, and let me inside. Once I was in, the bodyguard slammed the steel gate door behind me and slid a dead bolt across it. I followed him farther into the cage. Marcos sat behind a humongous desk, Scarface style, and I sat in the chair in front of him. The bodyguard, who had a gun in his waistband, kept his arms folded and his eyes on me the whole time.

I was pretty much petrified. Not only because of the King Kong, Bundy look-alike next to Marcos Vargas, with more guns than I could count—or dodge. Not only because of the steel bars on every conceivable opening, which would have prevented any escape. I was petrified because of the question that I just knew Marcos Vargas was going to ask.

"Would you like something to drink?" Marcos asked.

"Got any Absolut?" I asked.

He nodded and the bodyguard got up to get a bottle. He poured us a stiff one, and my heart was in my throat. I knew I couldn't pick up that glass! I never did in the beginning stages of a negotiation. Because my hand would surely shake from fear. So I switched into Crazy Jerry mode.

"You got a straw?" I asked.

Marcos again nodded to his bodyguard, who, sure enough, came out with a straw, which he stuck in the glass of Absolut. I leaned over and sucked up the whole glass through the straw in one single swallow. Marcos laughed. His bodyguard laughed. And my heart slowed down a little.

I started telling Marcos how I could provide transportation services for the load. I told the old stories from the traffickers I had busted. I threw names around. I talked credibility, prices, and strategies. Finally, Marcos said he wanted to transport cash and coke from Aruba to the States. We struck a deal, not only to transport a coke load from Aruba to the U.S., but also to launder a pile of cash.

It was a hell of a deal, more than I'd expected. I was ready to get out of that cage, and out of the country, before Marcos Vargas got wise.

"I have some business in New York that I need to take care of, so I'll be leaving Colombia tomorrow," I said.

We shook hands and Marcos said he'd be in touch soon. I rose from my seat. Marcos nodded to the bodyguard to open the steel doors, and I walked through the bars back into the street.

—————

A month later, I was back at Group 93 headquarters when Marcos Vargas called, saying he wanted to discuss the load.

"Let's meet in Aruba," he said.

We set a date: June 12, 1996. I flew to Aruba with John "Big Daddy" Saager. Marcos was to arrive a day later on a flight from Barranquilla on SAM Airlines. I agreed to pick him up at the airport.

As soon as Big Daddy and I arrived in Aruba, I called the embassy attaché, Gerry Francioci. "Where should we meet you?" I asked.

"Stay at the Marriott at the end of the island and look for me in the casino at about ten P.M.," he said.

"How am I going to recognize you?" I asked him.

"Don't worry, you'll know me," he said.

———

Big Daddy and I arrived at the casino at ten and immediately saw a big, heavyset Italian guy at the craps table surrounded by middle-age women. He was throwing the dice and screaming, "C'mon, eleven, c'mon, eleven." I looked at Big Daddy and said, "That's gotta be him."

I walked up to the table and said, "Are you Gerry Francioci?"

"Are you Speziale?" he asked.

"Yeah," I replied

"From here on in your name is Omar," he said.

"Omar?" I asked. "Why Omar?"

"Because you look like Omar Sharif," he said. "So from now on you're Omar."

From that day forward, Gerry Francioci called me "Little Omar." We sat down and had a few drinks in the lobby. I had learned that this was the custom when you first meet an embassy attaché—who, in my experience, was frequently a wild man or a drunk—in a foreign country. Gerry Francioci was a wild man; he loved to party. Big Daddy and I filled him in on the specifics of our operation, and he agreed to cover us.

We all retired to the casino. But first, I called Maggie on my cell, telling her that everything was going well, that I missed her, and that I hoped to be home soon. I considered myself quite the craps player, and I would always get very hyped up, very revved, very excited. That night, I hit the craps table with my new friend Gerry Francioci, and pretty soon I was throwing the dice, yelling, "Yo, eleven! Yo, eleven!"

The table was full, a mix of professionals, tourists and locals. I got the table smoking. When I didn't have the dice myself, I'd make up nicknames for whoever was throwing. "Come on doc," I'd yell at the doctor. Or, "Come on, baby, sweetie, come on, let's go, you throw one," I'd yell at the flight attendant. I was so obnoxious, so cranked on booze and ego that the pit bosses wanted me thrown out.

"Don't slow the dice down, let's go, let's go!" I'd scream whenever anybody tried to slow the action. "You're the kiss of death, let's go. Throw the dice." Then I turned to the cocktail waitress. "Gimme another vodka and cranberries," I demanded. "Let's go! Let's go!

Let's go! Then back me up with another vodka and cranberry. Come on, you, baby, come on, let's go!"

I probably lost a grand or two, but I was unfazed until late that night I got a call from Maggie on my cell, which apparently had inadvertently redialed my home number after our last conversation.

"What were you doing tonight, Jerry?" she asked.

"Oh, nothing," I said. "Just going to bed."

"Well, Jerry, have another vodka and cranberry and tell doc to throw you another 'yo' eleven," Maggie said. "And don't call me."

She hung up the phone.

I was in a foreign country, what was I supposed to do? Sit in my room and play canasta? I was Geraldo Bartone, an international drug transporter. I was in way too deep to realize that I was playing the part far too well.

Big Daddy was in the bunk next to mine. "Boy, did I screw up," I said, telling him the story of what happened with Maggie and the cell phone.

Big Daddy laughed. "And you're supposed to be such a big phone expert?"

———

The next day, I met Marcos at the Sonesta Hotel, not in the lobby, but outside on the street. There was a pink mini-mall next door, and for security's sake, Marcos insisted that I meet him there. Big Daddy waited across the street, in case anything went wrong.

When I walked over, Marcos was standing there, alongside his bodyguard. It was another perfect day in paradise, and Marcos and his humongous bodyguard were dressed in short sleeves and shorts. I said hello and shook his hand.

"Wanna sit down and get some coffee?" I asked.

"No, let's walk and talk," Marcos said. "The three letters are everywhere around here, listening to everybody."

The three letters—the DEA. "Yeah, la DEA, they're all over," I said, pronouncing it, Cali cartel style, *la daya*.

With Big Daddy tailing us, Marcos, his bodyguard, and I walked through the main streets and shopping areas of Aruba, which is always packed with tourists. Midway through our walk, as we passed crowded beaches and towering cruise ships, I told Marcos, "We're gonna do *tons* together!" echoing the words Paul Lir Alexander had told me so many times. I outlined our deal. I'd transport his kilos from Aruba to the U.S. on one of my boats, and Marcos would take it from there, distributing the load through his network. "We're ready to go whenever you are," I said.

"That's fine, Geraldo, but I want to do a hundred-kilo test shipment," he said. He told me the dope was coming from somebody named Chin Chin, a major trafficker who ran the Guajira, the jungle area of Colombia where all the coke planes took off. He said he wanted to do the hundred-kilo test load to work out any kinks. I knew he also wanted to make sure we weren't amateurs—or cops.

We shook hands and Marcos said he'd be in touch. The next morning I went back to New York.

———

A month later, late July 1996, Marcos called, saying he was ready to meet me again in Aruba and get to work on the test load. I called Gerry Francioci and told him I was heading back to Aruba with Big Daddy and our Group 93 compadres, who now included Kevin Scanlon and Mike "Muscles" McGurk, part of the crop of young, new guys who were always being sent to the group for training.

Scanlon was from NYPD. He was a city detective, 100 percent Irish, and always cracking jokes. Mike McGurk was from the DEA, an older Billy Baldwin type, on his way to becoming a good administrator, good with paperwork. Whenever anybody new started on a case with me, they'd follow along. I had a reputation for being a crazy renegade, but they were happy to learn however they could.

Before we left, the task force chief and good friend, Bill Mockler, called me in. Somehow he got wind that I had started this deal by meeting with Marcos in Bogotá. He was fuming.

"You lied to me, Jerry," Mockler said. "You broke the rules. You could have been killed. I'm sending an agent from the DEA division to keep an eye on you."

———

The babysitter's name was Mauricio Fernandez, a stocky agent of Mexican descent. He was from the DEA division upstairs and happy for a trip to sunny Aruba. The five of us—Big Daddy, McGurk, Scanlon, Mauricio, and I—flew back down to Aruba. Embassy attaché Gerry Franciosi told me he would be out of town but that I could work with his assistant, Mark Garcia. Mark worked out of headquarters in Curaçao, and he flew over to meet us.

We stood out from the moment we touched down. Five guys without women in Aruba is a rarity, because this is honeymoon country. Everywhere we looked there were couples, hand in hand. We got off the plane in our shorts and T-shirts, like five rowdy middle-aged surfers looking for a beach. We rented a car and drove to the Marriott, where we checked in.

We all met at the Marriott along with the Aruban chief of police. Over drinks in the bar, we ordered an appetizer of fried jalapeno "poppers"—deep-fried jalapenos, stuffed with cheese—to tide us over until dinner. Big Daddy must have been dealt a bad popper. All of a sudden, he turned green and got clammy and became violently ill. It turned out to be a commode-hugging case of food poisoning. He was burning up from fever and leaking from both ends of his body, effectively taking him out of the operation.

We had other problems as well.

"When Marcos flies in, you cannot leave the hotel because we had a drive-by shooting," Mark Garcia insisted.

It seemed a Dominican coke dealer on the island had been found responsible by the cartel for losing twenty-five kilos of cocaine. The bosses had sent an assassination squad to shoot the dealer. Upon finding him in Aruba, six Colombian *secarios* (assassins) formed a circle around him and started blasting away. The scene was straight out of *The Keystone Cops*. Their intended victim, the dealer, was in the intensive-care ward and wasn't expected to make it, Mark Garcia told me. But in the circle-jerk of gunfire, one of the Colombian assassins got hit by another.

"The bullet struck him in the nuts," said Mark. "Or at least near the nuts, in the groin. We can't take a chance that these are the people you're to meet with. So you gotta stay in the hotel."

"No worries, I promise," I lied. "We'll stay put."

Yeah, right. I was yessing Mark, telling him what he wanted to hear, knowing all along that I had agreed to pick up Marcos at the airport. I intended to keep my appointment, or, I knew, the deal would be off.

After Mark left with the Aruban chief of police I got a call from New York. Mark had called Chief Mockler and apprised him of the situation. "You better not leave the hotel, I'm warning you," Mockler said.

"No problem," I lied. "I'll be good."

I turned to Mike "Muscles" McGurk and my baby-sitter Mauricio and said, "You two better grow some balls. We're going to the airport to pick up Marcos—or let's go home now. Because without Marcos there is no deal."

———

When Marcos Vargas walked off the plane, down the jet bridge, onto the tarmac and passed through Aruban customs, I was there to meet him, with Mauricio alongside and McGurk and Scanlon watching from afar. I watched him walk down the steps, then toward the little terminal where we were waiting, just beyond customs.

I introduced him to Mauricio, telling him that he was my new assistant. "Everything is set," he said as we walked toward my rented van. He asked to borrow my cell phone to call the dealer who was going to give us the hundred kilos. We got into the van. "Take us to the Sonesta Hotel," Marcos said. "The guy is going to meet us there with the load."

When we arrived at the hotel, I told Marcos I'd wait in the van with Mauricio, but he wouldn't hear of it. He insisted that I come with him to meet the dealer. We took the escalator to the mezzanine level. The guy, whom Marcos called Juanito, was waiting for us in the bar. He was a big, heavyset guy, unshaven with dirty long brown hair. He looked like the typical dirt bag.

After the introductions—"Geraldo, meet Juanito"—were out of the way, Juanito stood up and dropped his pants. The next thing I knew, he was removing a gauze pad from the inner side of his left leg to show us a bullet hole. My heart skipped a beat. This was the assassin!

"*Mira*, Marcos!" he said. "Look!"

I looked around for an exit, wondering how I could get away before the other assassins showed up.

Marcos told Juanito we'd all get some rest and meet at the Marriott in the morning. Juanito invited Marcos to stay with him, so I started to leave. They stopped me.

"Where are you going, Geraldo?" Marcos said. "We need a ride, amigo."

As we drove, I was feeling paranoid. Their directions were leading to a desolate part of the island. We finally came to a little cantina/hotel. We said our good-byes and they got out. Mauricio started to drive away, but I saw Marcos chasing us down the road. He had left his suitcase in the van.

I climbed into the back of the van, which was rolling at thirty-five miles an hour, grabbed the suitcase, opened the door, and threw the bag onto the dirt road. "See you tomorrow, amigo!" I yelled. We kept driving.

Mauricio looked at me as if I were crazy. "What the hell is wrong with you?" he asked.

I had come to like Mauricio. He was a stand-up guy, and thus far he had followed me step by step. He was into having fun, a prerequisite for going on a job with me.

"You are not going to believe this," I said. "Marcos's dealer is the assassin!"

Mauricio's mouth hung down so low, I practically had to shut it for him.

It turned out that the assassin was Marcos's representative in Aruba. He would receive and store the dope and then turn it over to transporters that would bring it back to the U.S.

We got back to the hotel and decided to tell the Arubans that we'd found the wounded assassin. I'd learned an unspoken rule in undercover drug work—always follow the biggest lead. The Colombian hit squad was potentially bigger than Marcos—and, maybe, by busting the hit man, I could tie up Marcos, too.

I called Mark Garcia, the assistant to the embassy attaché, and told him the whole story. He picked me up and took me to the Aruban police headquarters downtown, where I told the cops everything.

Later that day, the Aruban prosecutor came to my room and said, "We cannot allow you to do a deal. We've got to take the killer down. Their target, the Dominican coke dealer, died today. You're in danger, Jerry."

I thought of various exit strategies. "Okay, I got it," I said. "We'll get them to my hotel room under the pretense of discussing the deal. We'll break for lunch, and when they leave you can take him down."

=====

By the time Marcos and the assassin arrived the next day to discuss the deal, we had the hotel room wired. We'd brought a special camera from New York, supplied by the DEA tech people. In the room where I'd meet with Marcos and the assassin, we had the camera linked to the TV in the adjoining room, where Big Daddy, Mike McGurk, and Kevin Scanlon would watch and record the meeting.

When Marcos and Juanito, the assassin, arrived, Mauricio and I frisked them for weapons. That was not standard practice in the drug-dealing world, where everybody carries a weapon, but we were dealing with a cold-blooded killer. I poured Bloody Marys for everybody and got them to take me through the whole thing.

Marcos outlined the Chin Chin plan, how we would put a hundred kilos on a cruise boat, and how it would be distributed. Hoping to get Juanito to confess on tape, I looked at him and said, "How the hell did you get a bullet hole in your leg? You a nice guy or what? How do I know I'm not getting set up to be ripped off?"

He seemed glad to unburden his mental load as he told us how he shot this Dominican dealer who lost a load, and how he was shot in the cross fire.

Next, I needed to implicate Marcos.

I looked at Marcos. "You still haven't told me how you are going to guarantee that I'll be paid," I said.

He gave me some lame answer, but it was enough. We had the killer's confession and Marcos's compliance, and it was time to take them down.

I let Crazy Jerry take over. I had an electric money-counter in the room so I grabbed the cord and tied it in a loop and shook it at the assassin. "I'm gonna wrap this cord around your neck and throw you off the balcony," I said.

Marcos looked at me as if I were crazy.

"You know what?" I said. "I need to calm down a minute. Let's break for an hour and meet back here. I've got to make some phone calls back to the States."

They walked out of my room, but the dim-witted Aruban cops

missed them. Marcos and the killer made it all the way to the parking lot, and the police still hadn't taken them down. I went running down and charged the assassin again. I grabbed him by the back of his shirt and wrestled him to the ground.

Next thing I knew, the Aruban police drove over the hedges in the parking lot, scattering the tourists who were everywhere. It was pure chaos. When the cops climbed out of their cars, I saw that they were wearing suits with white socks and black shoes. I had to laugh. But they got Marcos.

The Arubans prosecuted the assassin for murder and sent him to jail. Marcos was arrested on our provisional arrest warrant. But when we tried to expel him, the Arubans instead of helping us, extradited him back to Colombia, where he was eventually released.

Once again, we had gone to all the trouble of nailing a major drug dealer—only to see him freed to go back about his business. It was getting downright ridiculous.

19

Road Rage

Tocayo and Ricky were practically panting on my doorstep when I got home from Aruba.

Ricky was, of course, grateful to me for getting him out of Riker's Island on a $10 million bail in time to visit his father, who was dying in Colombia. To show his gratitude, he said, he'd brought Tocayo, who blew the whistle on the Salazar organization, to New York. So there they were, two clean-cut, young Colombians, eager to do a deal.

"We wanna give you some information for a wiretap, Jerry," Ricky said.

He said they knew a group that I could bust for money laundering. The leader was a major Cali bigwig named Diego Montoya.

We were in our DEA offices. Our meeting was late in the day, when most of my Group 93 colleagues had gone home, except for a new guy, Brian Schneticker, whom we called Sneed. He was an ex-military guy and was one wacky character. When he first came into the group, he was an oddball, just like the rest of us. He had a "gilly suit," a camouflage suit that makes a man look like a tree. When we'd be on surveillance, he'd say, "Do you want me to get the gilly suit?" And there he'd be, in the middle of Manhattan, dressed like a bush.

I told Brian that I needed his help as a witness. At that point, I had been betrayed by Paul, and I was still shell-shocked by all the internal affairs innuendoes and accusations. That's why I brought Brian into the conversation. "I've got these two informants who want to give me some information about the next case Group 93 is going to do," I told him.

We brought Ricky and Tocayo into a room where we could debrief them. Brian and I sat on one side of the desk, Ricky and Tocayo on the other. Tocayo was wearing cowboy boots.

"Diego Montoya is a major cocaine producer who runs laboratories in the jungles of Colombia," Tocayo said. "The sales of his coke generates huge sums of money that is collected and laundered by US-based money launders, who funnel the profits back to the Montoya organization in Colombia. They export the cash in bulk cargo out of the Port of Miami."

Sounded good, so I let him continue. When he started asking me stupid questions, my BS antennae shot skyward. Tocayo was asking me hypotheticals. What if we didn't touch Montoya's money-laundering cell and we just went after the New York drug dealers who were dropping off payments?

"Let's not talk in riddles," I said, at last. "What are you trying to say?"

Basically, he wanted me to allow the six guys in the money-laundering cell to receive money from drug dealers and only go after the drug dealers that were bringing the money in. Tocayo told me that if I went after the six in Montoya's group, they would know that he had flipped, and he would get whacked.

I had a funny feeling that Tocayo was up to no good. My sixth sense told me not to trust him. I didn't want to lose the deal, but I didn't want to commit to his terms. I pulled out a legal pad to document everything. I drew a diagram on the pad, showing how the operation they were describing worked. My diagram led Tocayo to believe that Montoya's money launderers were safe, but I didn't say anything in that regard. I didn't have any intention of leaving anybody out of the bust. I was going to take them all down.

"Okay, here's the deal," I said. "We'll try not to hit Montoya's money laundering group, but I'll have to get everything approved by the special narcotics prosecutor's office."

He nodded. "Fair enough," he said.

"Yeah, but I gotta warn you. There are a multitude of other agencies in New York that could end up stumbling on Montoya's organization, so Montoya's people are not gonna get away. If somebody else hits it, somebody else hits it. As if we get the money cells involved in this, we're going to hit the money laundering cells."

He shrugged. So far, so good.

Tocayo and Ricky gave me six phone numbers, which we turned over to the wiretap room for immediate surveillance. Meanwhile, I wrote a wiretap order for the phones of all six of the money launderers, the guys Tocayo didn't want us to hit. The wiretaps commenced on February 10, 1996, and we began listening to this group of money launderers controlled by someone called "Code 119." We quickly realized that millions of dollars were being moved through this money-laundering cell.

I had to find out where the money was being delivered. I was obsessed with trying to bring down Montoya's six money launderers, who Tocayo didn't want me to touch. But they turned out to be the most disciplined organization I've ever come up against. They would never talk outside their circle, never call a hard-line phone at someone's house, never call a pager. They would only call the six phones. So we couldn't find them. Their communication system made Caliche's look amateurish.

By then, I was an expert in cellular telephones. Bernie Kerik and I had written the "Use of Cellular Intercepts in Organizational Targeting" manual for the U.S. Justice Department, which was being used by investigators for wiretaps across the U.S. and abroad. But all I could discover was that there was one worker, obviously sitting in a stash house, because the other five guys were always talking about counting money. The guy never seemed to leave the house. Food was brought in to him by the other workers.

I did a comparison study of his phone and saw that it received incoming and made outgoing calls from the same cell site location every single day. The phone never moved out of the cell site, which was in Brentwood, Long Island. Because the phone was hitting off of that particular site, I knew the caller must have been within a couple of miles of the cell site tower. So I called my friend Gary Suttcliffe, an engineer at AT&T Wireless, the cellular carrier for the guy's phone, and asked for the exact location of the Brentwood cell site.

It was on Crooked Hill Road. I got a map of the area and asked where the cell sites would be in the adjoining area. Gary Suttcliffe told me that you could only be within a three-mile radius of the tower at

925 Crooked Hill Road, because cell sites have three sides to them, A, B, and C. I knew from Gary that this guy's phone kept hitting off of the B side, the north side of the tower. If he could only be three miles away from 925 Crooked Hill Road and his phone always hit off of the B side, he had to be due north of that address.

I sent Big Daddy and Jerry Neville out to the tower with a compass.

I told them to put a compass on the map and go directly north from 925 Crooked Hill Road. They found themselves in a fancy residential neighborhood with $2 million houses on Stonehurst Lane in Brentwood.

Next, I heard one of the money mules call the stash house. Again, the call came off of the B side, so I knew the guy still had to be in the same location. I worked late into the night, trying to figure out where he was. Meanwhile, I had our guys out on 925 Crooked Hill Road, riding around in a three-mile radius. It was like trying to find a needle in a haystack.

At around midnight, one of the monitors from the wiretap plant called me. "We just got another call and it appears that the boss is speaking to someone at a stash house," she said.

"What did they say?" I asked.

"The guy in the stash house said to pick him up at seven-thirty tomorrow morning and that they'd bring the money to the warehouse to go south," she said.

"Did they say anything else?" I said.

"The guy in the stash house said to pick him up an Egg McMuffin," the operator said. "That's the only other thing they said."

Group 93's Jerry Neville was out in the field going in circles around 925 Crooked Hill Road.

I called him. "Jerry, listen, I just heard this guy say that they're going to do a money drop tomorrow early in the morning," I said. "Is there a McDonald's anywhere near this radius?"

"Yeah, there's a McDonald's right on the corner," Jerry said.

"Okay, fine, let's get everybody, and we'll set up there at five tomorrow morning," I said.

The next morning, February 24, at 5:30, I was set up with Big Daddy and the rest of the group at the McDonald's. At 7:00 sharp, a gray

Oldsmobile driven by a Colombian-looking guy pulled into the Mc-Donald's and drove back out. We ran the license plate on the car; it came back to a post office box in Manhattan, a place we knew to be a mail drop.

"This is too much of a coincidence," I told Big Daddy. "That's got to be our guy. Let's follow him."

Big Daddy and I followed that car out of the McDonald's, and he drove right into the Stonehurst Lane neighborhood, which I'd staked out the night before. It was a cold, rainy morning, typical New York weather for February. So cold we could see our breath.

Two hours later, about nine o'clock, the guy in the gray Olds came driving out of the neighborhood. We followed him all the way over to Plainview, Long Island, where we watched him take two cases of canned tomatoes out of his trunk and walk into a warehouse for a company called PNC Tropicals.

I called for helicopter backup to assist in surveillance. The Colombian targets inside the warehouse became anxious when they heard the chopper, and we could hear them discussing the noise over our wire-tap. They thought they had been followed. I told the helicopter to get the hell away and everybody to lie back.

PNC Tropicals was in a U-shaped complex of warehouses. I went into the warehouse directly across from PNC's back door, identified myself as a policeman, and asked to borrow their back room for surveillance. The manager flashed me a big grin and said, "Anything you want." As usual, the civilians got excited. Most people love the excitement of being part of a police operation. They usually open their doors without even asking for ID.

From that vantage point, Big Daddy and I could see a Rowland's Rents tractor-trailer with Miami plates backed up to the back door of PNC Tropicals. Now I knew the laundered money had come out of the stash house and gone to the warehouse. I also knew that I had a big tractor-trailer backed up to the warehouse I figured the tractor-trailer had to be loaded with money. Not enough evidence for a warrant. But there had to be something going on.

More Colombians arrived at PNC Tropical. They started up a fork-lift and loaded the tractor-trailer with big pallets of boxes. Through my binoculars, I could see the label on the boxes. They were filled with cans of tomatoes. I could even read the fine print: whole, plum, crushed, and tomato paste. Each box contained six six-pound cans. Although I didn't know it at the time, there would turn out to be 5,400 cans of tomatoes onboard this tractor-trailer, a number that would soon become a major factor in the investigation—and my life.

Meanwhile, the entire Group 93 had arrived at PNC Tropical with me, all twelve of us, from Eddie Beach on down, along with some of the brass, watching and waiting for the tractor-trailer to leave. Around 9:30 in the morning, the tractor-trailer pulled out. We all climbed into our unmarked, undercover cars, and began radioing back and forth. My car was a green Monte Carlo with dark, tinted windows. We followed the rig onto the highway out of Long Island.

I thought I was headed out on a typical surveillance. Boy, was I wrong.

━━━

I had just begun following the tractor-trailer when my cell phone rang. It was Ricky. "Hey, Jerry, Tocayo called me from down in Colombia," he said. "He wants to know if anybody is watching a warehouse and tractor-trailer somewhere out in Long Island."

I played dumb. "I don't know about a warehouse," I lied. "Find out more about this tractor-trailer and this warehouse, wherever it is, and let me know. Then maybe I'll be able to find it."

I barreled after the tractor-trailer rig through New Jersey. Eddie Beach was in another car, ready to bust the rig right then and there. But I held him back. "No, we can't hit this thing until we get it at least a couple of states away," I said. "How about this for an idea? When the driver gets out of the truck for a break, I'll hot-wire it, jump in, and drive away. We'll let the driver think that his truck has been stolen. He knows he's carrying contraband. Who's he gonna call?"

Eddie said okay, but be careful. Are you sure you can do it?'"

"Without a doubt," I told Eddie, "But I need a little time."

While I was driving, I called Don Campanello, a friend of mine who knew tractor-trailers, over at Camp's Auto Wreckers in my hometown of Wayne, New Jersey. I gave him the make and model of the tractor-trailer and asked him how to hot-wire it. In ten minutes, I was ready to steal this truck as soon as the driver took his first toilet break.

Looking back on it now, I have to admit I was already a little out of control. I didn't think anything was out of whack—not when I tried to drop back and let somebody else from the group take the lead in the surveillance so the target wouldn't keep seeing the same car behind him; not when I made an illegal U-turn on the freeway; and not when I smashed into a woman's car as she drove through the toll booth.

In my mind, this was a major surveillance, warranting aggressive action. The woman had a little kid in the car. They were both okay, thank God, but my government car was totaled.

I called Big Daddy and said, "I hit a little snag. Can you come and pick me up?" He was there in ten minutes.

I called the New Jersey State Police on my cell phone. The second they showed up, I threw them the keys. "I'm leaving the car with you," I said. "Everything was all my fault. Write it up that way in the report, but I'm on a major case, and I've got to run."

I jumped in Big Daddy's car, and within a half hour we were barreling down the road, Big Daddy driving and me ranting and raving from the passenger seat. We were behind the tractor-trailer as it crossed into Delaware.

The driver pulled over at the first gas station across the Delaware state line. As soon as he went into the men's room, I jumped out of Big Daddy's car and tried to hot-wire the truck, but I didn't have enough time. The driver was back in a flash. I ducked out of the way before he spotted me. We continued tailing him. By now, it was Thursday evening. I hadn't slept in two days.

———

We followed the rig to Maryland. The driver pulled over at a state police weigh station, where he was checked out by the troopers, who by now knew exactly what was going on. We were looking for help to stop the tractor-trailer, so we could hijack the truck and bring it back. But everybody was giving us a hard time, because all of the local law enforcement agencies wanted to be in on the seizure. We were yelling over the radio, which I thought was point-to-point. But the radio transmissions were monitored by the local police station.

They looked through the rig, trying to find something to seize, but couldn't find anything but a load of tomato cans. So the guy got waved through. He drove through Virginia and pulled over in a place called Portville, on the Virginia-North Carolina border, where, we guessed, he planned to spend the night.

Because I was in Virginia jurisdiction, I called the local DEA and the Virginia State Police. I explained that we'd come upon a major money-laundering operation on a wiretap, and had followed a truck that we believed was filled with contraband cash into Virginia. But we had some informants who could get killed if the situation wasn't handled carefully.

"We have to take this truck under some sort of ruse, so they never know that law enforcement from New York actually intercepted it," I said. "We have to make it look like an accident."

I must have sounded like Paul Lir Alexander in full-bore "pin it back" mode. But the Virginia State Police went by the book. "If it's in Virginia, we're going to pull it over, seize the truck, and arrest the guy, and use the New York info as the foundation for the search" the Virginia State Police rep said.

"Forget it, buddy, that ain't gonna happen," I said.

"Then you ain't doing this in Virginia," he said.

It was typical. Law enforcement fighting with law enforcement, instead of working together as a team. I got in a battle royal with Ben Butcher, the acting resident agent in charge of the Virginia DEA field office in Richmond. I also got into an argument with the Virginia State Police assistant special agent in charge of narcotics. Finally, I told them all to go to hell. I called the DEA in North Carolina, where, I figured, the driver was heading next. They agreed to meet us on the Virginia-North Carolina border and assist us as soon as the tractor-trailer crossed the state line.

We came up with a plan. The North Carolina troopers in an unmarked car would stop the truck, I would steal it and drive it back to New York. By now I had gone three days without sleep.

———

Big Daddy and I, along with the other guys from Group 93, guarded the truck all night long. Bright and early Friday morning, the truck left Portville, Virginia, and the driver got pulled over at the first weigh station. The Virginia State Police worked with the Virginia branch of the DEA, and the DEA has a universal channel on the radio, so they had been monitoring all our radio transmissions. All day and night we had radioed back and forth. "Okay, it's at mile post number ten. . . . Okay, it's just going up onto the weigh station," and on and on. The

Virginia State Police had been monitoring everything. They even heard us call them "assholes."

We had led them right to the truck, and they decided to screw us. So they pulled the truck over, and while it was being weighed, they ran a drug dog on it. At the dog's first bark, they were ready to rip the cargo apart in a full search and seizure, burning me, Ricky and Tocayo in the process.

"We've got to get over there and stop this," I said.

Big Daddy and I raced over to the Virginia weigh station and I identified myself. I told one of the Virginia troopers what was going on, that we had a major investigation, that this tractor-trailer was loaded, and that we had to let it continue down the highway. Knowing the truth wouldn't be enough to persuade them, I added a lie. "We're going to let the truck go all the way to Miami, so we can locate the warehouse and the recipients. If you don't let it through, you're going to totally screw up a major investigation."

Finally, he called the DEA in Richmond and put me back on the phone with Ben Butcher, who had told me earlier that he couldn't assist us. This time, he relented.

"Ben, look, you know the deal, it's a major investigation," I said. "We've got wiretaps, and informants could be killed. This truck has got to be released."

Ben got back on with the state trooper and told him, "Look, let the truck go."

After about two hours of being jerked around, the driver was allowed to leave. The truck rolled over the North Carolina-Virginia state line. As soon as it did—*boom!*—North Carolina troopers pulled him over. I saw the troopers grab the driver and bring him back to their car. While they were talking to him, Big Daddy and I jumped into the tractor-trailer and, grinding gears, pulled a U-turn on I-95 and started barreling that babe north.

When we passed the same Virginia weigh station northbound on Route 95, the troopers came flying out like a nest of hornets to chase me. One of them pulled out in front of us to try and stop us. I swerved wildly and left him in the dust, grazing his car in the process. Big Daddy and I continued speeding down the road, leaving Eddie Beach and the others to try and calm the cops we'd left behind.

"You're crazy, Jerry," Big Daddy said.

"No, I'm not, look," I said, motioning to the other cars.

Everyone else had moved out of the way, fast.

"Shut down I-95 until we get to Maryland," I phoned back to my guys in Group 93, who were at various points on the road, trying to back me up. I was driving this eighteen-wheeler like a bat out of hell, convinced that it was loaded with a fortune in cash.

On the road, I kept getting calls from Ricky, telling me Tocayo said everything was okay and that the tractor-trailer he'd called me earlier about must have made its way safely on its journey. By then, I wasn't ready to play phone games.

"That's fine, Ricky, but you better tell Tocayo that he better not be dirty and he better not be lying to me," I shouted. "Because if he is, he's going to jail."

I was barreling north to New York, and the only route was I-95 through Virginia. I had just crossed the Virginia state line when I remembered the lie I had told the troopers, that we were going to follow the tractor-trailer all the way to Miami. As soon as I crossed back into Virginia, the troopers recognized the truck and started chasing me. Of course, I wouldn't pull over. Not having slept in what was now three days, I wasn't thinking straight. In my mind, this was a federal seizure, part of a DEA investigation, so I wasn't going to stop for anybody. I just kept driving, eighty miles an hour with one particularly aggressive trooper in full-chase mode, sirens and lights blazing.

I called Eddie Beach. "Surround that trooper and stop him from following me," I said. "Make sure he understands. If he gets in front of me, I'm going to drive over the top of him."

Eddie said, "Whatever you do, don't stop until you get into Maryland."

Eddie and the guys pulled the trooper over and explained it all to him. I was exhausted by the time I made it halfway through Maryland. I called Eddie and told him that I needed to stop and get a hotel for the night.

"Can't do that, Jerry," Eddie said. "Maryland law enforcement is friendly with Virginia law enforcement and they could make problems for us. You gotta get to Delaware."

When I got to the last tollbooth in Maryland, right before the Delaware border, I almost took out the tollbooth attendant, driving so fast that the truck's side mirror nearly slapped him in the face. By then, I was delirious.

I called Eddie again. "I'm so tired," I said. "I gotta stop, now. I just saw the inspection sticker move across the windshield. I'm hallucinating."

But Eddie said no. "Don't stop, Jerry, just keep going," he said. "It's only two more exits until the Holiday Inn in Delaware."

Just before I pulled into the Holiday Inn, Tocayo called me and said he had been told everything about what was going on. "You gotta let the truck go or we're gonna get killed!" he said.

"Screw you, pal," I said. "You're double-crossing me. You're dirty and you're going to jail. I just ran the tractor-trailer full of cash through the Virginia State Police, and this rig's headed back to New York."

———

It was about 8:00 P.M. Thursday when we parked at the Delaware Holiday Inn and got one room for Big Daddy and me. We had been going nonstop since Tuesday. Big Daddy went straight to bed. But I thought I'd unwind and wash my week-old clothes.

A few hours later, I was outside in the middle of the motel courtyard, causing a ruckus. Big Daddy peeked out to find me dressed in nothing but a bedspread. I still can't remember where I found that bedspread.

"What the hell are you doing?" Big Daddy asked.

"I'm washing my clothes," I said. My clothes were filthy. Once I got to the room, now delirious, I had wrapped myself in the bedspread, walked through the main part of the motel, and took my clothes to the motel laundry.

Meanwhile, Eddie Beach and the other guys were watching the truck to make sure that no one tried to steal it back.

It was 1:00 A.M. when I crawled into bed. But the booze kept me awake.

At 4:00 A.M., we hit the road again. I roared through Delaware and New Jersey and on toward the New York headquarters of the DEA.

———

We could see the Manhattan skyline as I came up on the turnpike. It was one of those brilliantly sunny New York mornings, and the city glittered bright, new, and welcoming. I tried to go through the Holland

Tunnel, but the truck was too tall. So I took the George Washington Bridge and River Road. I had already alerted headquarters, and they called the New York district attorney, who called the U.S. Attorney. Everybody from New York to Washington had been alerted that Group 93 was involved in a "major incident," which included a stolen truck and two car crashes.

"We made it," said Big Daddy with a sigh of relief, as we headed toward headquarters. "Now we gotta unload this stuff to see what we've got."

There were about a hundred people waiting for the truck by the time Big Daddy and I pulled into the big fenced parking lot that adjoined DEA headquarters on Tenth Avenue. Everybody in Group 93, along with anybody remotely connected to the DEA, from clerical staff to lab technicians to NYPD, State Police, *everybody* came out to greet Group 93, who'd blasted across four states, through cops and roadblocks, to deliver a truckload of what, I was certain, was one giant cash seizure.

I just hoped that I was right.

20

Knee Deep in Tomatoes

"I got it!" I was yelling to the waiting crowd as Big Daddy and I backed the tractor-trailer rig into the fenced lot down on 99 Tenth Avenue. It was a sunny but cold February morning at around eight o'clock. By then, I had gone almost five days without sleep and was far too out of it to know how truly crazed I'd become. "I got it! I got it!" I kept yelling. "I got it!"

By the time we pulled in to Manhattan, I had secured a search warrant for the contents of the trailer by telephone, through the special narcotics prosecutor's office. The prosecutor's reps ran over to the judge, explained the situation, and got an immediate search warrant for the truck and its contents. But when Big Daddy and I climbed down from the cab and opened the back door, all everybody saw was a truck filled only with . . . canned tomatoes.

"I got it!" I yelled again.

"Yeah, you got it, Jerry." Someone laughed. "Anybody want a pizza?"

I was convinced that the dealers had hidden the cash in the truck—or the tomato cans.

"Get me a forklift!" I said.

By now, the entire group, along with members of other groups, as well as bosses, secretaries, and various civilians from the DEA offices upstairs, were gathered around and looking out of windows to see what all of the commotion was about.

240

Nobody had a forklift. I raced over to Western Beef, a nearby meat-packing place, and borrowed one. I drove it down Fourteenth Street and back to the truck at the DEA office.

"We're going for it!" I yelled out on my return. I used the forklift to unload all sixteen pallets from the back of the truck. Boxes of tomato cans were shrink-wrapped onto the pallets.

"Rip them open!" I instructed once the pallets were on the ground.

Everybody began ripping open the shrink-wrapping off the pallets. Once that was done, we stood there looking at a parking lot full of boxes of tomato cans. I climbed up into the back of the truck with a flashlight. I asked Big Daddy, Eddie Beach, and Eddie O'Casio to come up into the trailer with me and we ripped that rig apart. Nothing. No drugs. No cash.

"I know it's there," I insisted. "Call the dogs."

It was 10:00 A.M. Friday when the two drug dogs arrived from NYPD. They sniffed here, there, everywhere, and came up with nothing. One of the dogs seemed so bored that he urinated on a box of cans.

The pressure was on me. I'd made everyone drive across the country. I'd burned bridges with the Virginia State Police. I'd spent a fortune in time and money on this operation. If the cans contained only tomatoes, then my name would be mud.

I stared at the boxes of tomato cans. They looked absolutely normal, but then something happened that made me even more certain that the cans were filled with cash.

My cell phone rang. It was Mike De Francisi, resident agent in charge of the Long Island office of the DEA.

"Jerry, you won't believe what I just found," he said.

"Tell me something positive," I said. "I need something, anything positive."

He said he'd just hit the mansion in the fancy Stonehurst neighborhood where we'd watched the guy from the McDonald's take the two cases of tomatoes. "Something strange is going on out here," De Francisi said. "There's a canning machine, a heat-sealing machine for plastic, a one-ton press, and tons of carbon paper. . . ."

"All right, the cash is definitely in the cans," I said, then turned to the guys again.

"Get me an X-ray machine!" I said.

Within the hour, a representative from U.S. customs pulled into the parking lot in a Ford Econoline van. The rep crawled out and opened the van's sliding side door. Inside, there was a elaborate X-ray machine. It looked just like one of those airport security machines, with a conveyor belt to run things through the scanner. The group formed a chain and began feeding carton after carton through the machine, while the customs agent watched a monitor.

After examining all eight hundred boxes, the customs agent shook his head. "Sorry, Jerry," he said. "There's nothing there."

"No, no, there's gotta be!" I insisted. "I want you to X-ray each can."

There were 5,400 cans of tomatoes. He shook his head, but said he'd do it if we'd unpack the boxes. We went to work, and soon 5,400 six-pound Hunts Tomato cans were being passed through the X-ray machine.

Again, nothing.

"I'm telling you, this is a two-hundred-and-fifty-thousand-dollar machine," said the customs agent. "It's worth its weight in gold, and it never fails. If there's anything but tomatoes in those cans, I'll give you the machine. I'm one hundred percent positive there's no money in those cans."

He started to pack up the machine, but I stopped him. "Send 'em through again," I insisted. Once again, we formed the human chain, passing 5,400 cans through the X-ray machine. Once again, the customs agent shook his head.

"Still, nothing but tomatoes, Jerry," he said, and this time he packed up for good and left.

I gathered the dozen guys in the group and looked at their tired and dirty faces. They all wanted to call it a day, to go home, and maybe they thought I'd come to my senses and was going to quit. Instead, I fished in my jeans and pulled a handful of bills.

"Here's some cash," I said. "Go buy thirty can openers and get a Dumpster over here. We're opening every one of these cans."

"You're absolutely nuts!" Big Daddy said.

"You gave it a shot, Jerry, now let's call it day," said one of the lieutenants who had come downstairs from the offices.

Eddie O'Casio, my trusty assistant, scurried up. "Okay, boss, I'll go get 'em," he said.

I think I heard the whole parking lot full of people groan in unison.

Within fifteen minutes, Eddie O returned with a sackful of manual can openers. We pulled over a Dumpster from the far side of the parking lot. I opened the first can, twisting the can opener around the big can, emptying out the contents slowly into a Hefty bag held by Big Daddy, each of us scanning the red slop for the telltale green of cash, and getting splattered with tomato sauce in the process. Sure enough, the can contained nothing but tomatoes. I put the can aside, then grabbed another. Everybody was looking at me as if I were crazy.

"C'mon, gimme a hand!" I said.

So the group gathered around once more, each of the twelve guys grabbing a can opener, twisting open can after can, pouring the contents into a Hefty bag, scanning the slop for green, then tossing the bag and its contents into the Dumpster, getting splattered with tomato sauce in the process.

By the time we'd opened half the cans, I turned to Big Daddy—or at least I thought it was Big Daddy. He looked as if he'd been in a gunfight; bloodred sauce soaked his hair, dripped from his beard, covered his clothes. Tomato paste, stewed, plum, skinned, every kind of tomato—you name it, he was wearing it, as was everybody else in the group.

Just then, a pizza delivery guy drove onto the parking lot, got out, and came over to us with two pizza boxes. "Who ordered the two large pies, no sauce?" he asked.

I looked up at the building adjoining the parking lot and could see the leering faces of the bureaucratic DEA loons above. Cop humor. "Fuck you!" I told the pizza guy, who looked around, oblivious.

To facilitate the disposing of the Hefty bags full of tomatoes, we'd built a set of makeshift stairs to the Dumpster, and, pretty soon, the stairs were covered in tomato sauce. On one of my many trips up the stairs to the Dumpster, I slipped and ruptured my Achilles tendon— which had already been injured years before. But that didn't stop me. I limped through the final cans, determined to find that fortune in drug money.

By the time night fell, we had huge floodlights set up in the parking lot, which lit the tomato sauce that covered everybody and made everything and everybody look like extras out of a horror movie. By 8:00 P.M., we had opened all but a hundred of the 5,400 cans, which yielded nothing but tomatoes. Finally, I threw down an empty can and pulled out my phone and called Ricky. He sounded more panicked than me.

"What the hell is going on, Jerry?" Ricky said. "Tocayo said a truck was taken in Virginia, and that we're going to get killed. They think we tipped off the cops to the operation."

I didn't let on that I knew anything.

"Why are they so interested in the truck?" I asked. "Is there something in it?"

"No, there's nothing in it," Ricky said.

"Then why are you so concerned?" I asked.

He wouldn't admit anything. I went over to Eddie Beach. "Eddie, something's not right," I said. "I think this guy, Tocayo, is double-crossing me, just like Paul did."

Eddie, covered in tomato sauce, waved me away.

"You're crazy, Jerry" was all he said.

Was Eddie Beach in on this? I thought. We'd been through everything together, but I was convinced that he was conspiring against me. "I'm sorry, Eddie, I gotta check you for a wire," I said, and I patted him down.

"You're nuts, Jerry," he said again, and he walked away.

After that conversation pushed me to the brink, the next one pushed me over. I called Maggie to check in. She barely said hello. "Are you ever coming home?" was her greeting. I tried to explain but must have sounded unintelligible.

"You sound exhausted, Jerry," Maggie said. "Please, just come home."

When I saw her last, I thought I was going to work for the day. Now it had been nearly a week. I was wearing the same clothes I'd left in.

"Are you going to kill yourself for this job?" she asked.

"Just mind your own business," I said, and I hung up on her.

When I got back the tomato cans, Brian Schneticker, the wacky ex-military Group 93 member who loved to disguise himself as a tree, told me that he'd gotten a call from the wire room, where our monitors where still covering the six phones.

"They kidnapped one of the guys and they're gonna kill him," Brian said.

A prosecutor was standing next to Brian, because this was a big case and the special narcotics prosecutor's office had sent someone over to observe everything. Seeing the prosecutor—and hearing Brian saying somebody, who I knew must be either Ricky, Tocayo or one of Montoya's money launderers, was going to get killed—really pushed me over the edge. Brian sounded crazy, like a cold, callous agent who didn't care if somebody got whacked.

"Screw them, maybe they will kill him," he said. "That'd be great if they killed the guy. He'll get what he deserves."

I thought that, by saying that in front of a prosecutor, Brian was sanctioning the death of either my informants or one of the money launderers, and I went nuts. From that point forward, I thought everyone was dirty. I went back to the truck, where there were still a hundred cans left to be opened. The tomato-splattered guys were opening them, can after can.

I heard somebody in the group yell out, *"Jerry! We got it!"*

There were still a hundred people in the parking lot, and all of them were gathering around me, cheering and pulling me over to the cans. "Jerry, Jerry!" they were yelling. "You did it, Jerry!"

I looked over and could see Big Daddy holding this black X-ray-proof paper. I must've just stood there with my mouth open, because Big Daddy rushed over, grabbed me, and led me to a laundry bin.

"You won't believe this," he said. "The money was wrapped in carbon paper, then sealed in plastic, then put in the cans, with water and sliced black olives." (Later, an informant would reveal that the Colombians had tested the cans with tomatoes, but the acidity, when repacked without the original vacuum packing, made the cans explode upon opening. Hence the olives and olive juice).

I couldn't understand, much less conceive of, what he was trying to tell me. He grabbed my head and pointed my face into the laundry bin, which was filled with cash. "Hey, c'mon, Jerry, you did it," Big Daddy said. "It's all good."

I couldn't see it. I was like a zombie.

All I could think of was that my informant was going to get whacked. "Each of the last hundred cans had twenty-five thousand bucks hidden in them," Big Daddy said. "That's a total of two-point-five million, Jerry, one of the biggest cash seizures in history!"

Big Daddy and Eddie Beach were on both sides of me now, trying to explain how the money had been hidden. They tried to show me the inside of the cans, tried to show me that they didn't contain tomatoes, but olives and olive juice. Big Daddy and Eddie Beach tried to explain to me that the Colombians had taken hundred-dollar bills in twenty-thousand-dollar packs and pressed the money flat. They wrapped it in carbon paper reversed with the black on the outside, heat-sealed it in plastic, then put the bills in the big six-pound cans. They tried to explain to me how the packing prevented the X-ray from spotting the cash, because carbon paper is X-ray proof.

"Hey, you got the money, you got the money!" Big Daddy kept saying.

But I kept saying the same thing. "I haven't heard from 'em," I said, meaning Ricky and Tocayo. "I haven't heard from 'em."

I turned to the other members of the group, who were gathered around. Their bloodred clothes and faces were now flashing me looks of concern as I kept spewing gibberish. "Have you heard from 'em? Have you heard from 'em?" I kept asking.

"Oh, they're probably dead," said Brian Schneticker. "Who gives a fuck?"

"Fuck you!" I screamed and lunged at him.

Big Daddy grabbed me. "Calm down, Jerry, relax, relax, let's take one thing at a time," he said.

I couldn't hear their explanations. I was sick of all the death, from my first shooting, Benjamin Clark, to Avelino and Alonso, to the meat-grinding of Javier, the assassination of John Lopez. I couldn't see the money. I was hallucinating. I was standing over the laundry bin, which was brimming with cash. I was looking in but couldn't see it. I couldn't put the picture together. Everyone was cheering my name, but I thought they were cursing me. My argument with Maggie, my fear that my informant had taped me, Brian's comments with the prosecutor beside him . . . everything was a train wreck inside my sleep-deprived brain.

I had lost my ability to think rationally about what was happening around me. Feelings of paranoia multiplied exponentially. The censors in my brain that would normally filter crazy thoughts were no longer working. I couldn't reason, I couldn't think. I just wanted to leave.

Eddie Beach turned to Big Daddy. "You better take care of him! You better do something with him!"

Big Daddy grabbed me by the arm. "Look, Jerry, you're tired, go home, and we'll meet to discuss everything tomorrow," he said.

It was 12:30 A.M., February 29. I turned and walked off, as if I were headed home. "Yeah, Jerry!" the group cheered. "You got it, buddy! Let's go celebrate this thing."

I didn't hear them. I thought everybody was sanctioning the murder. Every member of Group 93 was involved. So I ran. I ran from the cash, from the tomato cans, from Group 93. I ran exactly where Paul Lir Alexander had told me to run if ever things got rough. I ran to the subway and I jumped onto the first train.

———

I got off the train at Grand Central Station. I was sure that tails were everywhere, following me. Hoping to lose them, I walked through thousands of people in the busy commuter terminal. Then I took a train to the Port Authority Bus Station, where I did the same thing. I thought of my options, and I decided that I'd be safest if I headed toward home. I walked down to the entrance of the Lincoln Tunnel, always my passageway toward home. It was teeming with bumper-to-bumper traffic.

An eighteen-wheeler was coming down the ramp. I jumped on the running board of the rig and grabbed the mirror, thinking I'd get a free ride through the tunnel. But the driver spotted me and slammed on his brakes, sending me flying to the side of the road. I hadn't been there a second when a Port Authority cop skidded to a stop, jumped out of his car, and grabbed me. He pinned me up like he was going to arrest me, and had me spread-eagle on the car. I must have looked like a desperado, with several days' growth of beard and my rumpled, tomato-sauce-saturated T-shirt and jeans.

"I got my ID in my pocket," I said, using the old ploy I learned in Harlem whenever my disguise went over too well. "Hey, dude, I'm on the job, you're gonna blow a major undercover operation right now. Just check my right pocket, you'll see ID."

The Port Authority cop took my ID from my pocket and looked it over. "I got you, bro," he said. "No problem." Still, he looked me up and down as if I were some drug addict. He even inspected my cell phone, removing the battery and checking for contraband. Then he put the battery back and let me go.

I had to get out of the Lincoln Tunnel as quickly as possible. On the New York side, there's a three-story wall. I'd passed it a million times in my commute into the city. It's a big, tall, foreboding slab of concrete rising a hundred feet.

I climbed it like a cat. Perched up on the catwalk at the top, like some filthy gargoyle, I hunkered down. Cars passed below, and I thought every one of them was a surveillance car, out searching for me. I crawled down the wall and onto a construction scaffold. Finally, I spotted a gypsy cab.

I leaped out into the roadway, dropping a dozen or more feet, and somehow landed on the hood of the cab—or at least that's how I remember it happening. I climbed into the rear seat of the cab. The surprised driver, whose license and appearance suggested he was Haitian, turned around and stared at me startled, like you'd look at somebody who'd just risen from the dead.

"Listen, pal, NYPD, let's go," I said. "I'm on a big case. Just do what I tell you to do." I guess I looked crazy enough for him not to argue with me. He went where I told him to go. Down one-way streets, the wrong way. A hundred miles an hour. This poor guy was following my every order.

I heard his radio picking up static, and I thought he was one of "them." Adding the cabbie to the hundred tails I imagined behind me, I directed him to a route that I knew had a one-lane bridge. When you come around this bend, there is a cement funnel of sorts, allowing cars only inches to pass and then inch forward.

"Speed up!" I urged the cabbie, and he stomped the accelerator. Then I saw the cement funnel and changed my tune. "Slow down, you idiot, you're gonna crash!"

When he didn't slow down, I drew back my fist and socked him. I jumped out of the car and threw my last few dollars at him because I didn't want to get locked up for stealing a cab ride.

By now, it was a pitch-black night. I climbed down from the one-lane bridge into a ravine and crossed a little river. President Clinton was giving a speech at the Meadowlands, so I was right under the flight pattern. Choppers for Air Force One were circling over my head. Of course, I was thinking they were looking for me. How could they know where I was? I figured it out: my cell phone and pager! I dismantled the pager and I dug a hole and buried it. I dismantled the cell phone, dug a different hole, and buried that.

I walked until I arrived at a nursery. I found a truck and took a shovel, rope, and some camouflage tarp material. I kept walking. After a while, I found a tree that had fallen over. I dug a deep foxhole, draped the camouflage over the tree trunk, and dug myself into one hell of a hiding place. On the perimeter of my foxhole, I made a few snare traps in case Eddie Beach and the boys stumbled onto my camp. It was midnight by the time I settled in.

———

I couldn't sleep. It was freezing, probably thirty degrees. The rain began. Freezing rain. I was wearing only a thin sweatshirt, shivering from both the cold and lack of sleep. Time passed slowly, like some bad movie. I stayed in the foxhole from midnight to eight the next night.

Starving, I crawled out to find something to eat. There was only foliage and rainwater, but that was enough for me. Every moment I was watching for the enemies that, I was convinced, were out to find me. I'd see joggers pass by, and I'd write in the mud what they were wearing. I thought they were plants from the various agencies—or from Ricky and Tocayo.

My experience in the South American jungles had taught me not to move when the leaves were crisp, when someone could hear. I waited until the rain had saturated everything, and the ground was either wet or frozen, or both. Late on my second night in the foxhole, I moved.

After a few minutes outside of my camp, I found myself on Linden Lane, in a residential development near my hometown of Wayne, New Jersey. Avoiding the streets, I cut through a series of backyards. After a week without sleep and two nights underground, I looked like hell. I was crossing through one backyard when the homeowner stepped out of his house.

"What the hell are you doing?" he yelled.

"Nothing, nothing!" I replied. "Mind your business."

I kept going.

———

By now, Maggie and our daughter, Francesca, were frantic. From our last conversation, before the tomato can incident, Maggie knew something was seriously wrong. Whenever she called or beeped me, I always called right back. In our twenty years together, she never had paged me with a 911 emergency. But on the night that I was crossing through backyards, Maggie was pregnant with our son, Jerry, and Francesca was 10.

"Is Daddy gonna ever come home?" she asked Maggie. "Am I ever gonna see my dad again?"

"Yes, you'll see him, and soon," Maggie said.

"Promise me," Franki said.

At about one that morning, Maggie paged me with a 911 alert. When I didn't call back, she called my cell phone. Since both pager and phone were buried in a New Jersey field, I couldn't respond. Finally, she called the DEA dispatch.

The operator laughed. "You're calling at one in the morning wanting me to know where your husband is? He's probably with his girlfriend." Nobody would listen to her concerns.

Maggie stayed up all night, calling every hour. Nothing. The next morning she assured Franki that everything was okay, although she had no idea where I was, or whether my fingers were getting cut off by Colombian drug dealers—or worse. All she knew was that if I could, I would have gotten in touch with her. I always had. And I wasn't.

Next, she called Eddie Beach, who thought I'd gone straight home after he last saw me in the parking lot.

"Jerry never came home last night," Maggie told him. "Is he okay?"

Soon, everybody in the group was at my house. Bernie Kerik, Eddie Beach, Terry Hartman, the whole Group 93 crew. Maggie was screaming at them, "Why are you in my house? Go find him! Don't waste your time looking for him here."

Eddie Beach called Washington and spoke to DEA administrator Thomas Constantine. Eddie told him he thought I was delirious from lack of sleep.

"Listen, he taught surveillance to agents around the world," Tommy said. "Give it up. You're not going to find Jerry until he wants to come in."

———

I decided to call Maggie and let her know that I was okay. I had a special 800 number that would go to my Group 93 office, which I had forwarded to a Warwick, New York, number that forwarded the call to my home number. This way, I was able to call toll-free from anywhere.

I called the 800 number. But somebody must have taken the call-forwarding off of the phone by accident while they were trying to find me. The phone rang in the office. Everybody but Jimmy Grace was out looking for me. Jimmy answered the phone.

"Mag?" I said, thinking maybe she was disguising her voice.

"Jerry, it's you!" Jimmy screamed. "Oh, Jesus, thank God. You're alive!"

Poor Jimmy. I loved Jimmy. We were the best of friends. But I didn't even say hello. "They got to you too, huh?" I said. "I'm done with you!"

I hung up on him.

By now, the group was worried. Most of them knew that no amount of torture would get me to jump to the other side. But you never know what's going to happen to a drug cop. If I did flip, I could do serious damage. Everybody, and their families, could be in jeopardy, if I told the Colombians everything that we'd done to them.

They had to find me, fast. Eddie Beach came up with an idea. He knew that Robert "Boogs" Rikowich and Maggie's brother, Steve Reinhardt, were two of my best friends. He knew Boogs was my best friend when we were kids, and his father-in-law, Wayne Chief of Police Joe Alvino, got me in the DEA, and that I'd known Steve since I'd met Maggie. When Eddie realized I was delirious, he figured that Boogs and Steve would be the guys I'd contact to help me.

Steve was in bed, naked with a girlfriend, when they broke his door down at nine on Saturday morning, twenty-four hours after the tomato can incident. The door was old and dilapidated so it didn't take much to smash it. Seven guys from Group 93 came running in.

"What the hell?" Steve screamed.

"Just get up and get dressed," they told him. Then Steve heard the name "Jerry Speziale," and he knew that his brother-in-law was once again up to something, although he didn't know what. At first, he thought the Colombians had snatched me. Then he called Maggie, and she explained everything.

They searched Steve's house, from his kitchen to the dump trucks that he used in his business, Reinhardt Paving. They had traps on his phones. Any incoming call would be trapped and they'd know where it was coming from.

About an hour later, boom, they came back, kicking his battered door open again. This time, they had a Wayne cop with them. No search warrant, no nothing. They went through the whole house: closets, bedrooms, kitchen, even the pots and pans. The first time, Steve thought they were just worried about me. When they came back the second time, he started getting concerned about my welfare.

Eddie Beach was barking questions. "Have you seen Jerry? Did you talk to him? Is he here? We know that if he's going to call anybody, it's going to be you. If anybody knows where he is, you do."

When Eddie and the guys went back a third time, Steve and Eddie almost had a fistfight. Each time they left Steve's house, they left a couple of surveillance cars across the street, behind some bushes. They figured he'd leave and they'd follow him straight to me.

But they were wrong about Steve. I called Boogs instead.

———

I made it to a gas station in my old Wayne, New Jersey, neighborhood. I got to a pay phone, where Boogs and I used to hang out when we were kids. When Boogs heard my voice, he said, "Oh, my God, you're alive!"

I just grunted.

"The cops just kicked Steve's door down!" he said. "They're looking everywhere for you."

"Listen, Boogs, shut up," I said. "Don't say a word, and don't call Maggie! Don't call anybody!"

"Okay, Jerry, what can I do to help?" he said.

"Remember when we were growing up and we used to hang at the gas station by your house?" I said. "Just get there."

Boogs called Steve Reinhardt. He said he'd swing around to Steve's backyard, and for Steve to sneak out and jump into Boogs's backseat. Steve did as Boogs instructed. They took off and met me at the gas station.

When I saw them pull up, I jumped into the backseat and my two friends did a double take. By the time I had explained everything, they didn't know whether to help me or turn me in. But because of the way Steve had been treated by Eddie Beach and the Group, when I told them that Eddie and the guys were out to get me, Steve and Boogs bought it 100 percent.

We dumped Boogs off with a friend, and Steve and I took off in Boogs's car. So now Steve was driving my getaway car, and I was barking out directions, "Go here, go there."

I used a phone technique I'd learned from the drug dealers. I bought a bunch of five-minute phone cards, because nobody can trace a call less than five minutes. I went from pay phone to pay phone, making two-minute calls.

I had to call Bernie Kerik. I knew he was going crazy. I figured he'd be at the house with Maggie. So I went to a phone booth and called him there.

"Your wife's going to have a miscarriage if you don't come home," he said.

I thought it was a trap, but Bernie said he was serious. "You're my best friend, Jerry," he said. "You know I would never set you up. I swear on Joey's eyes that I'm worried about Maggie and I'm worried about you."

Joey was Bernie's son, so I knew he meant it. Still, I timed our conversation. Once two minutes were up, I'd say, "Time's up, Bern." And I'd hang up. I'd call back a few minutes later and talk to him again for another two minutes.

"What the hell is wrong with you?" he said. "I'm with you, Jerry. I swear to you, I'm with you."

I didn't believe him. "I can't believe they flipped you on me, too," I said. I didn't call back. But Bernie's comments about the miscarriage weighed on me. Once again, Maggie stepped in to save me. The last remains of my grip on reality pulled me back to earth and made me decide to surrender. Not for myself. But for Maggie and our unborn child.

I called Maggie. "Don't trust anybody" was the first thing I said.

"Oh, my God!" was all she said.

"Who's at the house?" I asked.

"Everybody," she said. "They're all here to help, Jerry."

"Throw 'em out! I mean everybody!"

I could hear somebody say in the background. "He's fuckin' crazy!"

I exploded. "Go to my mother's house, and wait to hear from me there," I said.

———

Steve and I drove around for two days. We stayed at a Holiday Inn in West Jersey, where I insisted that Steve sneak me through the motel's rear entrance. My eyes were bulging out of my head, looking everywhere for the cops and Colombians, who, I was certain, were out to kill me. The minute we walked into the room, I drew the blinds and started peeking out.

Steve called Domino's for a pizza. When the deliveryman arrived, I flew out of bed to check him out through the peephole. "Go to sleep, Jerry," Steve kept insisting. But I couldn't sleep. I was running on adrenaline. I just lay in bed, staring at the ceiling.

———

Back at my mother's house, Maggie didn't know if the Colombians had me, or if I'd done something illegal. She was afraid to talk on the phones. I got a message to Maggie to get my lawyer to meet me. She drove to the Garden State Plaza shopping center, where she called my personal attorney, Linda George. I can't remember if it was day or night, only that it was March 1, three days after I'd left the group and the tomato cans.

Linda wanted to meet me at the Tick Tock Diner. I thought they'd have the place surrounded by the time I got there. I had Steve drop me off at the motel next door to the diner, where I climbed on the roof to watch it. "There they are, there they are, there they are . . ." I kept saying to myself, and, sure enough, the parking lot was filled with DEA cars.

I insisted that the location be changed to the El Bandido Restaurant out in Fairfield, New Jersey. I guided Steve on a roundabout route—through the woods, in the mud, to an industrial park across the street from the parking lot of the restaurant. I could see Linda, sitting in her car, waiting for me. I called her on Steve's cell phone and sent her on a wild-goose chase. "Go here," I'd say. "Go there." After I was convinced that nobody was tailing her, I guided her into the industrial park.

I jumped out from behind a Dumpster, looking, acting, and smelling like a week in hell. I opened her car door, jumped inside, and said, "Start driving."

21

Sleep Deprivation

"**R**elax!" my attorney, Linda George, told me as we were driving through sunlit suburban New Jersey shopping strips. "This just doesn't make sense, Jerry. You have to relax. Trust me. We'll get to the bottom of it."

That made me feel a little better, but not much. Linda and I had met ten years ago, when she was dating a good friend of mine. When their relationship ended, Linda became a friend in her own right. Over time, she became like a sister, a fixture at family dinners and holidays. She helped us whenever we had legal issues. Regardless of where she was in her life or legal business, if I called her, Linda would be there for me. I would trust her with my life.

By the time she picked me up, she had spoken to Maggie as well as John Comparetto, my lieutenant at the New York Drug Enforcement Task Force. John was a good friend and he tried to convince Linda of his support for me. He told her I was suffering from sleep deprivation and he wanted her to turn me over to him the minute she found me.

Linda took me to the house of an assistant U.S. Attorney she'd known since law school and trusted implicitly, in West Caldwell, New Jersey. After I showered and swallowed the soup they insisted I eat, Linda ran the situation past her friend. They looked at me and I could tell both of them were wondering the same thing. Was somebody really trying to set me up?

"Linda, listen, here's the deal," I said, and I took them through the whole crazy week.

I told her I thought Tocayo taped me, and I suspected he was trying to set me up to say I'd sanctioned Montoya's money-laundering organization. I filled her in on my betrayal by Paul Alexander. I went over how internal affairs of every division in New York came at me with the false allegations that I'd taken a deposit from Oscar Pozo. Linda, in her logical way, said, "Jerry, I don't see anything you did wrong."

"But you don't understand, Linda, this is the government," I said. "They shoot down planes and they lie. What would stop them from framing me for trying to have an informant killed or condoning a money-laundering operation?"

"Jerry, I think you need to check into a hotel and get some sleep," she said. "Things will be clearer to you after that."

Before I left, I told Linda to contact the NYPD and the DEA. "Tell them I'll surrender tomorrow, but I want to see my wife and my kid one last time before then," I said. "Take my family to a secret location. I'll call you in the morning and meet you there."

———

Linda called representatives of both agencies. "I represent Jerry Speziale," she said. "You can stop looking for him. He's in my custody and he's safe, everything's okay. He will surrender tomorrow. So could you tell me why you're looking for him?"

Both reps said they were only trying to help me, not incarcerate me. I hadn't done anything wrong, they said. On the contrary, I had done something right in seizing $2.5 million in the tomato cans.

"If that's the case, then Jerry needs rest and you should have no problem if I take him to a place where he can get it," Linda told them. "If he is truly your 'hero cop,' you should allow his family to get him to a hospital where he can get some help."

She added, "If you don't agree to my terms, then I'll sue you and the NYPD for the ten years that you allowed Jerry to become rundown while you stood at press conferences in front of loads of coke and money."

The brass backed down on their insistence that I surrender to them.

———

Steve drove me to a nearby Holiday Inn. I didn't sleep a wink that night. I was still paranoid, checking windows for plants.

The next morning, Steve called Linda, and I listened to the conversation as closely as if I were monitoring a wiretap. Steve wasn't really saying much, and what he did say sounded like code. I grabbed the phone.

"Jerry, you don't have to surrender," Linda said. "You haven't done anything wrong. They just want you to check into a hospital and get some rest, and see a police psychiatrist so they can 'desensitize' you from undercover exposure and sleep deprivation."

"Okay, so where do I go?" I asked.

"They want you to go to a hospital in New York City," Linda said.

"I ain't going to New York," I said.

"That's what I told them," she said. "I said, 'I don't give a damn about DEA, NYPD, FBI, or any other letter in the alphabet. Jerry's not going to New York.' But they said, 'We can cite him for being AWOL.'"

Linda said she'd called the U.S. Attorney's office, just to see if they had anything against me, and their reps said they thought I was the greatest undercover around. They told her that I was overworked for years and needed to get some rest.

"Okay, we'll surrender him tomorrow," Linda told them. "But we want him to go to our own doctor, no police psychologist."

"I want us to be in control of the situation, Jerry," Linda told me.

———

The morning of my surrender was a Sunday. Linda gathered my whole family together. She had everybody picked up and taken to Maggie's aunt Paula's house, where I would meet them: my wife, my daughter, my mother, Maggie's brothers. Everyone had to go a different route, just to make sure they weren't tailed, to make sure nobody snatched me.

Steve drove me over to Aunt Paula's, and by the time I arrived I looked like Jerry Speziale again. I had slept a couple of hours, bathed, shaved, and changed into fresh jeans and a clean T-shirt. I walked into the living room and everybody was there. For a moment, they all just stared at me. Then they rushed around me, giving me one giant bear hug, and everybody started crying, including me. With the support of my family, I felt like I could return to the living.

"Oh, Jerry" was all most of them could say. Maggie and our daughter, Franki, wouldn't leave my side. Sami Harawi, who lived with Maggie's brother Charlie, was there, too. He was part of our family. He is the head doctor of pathology at Hackensack University Medical Center.

"Jerry, you have to go to the hospital now," Sami said. "You suffered from sleep deprivation—and prolonged exposure to cold weather. You're not in trouble. Everything went good with the case. But you lost a lot of sleep and you need to go and get checked out and rest."

Hearing Sami, someone I trusted, telling me what I needed to do made me feel there was some hope for me. It was as if a giant weight had been lifted. I thought I was either going to be facing down a Colombian hit man, or going to jail and losing everything. And never seeing my family again. Now all I had to do was check into a hospital for a few days?

"Great!" I said. "This is great! I'll retire. Who cares?"

But when I got into Sami's car to go to the hospital, I started getting weird again. Sami was driving and Maggie's brother Charlie was in the backseat. I had a feeling that they weren't taking me to a hospital. *You gotta ditch 'em,* I kept thinking. *Gotta ditch 'em!*

We were headed down Highway 202 toward Sommerville when I saw a CVS drugstore. "Could we stop in there for a minute?" I asked. "I want to get a couple of magazines."

Charlie knew I didn't read magazines.

"What kind of magazines, Jerry?" he said. I rattled off a few names, and he insisted that I stay in the car while Sami went in. Charlie watched my every move. By the time Sami got back with the magazines, I had calmed down. But when we pulled up to the hospital my head was swiveling, searching for escape routes.

They took me to the emergency room, where the chief shrink, a Dr. Kraus, was waiting. He wore an immaculate white jacket and a look that somehow showed both calm and concern. I was still crazy, but not too crazy to tell my story. I recited what must have sounded like the movie version of my life, full of blood, guts, coke, and undercover craziness. Nobody had briefed the doctor about me. When I was finished with my story, he looked at me with skepticism.

"Let me try to get this straight," Dr. Kraus said. "You're Jerry

Speziale, but you're also Geraldo Bartone? You're really a DEA agent, but you're also a New York City detective who was loaned to the DEA? You're a cop, but also a coke smuggler?"

He laughed. "I guess the next thing you're going to tell me is that you flew the space shuttle, too!"

I jumped over the table and started swinging. I was ready to take him out right then and there. But before I could land a punch, a big guy in a white suit rushed into the room and hit me with a sedative. When I woke up, I was tied into a hospital bed.

———

By the time Dr. Kraus came in later that morning, I felt a little bit better, thanks to the tranquilizer-induced sleep. Dr. Kraus untied me and asked me about my story. Once again, I rolled it out like a movie. Once again, he didn't believe a word of what I was saying.

"Can you tell me about the tomatoes again, Gerald?" he kept asking, which got me thinking that he, too, was trying to set me up. The doctor had a beeper on his belt and it went off, vibrating the back of his jacket. Thinking he was wired, I bolted from the bed, shoved him up against the wall, and searched him.

"Call NYPD!" I kept ranting as he backed out of the room. I insisted that he call the medical division of the New York City Police Department. Every time an NYPD cop gets promoted, he goes to psychological services for an exam. I'd been promoted four times, so psychological services knew me and I knew them, and I even had a name, Dr. Regina Archibald. She'd know what was happening in my case.

"Call Regina Archibald!" I told Dr. Kraus. "She'll tell you everything! She's in charge of the unit!"

Dr. Kraus promised he'd call, but I could tell he didn't really trust what I was saying. He had me switched from the express three-day stay to the full-tilt seven-day stay.

———

The hospital was crazier than I was. On my second night, a woman patient crawled into bed with me. I awoke to find her, naked, beside me, eager for anything. I screamed until the nurses came running into the room. Later, at about 2:00 A.M., I heard a ruckus in the hallway. I got up and peeked out of the door. A big biker was telling the nurses, "I want my keys and you're gonna give 'em to me now! I'm leaving now! I want nothing to do with this place!"

"Relax, relax, everything's gonna be okay," the nurses said, trying to calm him. "The doctor will see you tomorrow, and we'll talk about everything then."

The biker wouldn't listen. "You see that clock right there?" he said, pointing to a wall clock. "You got thirty seconds to give me my keys or I'm jumping over that counter, and I'm gonna rip your throat out."

That did it. I was run down, but I was still a cop. I came running out of my room and clobbered him. I was rolling on the floor with this guy and the orderlies had to shoot him with a dart to sedate him and get him off of me.

The next morning, Dr. Kraus returned to my room and tried to blame the whole brawl on me. He also said he'd talked to Dr. Regina Archibald at NYPD psychological services.

"She said she didn't know anything about your case, Gerald," he said. "She said they don't let cops go to New Jersey, let alone Colombia. But she said she'd check it out and get back to me."

The next day, Maggie was in the room with me when Dr. Kraus came back and said he hadn't heard from Dr. Regina Archibald. "Gerald, I want to do some tests," he said.

"What kind of tests?" I asked.

"Bipolar, schizophrenia . . ." he said.

Once again, my temper got the best of me. I grabbed his shirt, tugging him closer to me. "Doctor, this is not BS," I said. "Everything I'm telling you is true!"

"Calm down, Gerald," he said, once again backing out of the room, this time with Maggie following.

When she came back, Maggie was crying. "Please, Jerry, you've got to calm down, not only for your own sake, but for the health of our baby," she said.

My best friend, Bernie Kerik, had warned me that Maggie was in danger of having a miscarriage because of my escapades. I thought he was just telling me that to get me to calm down and face reality. But when Maggie said it, I thought the danger could be real. Maggie said nobody believed my story, and they were ready to use the most stringent course of treatment. "They're going to use mind-altering drugs on you, and you'll never be the same."

"Mag, you know what I've been doing for the last ten years," I said. "Get somebody to explain to these people that I'm telling the truth."

"Okay, I'll do it, but you've got to calm down," she said. "You have to at least try to calm down."

I insisted that Maggie take me to a pay phone in the hallway so we could call Sami Harawi, the doctor who got me into all of this.

"You know what I've been through," I told Sami. "I trusted you. I came to this place. But everybody here thinks I'm crazy, that my whole career is a fantasy. You've gotta call Dr. Kraus and convince him that I'm telling the truth and to get in touch with task force chief Bill Mockler."

Sami said he'd do as I'd asked. When I hung up the phone, I turned to Maggie and gestured out the hospital window into the courtyard. The building was only one story high.

"Listen, Mag, either you get these people straightened out or I'm going over that wall and I'll never be found again," I said. "I just scaled the wall of the Lincoln Tunnel so don't think I can't do it."

The next morning, the doctor ran a full battery of psychological tests, for bipolar disorder, schizophrenia, everything. The tests spoke better for me than I ever could. Every test showed me to be 100% normal, but severely sleep deprived and traumatized. There was nothing psychologically wrong with me, other than the fact that I was sleep deprived.

Sami Harawi got in touch with Bill Mockler. He called Dr. Kraus and said, "Whatever Jerry Speziale tells you is true," and I was released from the hospital on Friday, March 7, five days after I'd arrived.

———

If I had been shot, everybody would have sympathized with my traumas. They would have been crying over me. But six days of sleep deprivation is something few people understand. When I reported to the NYPD Medical Unit to see the departmental shrink on Monday, March 10, they didn't know if it was the lack of sleep or if I really was crazy—and, deep down, I didn't really comprehend what had happened, either. I wanted to get my own evaluation before I went back to work.

I started meeting with an NYPD psychologist, Dr. Linda Intranova. I told her the whole story, because the police department needed to document everything that had happened between Ricky and me. After two days of sessions, Dr. Intranova said she was going to officially classify my condition as "a brief reactive psychosis from the sleep deprivation." She said she would conclude that the condition would not be recurring.

Because the NYPD has a great pension system, a lot of officers go to the psychologist and fake stress-related disorders in order to secure early retirement. I think I was the first "patient" that Dr. Intranova had treated who wasn't faking. She seemed mesmerized by the story of my journey into temporary insanity. Later, she told me I was her greatest NYPD case.

"I'm going to approve you for light duty," she said. "I think you're okay, psychologically. But I've gotta tell you something, Jerry. I've never dealt with a case like this, where someone has been put through such severe stress."

"Well, then, I'd like to see a specialist," I said.

The NYPD captain in charge said the department would pay for me to go to any shrink listed in the New York City phone book. But I wanted to go to the best cop shrink in the world, Dr. Richard Solomon of the Critical Incident Recovery Team in Baltimore. Dr. Solomon had helped the agents in the Ruby Ridge incident, when four hundred agents stormed what they believed to be a white supremacist group in rural Idaho, ultimately killing supposed leader Randy Weaver's dog, son, and wife. Dr. Solomon specialized in police traumas. NYPD wouldn't pay for me to go outside of the city for treatment, so I decided to pay for it myself. I started meeting with them on March 15, 1997.

Dr. Solomon and his team desensitized me with hypnosis, eventually delivering me from the undercover paranoid world where I'd spent the last ten years. He explained to me that sleep deprivation was a serious condition. In the Vietnam War, it was a common method of torture used to break down prisoners. Dr. Solomon and his team were the best people I've ever had the pleasure of coming into contact with.

They spent countless hours helping me get squared away, and when they learned that the NYPD wouldn't pay, they didn't charge me a dime.

Next came group therapy sessions. Dr. Solomon's Critical Incident Recovery Squad had a hotel room set up near Baltimore's Inner Harbor. They would bring in police officers that had shot someone and firefighters who had seen families burned to death for group therapy sessions. We talked about our experiences and how we could best deal with our traumas. We talked about how we'd watched lives slip through our hands, and how we could still save our own.

Through it all, one question remained in my mind. Could I go back to the career I loved? Dr. Solomon said yes, I could go back to undercover work. But he didn't think it was a good idea. He encouraged me to start thinking about other avenues of law enforcement.

"Gerald, your real problem is that you're an overachiever, a classic workaholic," Dr. Kraus told me. "You should never have let yourself be put through all of this. You need to start thinking about ways to relax."

I decided to learn how to spend time with my family. With the seaman skills I had picked up as a drug transporter, I thought that a boat might be a good way to start. I bought a forty-foot Sea Ray Sedan Bridge with twin diesels and two bedrooms, and began boating off the New Jersey coast with Maggie, our daughter Francesca, and our new baby, Jerry Jr.—my beautiful son, who had arrived healthy and hearty, relieving my concerns with his nonstop appetite and alert, intelligent eyes.

After a few months of recuperation and rest, I was ready to go back to work.

———

On April 1, 1997, I returned to Group 93. When I walked off the elevator into our cubicles, all of the group came out to greet me.

"He's back!" Eddie O'Casio said.

Everybody was all smiles. Somebody yelled, and they all greeted me with a mass bear hug.

"Craze!" said Big Daddy. "Craze is back!"

Big Daddy led me over to my cubicle, where he had taped hundreds of walnuts to the walls. "Because you're nuts!" he said.

"Fuck you!" I said.

I went right back into doing wiretaps and the usual stuff. But everyone was walking on eggshells around me. The phone would ring and I'd reach to grab it, and six guys would run to answer it. "Relax, Jerry, we got it!" they'd say. "Slow down, and don't worry about anything."

On April 8, eight days after I went back to work, I got a page from Ricky. He wanted to talk about the money-laundering operation. He demanded that I get the DEA to wire $2.5 million to Colombia immediately as repayment for losing the cash in the tomato cans—or Tocayo was going to get killed.

"Look, I know you and Tocayo are up to your eyeballs in dirt," I said. "I don't want to talk to you or see you. Tocayo was trying to scam us. He was part of that network all the time."

I hung up on him. Ricky called Eddie Beach. When Eddie wouldn't get Tocayo reimbursed, Ricky gave him a tape from our January 30 meeting, proving that I was right in my hunch that they'd taped me. He was hoping that the tape would somehow prove that I'd sanctioned Tocayo's money-laundering cell, which packed the tomato cans with cash, and that the cell wouldn't be touched. Ricky thought he'd use the tape to make me, then Eddie get the DEA to pay for the $2.5 million we seized in the tomato cans.

The next morning, Eddie Beach picked me up at my house. We were riding to work, like we always did. Eddie reached over and put his hand on my arm. "Listen, pal, you've been double-crossed again."

"What are you talking about?" I said.

"That scumbag Ricky taped your conversation and he's claiming that you sanctioned his and Montoya's money-laundering cell, then took it down," Eddie said.

I exploded. "Fuck him and fuck you, Eddie," I said. "I'm sick of dirty informers like Paul and Ronnie and Ricky. I've had enough of the double-dealing, backstabbing informants to last me a lifetime. Take me home, right now. I'm taking the day off."

"No, no, calm down, Jerry," said Eddie. "Just chill, chill."

I insisted that he turn the car around. When he got back to the house, I jumped out of the car.

"What are you doing?" Eddie asked as I was walking toward the house.

"I'm gettiin' the fuck out of here," I said. "Transcribe the tape and send it to the DA. But I'm done."

The next day, Eddie called me at home. "The tape is BS," he said. "Nothing on it. You were completely aboveboard. So why'd you get so pissed off?"

"Because I'm sick of dealing with scumbags," I said.

———

My beaten body was my passport to retirement. I had twice ruptured my Achilles tendon, most recently in the tomato can incident. I had undergone surgery on both my knees. I had been shot. I had nearly died from sleep deprivation. I knew it was time to do the administrative thing. There was no such thing as being a light-duty officer in the NYPD. There was no desk duty. You have to have the body of a twenty-one-year-old—or be crazy enough to fake it.

I filed my retirement papers with the medical division based on my physical injuries, and after an evaluation I was approved for a three-quarters disability pension. Because I had fifteen years with the force and several injuries, I was allowed to retire and receive my pension five years early.

Once my retirement was approved, I invited the whole group to join me on my boat. It was a beautiful sunny New York day when I sailed up from the Jersey shore and docked near the DEA building at the Chelsea Piers at Twenty-third Street, where I picked up everybody. We sailed into the Hudson River and I cracked open a few bottles of champagne. I raised my glass. Everybody expected me to toast to being back in business and getting back to busting the cartel.

"Well, guys, I'm hanging it up," I said. "It's been a good run."

Everybody turned silent.

"No problem, Jerry," Eddie Beach said at last. "It'll take you two years to get approved and get out."

"No, Eddie," I said. "I was approved today."

"Good for you, Jerry!" Big Daddy said. "Excellent! You deserve it!"

Eddie wished me luck. "Congratulations," he said and he shook my hand. "We're gonna miss ya, Jerry."

I sped back to the pier and dropped off the group, then turned the boat back toward Atlantic City. Undercover work had become an unhealthy addiction for me, a habit that could never be satisfied. But cruising home that evening, I knew that the chase was over for me. I had to stop—or it was going to kill me.

Epilogue

I stayed retired for five days.

Back home, I started going truly crazy. I hadn't really been home for fifteen years, so I had to learn how to do everything—wash dishes, take out the garbage, water the lawn. Everything that I should have known but was never around for. After Maggie dropped off our son, Little Jerry, at my mother's and our daughter, Franki, at school, she would go to her job at the dentist's office. I would get in my car and drive around in circles, trying to figure out what I was going to do with my life.

I went through two tanks of gas a day just driving around with nowhere to go. I had lost touch with all of my old high school friends. My only friends were the guys in Group 93, of which I was no longer a part, and whose members were moving on or retiring. I felt lost, confused, and for the first time in my life, lonely.

One day in the fall of 1997, I drove over to the Passaic County, New Jersey, sheriff's office near my home. The sheriff, Edwin Englehardt, had been up for reelection during the Salazaar case. When I needed to hide the two hundred kilos we had transported from Los Angeles, I had told him, "We're going to put two hundred kilos in a car and deliver it to a guy. When he takes it, build your own probable cause and lock him up."

The sheriff had agreed to help me. Later, he was reelected in a landslide due in no small part to the fact that this bust was the biggest seizure they had ever had in Passaic County.

"Remember me?" I asked the sheriff.

"Yeah, Jerry, of course I remember you," he replied.

"I want a job," I told him.

He flashed a big grin. "You can be the commander of my narcotics division," he replied.

I accepted on the spot.

———

This time, I did things different. I sat back and became the director of a group of younger guys. I assembled my own Passaic County version of Group 93 and began busting the bejesus out of dope dealers who were affecting Passaic County, which meant I was back to busting the cartel again. At the same time, I was able to prove to everyone who thought I was burnt-out, crazy, or in some nuthouse that I was still at the top of my game.

Our jurisdiction included the city of Paterson, and when I went to work the whole county was buried in Colombian Cali coke. Our new group began working with the Newark office of the DEA. There were about ten of us in the group, including Chris Roberts, a new, young DEA special agent who became our star, and two Passaic County identical twins, Jose and Lazaro Correa, and DEA group supervisor Mike Agrifolio, who is the best, bar-none. Chris Roberts went on to become the Jerry Speziale of the DEA, picking up where I left off. I taught him everything I knew.

We were very successful in busting the Cali cartels' operations out of New Jersey—in two years we seized approximately $30 million in fresh Cali cash. I'd been working with some old informants from Colombia. They helped me set up several successful busts in my new Passaic County assignment. One day, one of the informants called me and said, "I got a call from some big Cali guys who want to arrange a meeting with you."

The meeting was scheduled for the Marriott at the Newark Airport. I went up to a room and met with an attorney. "I represent Juan Carlos Ramirez and Victor Patino," he said in greeting.

I knew the names. Victor Patino was the head of one of the main families of the cartel, and Juan Carlos was his partner and right-hand man. The attorney told me that the Cali kingpins had a lot of respect for me, especially when they realized that Jerry Speziale in Passaic County was the legendary Geraldo Bartone from New York, who had traveled the world and taken down so many of their associates, a guy who would climb across an ocean and suck a dope dealer out of a window to bust him.

"They've asked me to talk to you, Jerry," said the attorney. "They've asked me to recruit you, to invite you to join our business."

He laid out a plan. First, they'd pay me a $250,000 signing bonus. Then they'd send me to law school. Once I got out, they'd open law offices for me in Bogotá, Miami, and New York. My mission would be to do legal work to discover why loads of coke and cash were being seized and to advise them on how to stop it.

"We feel your expertise is invaluable," the attorney told me. "You'll make millions."

"Let me get this straight," I said. "You not only want me to defend your associates, but you also want me to investigate, to figure out how the loads that the cartel is losing are being taken down?"

"Exactly, we want you to hire private investigators, so you can determine when we lose a load somewhere, how it was lost, everything," he said. "There's nothing illegal. You won't touch any drugs. You'll be rich."

I walked out, and went home to Maggie.

"You aren't gonna believe this," I said. "I met with a lawyer for Juan Carlos Ramirez and Victor Patino, and they offered me a job."

"Oh, my God!" she said.

I told her about the money they'd promised, the millions, the easiest money in the world, all just waiting for me to say yes.

"You gotta be kidding," she said. "What did you tell them?"

"What do you think I told them?"

"No," she said.

"I told 'em to go fuck themselves," I said.

We ordered a pizza and went to bed. I was back. I was home.

———

Sometimes, I think about Paul, my mentor in the drug trade. He's serving twenty-three years to life in a federal maximum-security prison in the U.S. I haven't had any contact with him since his arrest and most likely will never see him again. The work we did together put a huge dent in the Cali cocaine trade, but the trade rolls on, like a hydra-headed snake that you just can't seem to kill.

When one kingpin is taken out, another rises to the top. Even if we could take down all of the leaders of the cartel, the cocaine trade isn't going to disappear. No, a younger generation always rises up and takes over. Until somebody, or some government, goes to Colombia and wipes out the coke laboratories, the problem will never be completely solved.

Here's where the major players that we hunted are now:

- Pablo Escobar broke out of jail in Colombia and went on the run. He was tracked to a house in Medellín, where he was shot by the Colombian police.
- Victor Patino, who was one of the main suppliers in our Salazar investigation, was released from jail in Colombia in 2002. He was recently rearrested, and on December 10, 2002 was extradited to the U.S., where he is awaiting trial in Miami on Federal Title 21 drug importation charges.
- Juan Carlos Ramirez, also a major supplier for the Salazar case, was also released from prison in Colombia. There are numerous arrest warrants in the U.S. for him, but he is apparently still at large and most likely still in business.
- Helmer Herrera, the Cali kingpin whose nephew Freddy was the first major conduit for our success, was assassinated by what was believed to be a rival Cali associate while serving time in prison in Cali, Colombia.

When Group 93 was hammering the cartels, the United States pressured the Colombian government to establish an extradition treaty. Although a treaty was eventually ratified for new crimes committed by Colombian traffickers after 1997, the Colombian government decreed that anyone who committed trafficking crimes prior to 1997 would not be subject to extradition.

Even that flimsy treaty came with a catch. Drug traffickers could only be extradited if they hadn't been charged with any crimes in Colombia. If they had been charged by Colombian law enforcement, they'd have to remain in Colombia. That gave the cartel kingpins and their associates a giant loophole. If they hadn't been charged with a crime by the Colombian government, they turned themselves in before the treaty was signed. So the major players, Pablo Escobar, Victor Patino, Juan Carlos Ramirez, did their usually short jail time in Colombia, never to be extradited to the U.S.

And the jails? Give me a break. The Colombian government had a program where the prisoners paid to build their own jail. The jails were like palaces. Inmates were allowed to have visits from their wives, girlfriends, and private chefs. They had servants in their cells. They controlled the guards. Mondays they had their wives. Tuesdays, their girlfriends. Wednesdays, their kids.

After I left Group 93, the remaining members began to leave one by one. For some, our success parlayed into careers in other areas of law enforcement. Others left law enforcement altogether.

- Eddie Beach retired for a while and is now the New York State representative for the National Drug Intelligence Center (NDIC), serving as the liaison between law enforcement and the NDIC. He studies drug trends and patterns, new crimes, new drugs, and brings the intelligence back to Washington.
- Bernie Kerik became the fortieth police commissioner of New York City, serving from 2000 to early 2002. His autobiography, *Lost Son,* became a best-seller. He is now a partner in Rudolph Guiliani's law enforcement consulting firm, Guiliani Partners, in a subsidiary known as Guiliani-Kerik.
- John "Big Daddy" Saager retired from the NYPD and returned as a consultant, handling training for the federal agencies across the country, along with Bill Mockler and me. We work for the Department of Justice, Special Operations Division out of Washington, doing the wiretap seminars and lectures. We also do work for a company called Orion Scientific, which has a contract with the Department of Justice to teach wiretaps and techniques and case management and multijurisdictional investigations.
- Jimmy Grace is the country attaché to Denmark for the DEA. He now lives in Copenhagen with his wife and children.
- Eddie O'Casio is still with the New York State Police, running the state police administration of the DEA task force in New York.

- Terry Hartman went on to become the bodyguard for the DEA administrator Thomas Constantine. He was recently appointed the DEA country attaché to Madrid, Spain.
- Jack Higgins retired from the New York State Police as an investigator. Under a new program to bring experienced officers back to the force after the 9/11 tragedy, Higgins returned to the job. He is working out of the New York State Police, Fort Skylar Command, in an administrative capacity.
- Jerry Vetrano retreated to the mountains. He lives in a cabin in upstate New York in the middle of the wilderness.
- Our former lieutenant James Wood retired and became the partner in a major New York City corporate security agency, called Copstat.
- Bruce Stokes retired from law enforcement and is running a construction company in upstate New York.
- Steve Morse is semi-retired, but still works as an investigator with The Suffolk County District Attorneys office.
- As for me, I'm the sheriff of Passaic County, New Jersey, still on the streets, still doing what I love best: law enforcement. I see my mission as allowing my officers to do their job as they were sworn to do, free from the frustration that I felt for so many years because of bureaucratic roadblocks. As long as I'm sheriff, there is no criminal safe in Passaic County. I'll be out there personally hunting them down. Whether they're across a state line or an ocean, I'll reach out, grab them, and bring them back to justice.

Authors' Note

This is a true story. Every event recounted here really happened. Some names have been changed to protect the individuals involved. On occasion, the narrative has been related thematically, instead of strictly chronologically, for the sake of clarity. Dialogue has been reconstructed with the aid of memory, notes, and interviews.

About the Authors

JERRY SPEZIALE is a career cop who has attended three police academies and is a certified police officer in New York, New Jersey, and Pennsylvania. He served fifteen years with the NYPD, including tours in the South Bronx and the Organized Crime Control Bureau. For three years in the early 1990s he and Bernard Kerik were partners in an elite NYPD narcotics task force. Recruited by the Federal Drug Enforcement Task Force, Speziale was responsible for initiating, coordinating, and supervising some of the largest investigations ever conducted by the Drug Enforcement Agency. He has been credited with saving the victims of two separate kidnappings; he is recognized as the world's leading expert on multijurisdictional wiretap investigations (a subject on which he has written a manual for the Department of Justice); and he has been an instructor on major investigations for the FBI, DEA, IRS, and U.S. Customs Service. He has received numerous departmental recognition awards including the Michael John Buczek Medal of Honor, twenty-two New York City Police Department Commendations, and other awards, including two DEA Administrator's Awards, the U.S. Attorney General's Letter of Commendation, the NYPD Organized Crime Control Bureau Excellence Award, and the New York City Special Narcotics Prosecutor's Award. He has served as chief of police in New Hope, Pennsylvania, and Bergen County, New Jersey. In November 2001 he was elected sheriff of Passaic County, New Jersey, a role in which he continues to command media attention. A proud husband and father, he lives in northern New Jersey.

MARK SEAL has served as collaborator on ten nonfiction books. His work has been published in *Vanity Fair, Town & Country, Golf Digest, Texas Monthly*, and other magazines. His column, "Celebrated Weekend," appears regularly in *American Way*.

Acknowledgments

I met Maggie Reinhardt in November of 1978, and we immediately became one, a team able to conquer anything together. Maggie was always there for me: wiping my tears when my good friend and brother officer Michael Buczek lost his life; holding my hand at my bedside before and after my many surgeries. She has always been the voice of strength and reassurance, regardless of how long I was gone or how tough things really were during my absence. She always treated me as a hero when I returned home. Maggie, I love and adore you. Without your unselfishness, words of encouragement, and your steadfast belief in my abilities, I would have been lost.

My daughter, Francesca, "Franki" was born a year after Maggie and I were married. Francesca is "Daddy's little girl" and the love of my life. She has grown up to be a beautiful little lady who makes me so very proud each and every day. My love for you, Franki, is so deep.

My son, Jerry, "Lil Jer" was born the year I retired. Jerry's addition to the family changed all our lives. As with Maggie and Franki, Jerry is another love of my life. I would give anything to slow my children from growing up too fast, because I cherish every moment.

To my daughter, Paige, who will be born by the time of this book's publication, I love you.

To my dad and mom, Jerry and Barbara Speziale, you are the greatest two people on earth. My success is because of your love, support, confidence, concern, compassion, direction, friendship, faith, and strength. You are my role models, and I follow your guidance every-day as a parent and partner.

A special thanks to my sister and best friend, Debbie, who has always supported me regardless of the consequences. I am so proud of you. I love you dearly, little sister.

With much love and thanks to my brother-in-law, Tommy, and my niece, Britteny, for always being there.

To my late mother-in-law, Gloria Reinhardt, you became my sec-ond mom from the day I met you in 1978. Thank you for all your love and support and especially those late night meals. We miss you dearly.

To my brothers-in-law, John, Charlie and Steve Reinhardt, you are the brothers I never had. I thank each one of you individually for all you have done for your sister and me through some of the toughest times of our lives.

A special thanks to my attorney, sister, and best friend, Linda George, who always dropped whatever she was doing regardless of its importance when I called. Linda, I will never forget all you have done for my family and me.

A special thanks to my partner and best friend Bernard B. Kerik, retired Commissioner of the New York City Police Department. Thank you for your courage, friendship, humor, strength, tireless work ethic, support and knowledge. The successes of the investigations grew out of our teamwork. I am so proud of our accomplishments, what we stood for back then and today. I couldn't have done it without you!

Special thanks to Dr. Sami Harawi for his calm and compassionate voice when I needed it most.

To Chief Joseph Alvino, thanks for your help in being my reference and hook-up to the New York Drug Enforcement Task Force.

A special thanks to my lifelong friend, Robert "Boogs" Rikowich, and his wife, Laura, for thirty years of loyal friendship.

A special thanks to the New York City Special Narcotics Prosecu-tors Office, Special Narcotics Prosecutor Robert Silbering and Bridget Brennan, and Assistant District Attorneys Kevin Suttlehan, Mari Ma-loney, and David Hennessey. You are the unsung heroes of this story, and your tireless efforts led to our success.

A special thanks to the greatest jurist in the country, the Honorable Leslie Crocker Snyder, who's clear definition and knowledge of the law was the catalyst for the hundreds of wiretaps employed in these investigations.

To a true American hero and friend NYPD officer Michael John Buczek, who lost his life in the war on drugs in October 1988. May you rest in peace little buddy.

Thank you to the Buczek family for all of your support and friendship throughout my career.

Thank you to DEA Administrator Thomas Constantine and Task Force Chief John Maltz for believing in Group 93.

Thank you to Special Agents in Charge, William Mockler and Joe Keffe of the Special Operations Division for all your knowledge and support of the multi-jurisdictional concept.

A special thanks to the late Group 93 member Mike Kealon, whose tragic loss still saddens us all.

A special thanks to Retired Lt. James Wood, who believed in me and allowed me to take my first international action that began our success.

A special thanks to my pals and partners "Big Daddy" John Saager, Jimmy Grace, and Terry Hartman for their tireless contributions to the investigation.

A special thanks to my dear friend Danny Brown who stood with me from the beginning and always believed in me. Danny was the creator and first supervisor of Group 93.

A special thanks to Eddie Beach, who was with me from my first day in the Task Force. Eddie, your knowledge, guts, steadfast abilities, management skills and friendship are something I will always look up to. You are a friend and brother who I will never forget.

A special thanks to the following members of the Drug Enforcement Administration and New York Drug Enforcement Task Force who provided significant support in the referenced investigations:

Lt. Steve Krajci, Sgt. Jerry Neville, Sgt. Bruce Stokes, S/A Terry Hartman, Det. Kevin Scanlon, Det. Ron Nicastro, Inv. Jack Higgins, Inv. Eddie Ocasio, Sgt. Steve Morse, Lt. John Comparetto, Lt. Glen Morrisano, Inspector Ken O'Brien, Inv. Kent Fullenwieder, S/A Mike Furgason, S/A Dave Marzullo, S/A Mike Agrifolio, S/A Chris Roberts, Det. Bobby Mistretta, S/A Alfredo Cristolieb, S/A John McCormick, S/A John Chase, S/A Mike McGurk, Lt. Kiran Timoney, Lt.

Mike Gervasi, S/A Mike Defrancisi, Sgt. Chris Koehler, Det. Tommy Selvaggi.

Mark Seal would like to thank writer Rayce Boucher, assistant Jennifer Blocker and her talented TV sports broadcaster husband, Brandon, and invaluable transcriptionist Sheri Thompson.